*f*P

The Cult of Personality

■

How Personality Tests Are

Leading Us to Miseducate Our Children,

Mismanage Our Companies, and

Misunderstand Ourselves

■

Annie Murphy Paul

FREE PRESS

NEW YORK   LONDON   TORONTO   SYDNEY

FREE PRESS
A Division of Simon & Schuster, Inc.
1230 Avenue of the Americas
New York, NY 10020

For information regarding special discounts for bulk purchases,
please contact Simon & Schuster Special Sales at
1-800-456-6798 or business@simonandschuster.com

Designed by Joseph Rutt
Manufactured in the United States of America

1   3   5   7   9   10   8   6   4   2

Library of Congress Cataloging-in-Publication Data
Paul, Annie Murphy.
The cult of personality : how personality tests are leading us to miseducate our children,
mismanage our companies, and misunderstand ourselves / Annie Murphy Paul.
p. cm.
Includes bibliographical references and index.
1. Personality tests—United States. 2. Personality tests for children—United States.
3. Employees—Psychological testing—United States. I. Title.

BF698.5.P38 2004
155.2'8—dc22   2004047186

ISBN 0-7432-4356-0

To my parents, John Timothy Paul and Nancy Murphy Paul

Contents

The Cult of Personality

Introduction

Hello. Nice to meet you. Please allow me to tell you who you are.

Such is the introduction, polite but firm, extended by personality tests. When we first encounter them we are strangers (even, as some tests would have it, to ourselves). When we part some time later, we're a known quantity, neatly tagged. Personality tests take wildly different forms—questionnaires, inkblots, stories, drawings, dolls—but all make the same promise: to reduce our complicated, contradictory, changeable selves to a tidy label. These tests claim to measure not what we know, but what we're like; not what we can do, but who we are.

Today, personality tests are a startlingly ubiquitous part of American life, from the thousands of quizzes popping up online, to the personality types assigned in seminars and workshops, to the honesty tests and personality screens routinely required of job applicants. Millions of our nation's workers—from hourly employees to professionals like managers, doctors, and lawyers—must take personality tests to obtain a position or to advance in their careers. Citizens seeking justice in our courts may be compelled to take personality tests to secure parental custody or receive compensation for emotional distress. Even children are obliged to take personality tests: to gain admission to private schools and programs, to diagnose academic or behavioral problems, to guide the way they're taught or the kind of projects they're assigned. But where did these tests come from? And just what are they saying about us?

This book tells the surprising and disturbing story of the tests that claim to capture human nature. It goes behind the scenes to discover how personality tests are used—in America's companies, its courts, its schools, and in organizations from churches to community centers to dating services. Drawing on the latest scientific research, it exposes the serious flaws of personality tests, explaining why their results are often invalid, unreliable, and unfair. And it delves into the extraordinary history of the tests' creation, revealing how these allegedly neutral instruments were in fact shaped by the demands of industry and government—and by the idiosyncratic and often eccentric personalities of their creators.

The story begins with Hermann Rorschach, a Swiss psychiatrist possessed by a desire to create "a key to the knowledge of mankind." The inkblot test that bears his name, though one of psychologists' favorite tools for more than fifty years, has come under increasingly intense criticism over the past decade. The test's numerous detractors charge that the Rorschach—originally designed for use with psychiatric patients but now frequently given to normal people—"overpathologizes," making healthy individuals look sick. Multiple investigations have concluded that many of the test's results are simply not supported by evidence. Yet the Rorschach is still used by eight out of ten clinical psychologists, administered in nearly a third of emotional injury assessments and in almost half of child custody evaluations.

Even more popular is the Minnesota Multiphasic Personality Inventory, a 567-item questionnaire created at a Midwestern mental hospital in the 1930s. The MMPI, as it's known, was assembled in a highly unusual way: in the words of Starke Hathaway, one of its authors, "we permitted the patients to design their own test." Today it's administered to an estimated 15 million Americans each year, in spite of the fact that it features invasive questions about test takers' sex lives and bathroom habits. Like the Rorschach, the MMPI was intended for use with the mentally ill, but it is now given to a broad range of normal people, including aspiring doctors, psychologists, paramedics, clergy members, police officers, firefighters, and airplane pilots. It has also become a template for personality questionnaires that are used even more widely in the workplace: a 2003 survey shows that personality tests are now administered by 30 percent of American companies, from mom-and-pop operations to giants like Wal-Mart and General Motors.

The corporate world has seized on the innovations of another personality test creator: Henry Murray, a brilliant Harvard professor whose charismatic ebullience disguised a dark secret life. In collaboration with his mistress, he designed the Thematic Apperception Test, which asks the taker to tell stories about a set of ambiguous drawings. Despite falling "woefully short of professional and scientific test standards," the technique is popular with psychologists (it's used by 60 percent of clinicians, according to a recent survey) and also with marketers, who use its insights about personality to shape their product pitches. During World War II, Murray was enlisted to select spies for American intelligence operations, and from this work emerged another tool for evaluating personality: the assessment center. These centers, which put participants through a series of simulated tasks, have received mixed reviews from researchers—but they are used today by thousands of American companies, along with two-thirds of police and fire departments and state and county governments.

Perhaps no other personality test has achieved the cult status of the Myers-Briggs Type Indicator, an instrument created in the 1940s by a Pennsylvania housewife. Fiercely proud of the test she called "my baby," Isabel Myers believed that it could bring about world peace—or at least make everyone a little nicer. The Myers-Briggs, which assigns each test taker a personality type represented by four letters, is now given to 2.5 million people each year, and is used by 89 of the companies in the Fortune 100. Employed by businesses to "identify strengths" and "facilitate teamwork," the Myers-Briggs has also been embraced by a multitude of individuals who experience a revelation (what devotees call the "aha reaction") upon learning about psychological type. Their enthusiasm persists despite research showing that as many as three-quarters of test takers achieve a different personality type when tested again, and that the sixteen distinctive types described by the Myers-Briggs have no scientific basis whatsoever.

Personality testing begins early, when children are in elementary school or even before. One of the first instruments to be used widely with youngsters was the Draw-a-Person Test, designed by Karen Machover, a New York City therapist who had herself endured a singularly bleak childhood. Psychologists administering it or a related technique, the House-Tree-Person Test, make judgments about children's personalities based on the style and content of their sketches. Although decades of research have shown these tests to be all but worthless—"again and again," write two respected scientists, the results of drawing tests "have failed to hold up"—the Draw-a-Person Test is still used by more than a quarter of clinicians, the House-Tree-Person Test by more than a third. More recently, a fad among educators for teaching to each student's "learning style" has led to the development of at least half a dozen tests that label children by their personalities: feeling or thinking, imaginative or practical, flexible or organized. While proponents of the concept contend that its application can reduce delinquency, prevent dropouts, and even alleviate attention-deficit disorder, they offer scant evidence for such claims.

More scientifically minded were the studies of Raymond Cattell, a British-born psychologist who used sophisticated statistical techniques to reduce the vast array of human qualities to a more manageable number. Originally trained as a chemist, Cattell aimed to construct a precise "periodic table" of personality (though ultimately, as we'll learn, he became notorious for far more dangerous ideas). Cattell's research led to his Sixteen Personality Factor Questionnaire, still widely used for career counseling and employee selection, and to what those in the field call its biggest development in decades: the "discovery" of the five essential dimensions of personality. A test that measures the so-called Big Five, the NEO Personality Inventory, already dominates current research on personality, and is fast moving into the wider arena of workplace, school, and courtroom. There's just one problem: the lofty abstractions of these tests have left out the human being herself, partaking in what one critic calls "a psychology of the stranger."

The tests described here are together taken by tens of millions of people every year—and there are some 2,500 others on the market, each offering to explain us to ourselves (or to a boss or a teacher or a judge). Today personality testing is a $400-million industry, one that's expanding annually by 8 percent to 10 percent. Yet despite their prevalence—and the importance of the matters they are called upon to decide—personality tests have received surprisingly little scrutiny. That's in sharp contrast to aptitude, intelligence, and achievement tests, each of which have been inspected under the glare of political and popular attention (and which have often been found wanting). Personality testing has thrived in the shade of casual neglect, growing unchecked along with abuses like invasive questions, inaccurate labels, and unjust outcomes.

But perhaps the most potent effect of personality testing is its most subtle. For almost a hundred years it has provided a technology, a vocabulary, and a set of ideas for describing who we are, and many Americans have adopted these as our own. The judgments of personality tests are not always imposed; often they are welcomed. And what, some will ask, is wrong with that? Human beings are complex creatures, and we need simple ways of grasping them to survive. But *how* we simplify—which shortcuts we take, which approximations we accept—demands close inspection, especially since these approximations so often stand in for the real thing. This book tells the story of one very powerful and pervasive way of understanding ourselves: where it came from, why it flourished, and how, too often, it fails us.

ONE

A Most Typical American

On July 16, 1849, a young man arrived at the offices of Fowler & Wells on Nassau Street in Lower Manhattan. Six feet tall, strong and clever, he had tried his hand at a number of trades: printing, carpentry, even poetry. Now, two months past his thirtieth birthday, he found himself with more questions than answers, restless energy to spare and no place to apply it.

Entering an examining room, he took a seat before the man he'd come to see. Lorenzo Niles Fowler had serious eyes, an impressive beard, and an air of calm authority; with practiced skill he began running his fingers over the young man's head. A stenographer sat close by, recording his every word.

"Combativeness, six," Fowler pronounced. "Secretiveness, three . . . Self-esteem, six to seven . . . Conscientiousness, six . . . Mirthfulness, five"—on and on, more than three dozen scores in all.

The young man paid his three dollars and stepped back out into the bustle of Nassau Street. Though he might have looked the same to the merchants and newspapermen hurrying past, he knew he was profoundly changed. At last he'd been seen for who he was, and proof was in the report tucked under his arm. "You are one of the most friendly men in the world and your happiness is greatly depending on your social relations," Fowler had written. "You are familiar and open in your intercourse with others but you do not by so doing lose your dignity.

"You are no hypocrite but are plainspoken and are what you appear to be at all times . . . You have your own opinions and think for yourself . . . Your sense of justice, of right and wrong is strong . . . You are a great reader and have a good memory of facts and events . . . You can compare, illustrate, discriminate, and criticize with much ability . . . You have a good command of language especially if excited."

It was an uncannily accurate description of the young Walt Whit-
man, and Whitman took from it both reassurance and inspiration. The
American Bard, the Great Gray Poet who would go on to write "Song of
Myself," "When Lilacs Last in the Dooryard Bloom'd," and "O Captain!
My Captain!" had found an unlikely muse—in phrenology.

Phrenology, or the "science of mind," was a wildly popular way for
nineteenth-century Americans to understand themselves and others.
Lorenzo Fowler and his brother, Orson, were its leading proponents in
this country, and they taught their legions of followers that every human
attribute sprang from a particular structure in the brain. When well
used, these organs would expand, pushing up the skull just above to produce a palpable bulge. By feeling a person's head, the expert phrenologist could read its rugged topology like a map of what lay within.

The Fowler brothers and their partner, Samuel Wells, identified a
total of thirty-seven faculties, from Cautiousness to Intuitiveness, Destructiveness to Benevolence, each with a corresponding bump rated in
size from one to seven. They called many of these traits by unusual or
invented names: "Adhesiveness" indicated one's capacity for devotion
and commitment; "amativeness" described the proclivity to feel
amorous and sexual; "alimentiveness" was their term for a love of food
and drink.

They had no more faithful student than Whitman. He spent hours at
the Fowler & Wells Phrenological Cabinet, wandering among its
ghostly heads. (The cabinet, a kind of museum, displayed nearly a thousand plaster casts of such notable specimens as savages, murderers, and
madmen.) He read and underlined phrenological tracts, copying pas-
sages into his journal. He even wrote about the practice himself, ex-
tolling its virtues in the pages of the *Brooklyn Daily Eagle*. "Breasting the
waves of detraction as a ship dashes sea-waves, Phrenology, it must now
be confessed by all men who have open eyes, has at last gained a position, and a firm one, among the sciences," he proclaimed.

The Fowlers repaid his devotion with generous patronage, making
Whitman a staff writer on one of their many periodicals. When in 1855
he self-published his first book, *Leaves of Grass*, they sold it at their shop;
when a second edition came out, Fowler & Wells was its publisher.
Bound into each volume was Whitman's "chart of bumps," which he re-

garded as a credential, evidence of his claim to be a new kind of poet and a new kind of man. Flattering though his reading had been, Whitman saw room for improvement and augmented several of his scores. (He also wrote rhapsodic, and anonymous, reviews of his own work: "An American bard at last!" he raved in *The United States Review*.)

The phrenologists' early appreciation of his gifts gave Whitman the confidence to pursue his bold project of creating a truly American literature. But the concepts and vocabulary of phrenology also imbued the poetry itself. "In America," he jotted in his notes, "an immense number of new words are needed." Whitman found these words in the phrenologists' catalogue of human qualities and used them to sing of himself:

> Never offering others, always offering himself, corroborating
>   his phrenology,
> Voluptuous, inhabitive, combative, conscientious, alimentive,
>   intuitive, of copious friendship, sublimity, firmness,
>   self-esteem . . .

The new breed of Americans he anticipated were best described and explained through the miraculous medium of phrenology:

> They shall arise in the States,
> They shall report Nature, laws, physiology, and happiness,
> They shall illustrate Democracy and the kosmos,
> They shall be alimentive, amative, perceptive . . .

Phrenology, in short, was an indispensable tool for the still-young country that Whitman championed. Of those who would "talk or sing to America," he asked,

> Have you studied out the land, its idioms and men?
> Have you learn'd the physiology, phrenology, politics,
>   geography, pride, freedom, friendship, of the land?

In time, Whitman's exuberant vision of America and its people—a vision borrowed heavily from the nineteenth century's "science of mind"—would become one of the touchstones of our national identity.

It may be no exaggeration to say that a vital part of the modern American self came into being one summer day in the offices of Fowler & Wells, Phrenologists.

Human beings have long looked for signs of order in the unruly variety of our own natures. Today this need for coherence is met largely by theories about personality—as measured, usually, by personality tests. In Whitman's time it was answered by phrenology, and before that by a profusion of schemes notable for their inventiveness and their (to our eyes, at least) utter implausibility. All these systems serve the same clutch of deeply felt needs: They subdue the blooming, buzzing hive of differences among people. They allow predictions to be made and advice to be dispensed. They permit swift judgments about strangers. They authorize the assignment of individuals, ourselves included, to the comforting confines of a group. They often justify social arrangements as they are, extending a reassuring (to some) sense of stability. Most important, they offer to explain *why*—why we are the way we are.

The earliest such system was astrology, the idea that the order of the stars and planets at the time of our birth gives a glimmer of the people we will become. By the fifth century BC, Greek astrologers were consulting the heavens as they composed character descriptions and predicted fates far into the future. People born at the rising of the star Spica, for example, will be "very learned and erudite, fond of philosophical dissertations, eloquent, creative, perspicacious, ingenious and clever, keen on music and arts," prophesied one sky watcher in the year 379.

The ancients believed that climate and diet did their part, too: the heat of the sun, the lushness of trees, the fullness of rivers could mold the character of an entire people. "The chief reason why Asiatics are less warlike and more gentle in character than the Europeans," asserted the fifth-century B.C. Greek physician Hippocrates, "is the uniformity of the seasons, which show no violent changes either towards heat or towards cold, but are equable. For there occur no mental shocks nor violent physical change, which are more likely to steel the temper and impart to it a fierce passion than is a monotonous sameness." (These early "environmental" explanations of human nature never mention the influence we moderns consider so important: childhood experiences.)

The source of differences among people migrated inward with the theory of the "humors," our bodies' elemental essences. Hippocrates' intellectual heir, the second-century physician Galen, claimed that the balance of these fluids determined our characteristic mood: the gloomy melancholic had an excess of black bile; the sluggish phlegmatic, of phlegm; the irritable choleric, of yellow bile. "Those maddened through bile," for example, "are noisy, evil-doers and restless," while "those who are mad through phlegm are quiet, and neither shout nor make a disturbance." Likewise, an excess of the "moist" humors swamped women and children in irrationality and impulsivity.

Flesh and bone also held hints to one's psychological complexion. "Character" comes from the Greek word for "distinguishing mark," and the ancients believed that nature bestowed such marks in the shape of a prominent nose, jutting chin, or lofty brow. "Persons who have a large forehead are sluggish," declared Aristotle in the fourth century B.C., "those who have a small one, fickle; those who have a broad one are excitable, those who have a bulging one, quick-tempered."

Ancient as they were, each of these systems had its adherents in the nineteenth century (and some, such as astrology, remain popular today). But for a time they were all swept aside in the passionate craze for "bumpology." Phrenology had the sheen of science, the glamour of European origins, and the seductive claim to comprehensiveness. It's no wonder that Walt Whitman, along with a great many of his countrymen, embraced it without reservation.

Phrenology began, not as an ambitious plan to classify all mankind, but as a salve to one man's uncomfortable emotions. Franz Joseph Gall was jealous. The young German, studying medicine at the University of Vienna in the 1780s, saw himself bested again and again by students who were less intelligent than he but better able to memorize large amounts of information. Scrutinizing his resented rivals, Gall noticed a striking fact: all of his competitors seemed to have bulging eyes and prominent foreheads. Perhaps, Gall speculated to himself, the faculty for verbal memory was located behind these features, causing them to protrude when that capacity was especially well developed.

Intrigued, and perhaps consoled, by this evidence of their peculiar endowment, Gall looked around him for other such associations. He pursued the investigation in earnest once he became a doctor, beginning his research with servants, beggars, criminals, and mental patients. Their unsubtle tendencies, he thought, would be easy to identify (and their heads could be felt without much fuss). "I collected in my house . . . quite a number of individuals of the lower classes of society, following different occupations; such as coachmen, servants, etc.," Gall reported. "I obtained their confidence, and disposed them to sincerity by giving them beer, wine, and money; and when favorably inclined, I got them to tell me of each other's good and bad qualities, and most striking characteristics."

He then carefully examined the skull of each, and in this fashion established the bumps for quarrelsomeness, cowardice, and pride. In pickpockets, Gall detected signs of the Organ of Theft; in killers, the Organ of Murder. Another useful opportunity arose when one of his patients, a lady so libidinous that she became known as "Gall's Passionate Widow," suddenly fainted into his arms. Helping her back to her feet, the doctor could not avoid noticing a bulge at the base of her skull: thus was the faculty of Amativeness discovered.

Fingers ranging over hundreds of heads, Gall eventually counted twenty-seven different bumps, including those indicating "mechanical aptitude," "metaphysical depth," and "sense of the ridiculous." His youthful envy had unexpectedly yielded a key to human nature—one that had resided there all along, curtained by hair and hidden under hats. Gall's breakthrough brought him honor and fame throughout Europe, along with a flock of disciples. First among these was Johann Spurzheim, who in 1832 decided to carry the new science to America and to see what kind of heads the New World had to offer (he was especially curious about the skulls of Indians). But much to his teacher's displeasure, the system that disembarked along with Spurzheim was different from the one Gall originally devised.

For one thing, Spurzheim changed its name. Gall had called his science "cranioscopy," a term his student discarded in favor of the vaguely Greek coinage "phrenology." Spurzheim also shed a sunnier light on some of the dark qualities Gall's explorations had uncovered: the Organ of Murder, for example, became the less-fearsome "Destructiveness," and the Organ of Theft became mere "Acquisitiveness." Gall had imagined himself a disinterested scientist in search of truth, while Spurzheim eagerly advertised phrenology's many useful applications. Here was a "practical system of mental philosophy," he claimed, whose insights would improve the education of children, the reformation of criminals, and the treatment of the insane.

Spurzheim's message was pitched perfectly at the American ear. Within a week of his arrival on August 4, he was lecturing at Yale University, where, an observer noted, "the professors were in love with him." Then on to Harvard, where he was equally well received, and to a whirlwind series of public lectures and demonstrations. "When Spurzheim was in America, the great mass of society became phrenologists in a day, wherever he appeared," one onlooker marveled. "All caps and wigs" were pulled off, and "all fair tresses disheveled, in the search after organization."

So intense were the demands upon Spurzheim that after three months of frenzied proselytizing, he simply dropped dead. The crowds who had ardently welcomed him and his teachings now keened over the passing of what Ralph Waldo Emerson called "one of the world's greatest minds." Spurzheim's death was "a calamity to mankind," the Massachusetts Medical Association noted somberly, and certainly his funeral was befitting that of a very worthy man. Arranged by the president of Harvard, attended by three thousand mourners, the service included a stirring performance of "Ode to Spurzheim," a dirge composed especially for the occasion.

The many who grieved the loss of "Nature's priest" could not have known that phrenology was only beginning its glorious ascent in America. Its apotheosis awaited the special genius of two odd but brilliant brothers named Fowler.

When Lorenzo Fowler set out for college from his hometown of Cohochton, New York, it was understood that he would become a minister. What he found at Amherst College, however, was not God but phrenology. He arrived in 1832, the very year that Johann Spurzheim was electrifying audiences all over New England. Lorenzo and his older brother, Orson, who was already enrolled at the Massachusetts college, became deeply interested in the new science, and proposed a public debate on the subject with Orson's classmate and friend Henry Ward Beecher.

Though Beecher was meant to present the opposing point of view, his readings in preparation for the debate ended up convincing him of phrenology's merits. He submitted to a reading by the fledgling phrenologists, who declared him the possessor of "a strong social brain" and "an impassioned temperament," with "very large Benevolence" and "Amativeness fully developed." (Later, when Beecher became a famous preacher, he advised his congregants that the best preparation for a Christian life was "a practical knowledge of the human mind as is given by phrenology.")

Beecher was only the first of the brothers' many converts. Soon they were providing phrenological readings to their classmates at two cents apiece. After graduation, plans for a churchly life were put aside in favor of another kind of missionary work: "Phrenologize Our Nation, for thereby it will Reform the World!" the Fowlers exhorted. Lorenzo and Orson became professional lecturers and practitioners of the science of mind, opening an office in New York City in 1835 and producing their first publication, *Phrenology Proved, Illustrated, and Applied*, a year later. The two men brought an evangelical fervor to the enterprise, promising that phrenology would improve "the prosperity and material good of the next generation and greatly enhance the happiness of the race, besides abolishing poverty and nearly abolishing crime."

Along with such crusading zeal, the Fowlers exhibited a canny business sense and a showman's dramatic flair. Their sales pitches were all but irresistible: "Surely, [a reading] will point out, and show how to obviate, at least one fault, and cultivate one virtue, besides reinvigorating health—the value of which ASTOR'S MILLIONS can not equal! Shall, then, the trifling examination fee prevent what is thus INFINITELY valuable? Will you allow this to intercept your MENTAL progress, especially if just starting in life? In no other way can you even obtain for your self, at such a trifle, as much good—as great a luxury."

They advertised free lectures, charging only for a personal consultation, and drew overflowing crowds. These "two wizards of manipulation" delighted audiences by feeling out fakes among those who volunteered for a public demonstration. The village idiot presented himself as the mayor; the county judge dressed up as a beggar; the local doctor impersonated a raving lunatic—but there was no deceiving the Fowlers' sensitive fingers. "No Conscientiousness! Not a bit! No Approbativeness!

No feeling of shame!" Orson once cried out, recoiling from the touch of a particular head "as from a serpent." The man, it turned out, was a criminal charged with manslaughter.

So persuasive were the Fowlers' performances that they began to attract an illustrious clientele. Future U.S. presidents James Garfield and John Tyler had their heads read. (Orson coyly informed Tyler that he "would veto bills" one day.) Statesman Daniel Webster received the gratifying report that his skull was to ordinary heads "what the great dome of St. Peter's is to the small cupolas at its side." A young Clara Barton attended four weeks of courses taught by Lorenzo and became a teacher on his advice. "How can the value of the results of that month, extending through a lifetime, be put into words?" swooned the woman who founded the Red Cross. "How measure the worth of the ideas, the knowledge of one's self, and of others, growing out of it?" Charles Dickens, Edgar Allan Poe, and Oliver Wendell Holmes were also among the Fowlers' satisfied customers. Even the famously conjoined twins Chang and Eng (each) had their heads read.

Of course, phrenology had its doubters, including the reliably skeptical and acerbic Mark Twain. As a child he watched a phrenologist manipulate the heads of his neighbors in Hannibal, Missouri. "It is not at all likely, I think, that the traveling expert ever got any villager's character quite right, but it is a safe guess that he was always wise enough to furnish his clients character charts that would compare favorably with George Washington's," he noted dryly. "It was a long time ago, and yet I think I still remember that no phrenologist ever came across a skull in our town that fell much short of the Washington standard." His opinion of phrenology was not improved by a reading he received as an adult from Lorenzo: his was a generally mediocre head, Fowler told him, and one utterly lacking the Organ of Humor.

But as even Twain had to admit, his wariness of phrenology and its "outlandish" vocabulary was not widely shared: "By and by the people became familiar with the strange names and addicted to the use of them and they batted them back and forth in conversation with deep satisfaction—a satisfaction which could hardly have been more contenting if they had known for certain what the words meant," he cracked. Where the famous and prominent had gone, ordinary men and women followed: into the offices of the Fowlers, who soon set up branches in Boston, Philadelphia, and London, or under the fingers of the itinerant phrenologists who now traipsed the country, traveling salesmen for the truths of the day.

If Johann Spurzheim had not delivered phrenology to America's shores in 1832, the country would have had to invent it. This was a place and a time of momentous change, felt most acutely by those ordinary people satirized by Twain and served by the Fowlers. As they left family farms and workshops, as they traded the country for towns and cities, Americans were encountering something unfamiliar: choices. Whom to marry? What job to pursue? Which way to achieve distinction? These were new questions for many, and phrenology promised authoritative answers. "A correct Phrenological examination will teach, with SCIENTIFIC CERTAINTY, that most useful of all knowledge—YOURSELF; YOUR DEFECTS, and how to obviate them; your EXCELLENCES and how to make the most of them; your NATURAL TALENTS, and thereby in what spheres and pursuits you can best succeed," pledged one of the Fowlers' publications. The brothers took Spurzheim's practical orientation one step further, transforming phrenology into an individual oracle, a source of highly personal advice on the choice of a career, a spouse, a life's path.

"A most typical American," Walt Whitman called himself, and in seeking phrenology's reassuringly firm guidance, he surely was. Like Whitman, Americans seem to have greeted the phrenologists' counsel with relief and gratitude (while ignoring those recommendations that missed the mark, as Whitman slighted Lorenzo's suggestion that he become an accountant). One phrenology client spoke for many when he noted that though he had been suffering "painful confusion's derangement," after his reading, "doubts and perplexities fled like morning vapors chased away by the rising sun." This was metaphysics for the man on the street, wisdom on sale for a few dollars a head.

There was one other way that phrenology made itself indispensable. The country's growing businesses now needed a way to appraise the workers they hired. Phrenology, which claimed to provide "a complete mental daguerreotype," seemed just the thing, and many firms began requiring a phrenological letter of reference. An advertisement appearing in the *New York Sun* read: "AN APPRENTICE WANTED. A stout boy not over fifteen years of age, of German or Scotch parents, to learn a good but difficult trade. N.B. It will be necessary to bring a recommendation to his abilities from Messrs. Fowlers and Wells, Phrenologists, Nassau Street." In an expanding economy that could no longer rely on reputation or word of mouth, the impartial accuracy promised by phrenology was a boon to business. For America's employers, as for all its many proponents, phrenology was just too useful not to be true.

———■———

Three thousand miles and a hundred and fifty years away from Fowler & Wells, the offices of today's phrenologist are located on another bustling thoroughfare, San Francisco's Market Street. But today there's no exotic cabinet to draw passersby, no hovering stenographers to smilingly suggest a reading. To get there the curious must enter a blank-featured office building, ride an elevator to the third floor, and head down a long hallway redolent with the smell of new carpet. At the end they'll find not a clamorous carnival of gawkers and sightseers, but a dozen young people in a large open room, typing soundlessly at sky-blue iMacs. The clients of this venture, millions of them, are spread all over the country and the world.

Welcome to Emode, "The #1 Destination for Self-Discovery," as its Web site proclaims. This dot-com operation, offering more than two hundred online personality tests, has ministered to more people than Lorenzo Fowler could ever have dreamed: Fifty million individuals have taken one of its tests since the site launched in 2000. Like the itinerant phrenologists of old, this is a movable oracle, coming right into its customers' homes.

Just off the main room is the director of this ambitious organization, seated behind a desk in his sunny office. James Currier, thirty-five years old, is tall and lean and wears a blue shirt that matches his eyes. Nominated as a "Man of the Internet" by Women.com ("like his Web site, he knows how to ask lots of questions"), he exudes a cool confidence. Currier, who grew up in New Hampshire, got the idea for Emode in 1998 when he was studying at Harvard Business School. The school offers the Myers-Briggs Type Indicator, a popular personality test, to all its students.

"I saw that it was a tremendously meaningful experience for people," says Currier. "People fundamentally want to know about themselves and their place in the world." When his classmates received their results, "they were laughing and pointing and talking, just opening up to each other more than they had done before." Currier spotted an opportunity: "I realized that I could provide a life-discovery service to people that had never before been possible."

A year later, Currier opened for business in a leaky brick basement in Cambridge, Massachusetts, employing graphic artists to design the site and psychology PhD's to create the tests. While some of the tests purport to offer a comprehensive report on the taker's personality, others are "just for fun," he says, like "Who's Your Inner Rock Star?" and "What Breed of Dog Are You?" (Currier is a golden retriever.) The site offers these lighthearted tests for free while charging $14.95 for feedback on the more in-depth exams. Emode was an immediate hit, attracting three million visitors within its first two weeks, and Currier realized that his company's growing needs required a move to the epicenter of dotcom activity, San Francisco.

Although it all happened just a few years ago, the story of Emode's founding already has the hoary feel of a Gold Rush legend. The difference is in the ending: Emode continues to flourish even as innumerable other dot-coms withered and died. Currier has a simple explanation for his site's success. "Everyone is interested in themselves," he says. "Since the beginning of man, we have always wondered, 'Who am I?' and 'Where do I fit into this world?' I think these online tests are going directly to the heart of the question."

Currier's vision of his project is grandiose enough to rival the Fowlers': the company's mission statement announces that "Emode will use Internet technology to create a revolution in how people learn about themselves and how they improve the quality of their lives," and he is already expanding the business in several directions. In early 2003, he rolled out a service intended to match romantic partners through their personality profiles; prospective couples are rated on a "compatibility index" of 1 to 100. "It takes a really distracted and imprecise, scary process and makes it cleaner, simpler, deeper, and more entertaining," says Currier. He's also planning a career-finding function. "We take information about people's personalities and help them do something with it—like, 'Here's a job you should take, here's a person you should date, here's a trip you should go on,' " Currier explains. "We want to help them make those changes, help them go from A to B."

High-tech though they are, the goods peddled by James Currier are essentially the same as those advertised by Lorenzo Fowler a century and a half earlier: gleanings of self-knowledge, along with guidance through a thicket of choices that has grown ever more tangled since the phrenologists' time. And Emode is only one purveyor of this extraordinarily popular form of information and instruction. Thousands of online personality tests—from frivolous fare like "Which *Star Wars* Character Are You?," to ostensibly serious exercises "designed by psychologists"—have now joined the innumerable personality questionnaires already being printed in books and magazines.

Of course, many of the best known and most important personality tests are clinical instruments that can be administered and interpreted only by psychologists or other trained personnel. These are the tests this book will examine most closely, in part because they are often the models on which the more informal tests are based. But the ubiquity of personality tests in all their forms suggests that they have become our era's favored mode of self-understanding, our most accessible and accepted way of describing human nature.

This was the position held by phrenology, of course, until science came along to knock it off its perch. From the height of its popularity in the mid-nineteenth century, the decline of phrenology's reputation followed swiftly on a series of newly sophisticated studies of the brain. Though this research provided evidence that some mental functions, such as vision and speech, were in fact confined to particular parts of the brain, these parts were almost never where the phrenologists professed they would be. In addition, such localized functions were invariably highly specific, not the global characteristics claimed by the phrenologists. And there was no evidence at all that their placement or size was manifested in bumps on the skull. By the end of the century, phrenology had taken a place alongside astrology and the humors, another wrong answer to the riddle of human nature.

Is it possible that its modern counterpart, personality testing, will meet the same fate? Science has again issued a challenge, finding many of the personality tests in use today invalid and unreliable. At the same time, other alarms are being raised: about the tests' propensity to invade workers' privacy, label students in limiting ways, and supply misleading evidence to the courts. The time has come to take a closer look at these tests, and to ask whether the answers they offer are correct—or just the ones their users want to hear.

Phrenology, of course, did not disappear just because science had declared its moment past. Fowler & Wells continued advertising its services until 1904; the *American Phrenological Journal* published fresh issues until 1911; the American Institute of Phrenology graduated new classes of students until 1925. During the Great Depression, phrenology was offered as vocational counseling to people out of work, and a "mechanical phrenologist," the Psycograph, was a popular attraction at the 1933 Century of Progress Exposition in Chicago.

But perhaps the belief in phrenology lingered longest and most powerfully in the hearts of those who had first recognized themselves in its flattering reflection. Walt Whitman remained one of the faithful. Throughout his long life, phrenology continued to provide him with a literary language, an aspirational self-image, and an expansive vision of human potential. It even gave him words for his most private and unconventional passions, as in an 1870 diary entry about his love for a man: "Depress the adhesive nature/It is in excess—making life a torment/Ah this diseased, feverish, disproportionate adhesiveness." Phrenology was no abstract doctrine but a cherished familiar, an extension of himself as necessary as his name or his body. Science, which built up and then debunked such systems in relentless succession, could do little to dislodge a faith so intimate and so certain.

Whitman remained a staunch adherent of the science of mind even as those around him grew doubtful. "I know what [Oliver Wendell] Holmes said about phrenology," he wrote to a confidant in 1878, "—that you might as easily tell how much money is in a safe feeling the knob on the door as tell how much brain a man has by feeling the bumps on his head: and I guess most of my friends distrust it—but then you see I am very old fashioned—I probably have not got by the phrenology stage yet."

When Whitman died in 1892, the phrenological reading performed by Lorenzo Fowler nearly half a century earlier was found among his most precious papers. "Not even his manuscripts were preserved as carefully," a biographer observes. All his life, Whitman had recalled his visits to the Fowlers' Phrenological Cabinet with fondness and genuine gratitude. "I went there often," he reminisced in a letter to a friend, "and once for myself had a very elaborate and leisurely examination and 'chart of bumps' written out (I have it yet)."

TWO

Rorschach's Dream

Hermann Rorschach was twenty years old, a medical student at the University of Zurich in Switzerland, when he had the dream. The day before he had witnessed his first autopsy, and he watched it performed—skin split, muscle parted, cavities opened—with the "respectful eagerness of a young student." He was thinking, he said later, of "the cutting up of the soul."

"The following night I had a dream in which I felt my own brain was being cut," Rorschach recounted, a dream so vivid that even after he woke he could feel the pierce of the knife. This extraordinary experience would eventually give rise to a kind of waking dream: a powerful desire to dissect human nature itself. The phrenologists had stopped at the skull, feeling along its contours like searchers fumbling in the dark. Rorschach wanted to shine his light deeper—as deep as the surgeons who pared away flesh with their scalpels.

Rorschach, of course, would go on to create one of the most recognizable images of our time: the amorphous inkblot test that bears his name. What has become a universal icon of ambiguity began as a dream of universal understanding, a "key to the knowledge of mankind." In a sense, Rorschach was first in a line of dreamers extending through the twentieth century, a succession of scientists who imagined they could take the measure of human nature. The consequences of that dream, flawed though it was, are with us today in the personality tests—including the Rorschach—that millions take each year.

In some ways it was surprising that Hermann Rorschach was present at the autopsy at all. As a child he had dreamed not of being a doctor, but an artist. Born in Zurich in 1884, Rorschach was the son of a failed painter who made his living as a drawing teacher at a boys' school. Like his father, young Hermann had an artist's temperament, sensitive and a bit otherworldly. He could interpret the pain of a toothache as a musical melody, and recalled famous paintings he had seen by translating them into a series of movements. A talented drafts-man, even his briefest sketches seemed to capture some unmistakable essence of his subject.

When Rorschach was twelve, his mother died; his father followed when he was eighteen. About to go off to university, Rorschach now faced a difficult choice: should he be an artist or a scientist? He had an abiding passion for art, but his parents' illnesses had also turned his in-terest toward medicine. This dilemma would become an insistent theme, recurring not only throughout Rorschach's life but throughout the unfolding story of personality psychology: is human nature a subject for art, or for science? Does it call for creative, subjective intuition, or cool, rational logic?

In 1904, Rorschach enrolled in medical school, deciding to specialize in psychiatry. It was at this time that he saw the autopsy, and the vision of his life's work.

Five years later, Rorschach was working as a resident at the Munsterlin-gen mental hospital in northeastern Switzerland. The young doctor was popular among the patients there, both for his gentle and unassuming manner and for the many entertaining diversions he arranged. He pro-vided them with paper and paints, then hung their artwork on the hos-pital's walls. He turned the institution's chapel into a theater, designing sets and costumes and even performing with shadow puppets.

These activities were not solely for the patients' enjoyment, however. Rorschach was intensely interested in how they responded to the world around them, and he suspected that such reactions revealed much about their illnesses and about their individual natures. He carefully observed each of his wards, sometimes sketching their likenesses directly into their case histories. And he began to elicit their reactions more deliber-ately, introducing new experiences and attending closely to their ex-pressions and comments. For several months Rorschach kept a monkey at the asylum, watching the residents respond to its antic gestures and grimaces. Searching for still more evocative stimuli, he began presenting them with surprising drawings of, say, a green cat or a red frog. It was in 1911 that he got the idea to show them inkblots.

Inkblots—accidental forms created by folding a piece of paper on which drops of ink have been placed—had occupied an odd corner of European culture for almost a hundred years. Frequently used as a prop for parlor games and fortune-telling, these splotches were even made into literature. In 1857, the German poet and physician Justinus Kerner published a volume of inkblots and the rather ominous poems they inspired (Kerner was convinced that the blots' dark shapes were determined by "the other world"). As a child, Rorschach played with inkblots so frequently that his nickname was "Klex," or "Inkblot," and as a teenager, he likely encountered Kerner's book.

Now, at Munsterlingen, he fashioned some inkblots of his own and began showing them to patients, asking, "What might this be?" They invariably answered with fanciful images: "angels with fluttering wings," "carnival clowns dancing with each other," "waiters carrying a champagne bucket." Almost in passing, Rorschach noted that the interpretations offered by schizophrenics seemed different from the others, unusual and even bizarre, and he wondered briefly if the forms could be used as a diagnostic test.

The immediate needs of his patients were pressing, however, so Rorschach put his inkblots aside—until a startling development six years later compelled him to pick them up again.

By 1917, Rorschach was a husband, the father of a small child, and a full-fledged psychiatrist at a mental hospital in Herisau, near Switzerland's border with Austria. It was at the end of this year that a Polish medical student named Szymon Hens published his own work with inkblots, which he had administered to mental patients and to normal adults and children.

Reading Hens's paper, Rorschach felt the painful jab of professional jealousy—but also a gratifying flash of insight. Hens, he realized, had focused on the content of what his subjects discerned in the blots. For Rorschach, however, *what* his patients saw mattered less than *how* they saw it: Did they take in the entire shape, or did they concentrate on one part? Were the figures they saw moving or still? How did they react when colored blots were introduced? Such perceptual processes, Rorschach believed, revealed far more about the viewer than the simple content of their answers.

Rorschach returned with greater intensity to his inkblot experiments, recruiting patients and even colleagues as his subjects. Any staff member who wished to work with Rorschach had to submit to his "procedure" first. "The funny part was that everything I saw I connected with anatomy," one nurse recalled. "I saw the spine; that's all I could say." Before long Rorschach had tested 405 people, and the cards were growing grimy, he remarked, "by passing through hundreds of hands." All the while, he was developing his notions about what the results meant. Early on he'd grasped that an inkblot was a little piece of life, a stand-in for a face, a landscape, a situation. In each case, Rorschach reasoned, we approach things in our characteristic way, looking for the same features, responding to the same factors.

He began to refine that original insight, sifting differences in the way people talked about the blots. He noticed again, for example, that schizophrenics tended to give odd and idiosyncratic replies that bore little relation to the actual shapes of the blots. Normal individuals, on the other hand, seemed to choose their answers from the same stock of conventional images—a butterfly, a flower, a fox—and the figures they pointed out could be readily perceived by others. Rorschach named this aspect of inkblot interpretation "Form."

Another element that interested Rorschach was the reaction to color. Here he made an intuitive connection to personal style: "It has long been realized that there must exist a very close relationship between color and affectivity," Rorschach observed. "The gloomy person is one to whom everything looks 'black,' while the cheerful person is said to see everything through rose-colored glasses." The reaction to "Color," he concluded, was an index to one's level of positive engagement with the outside world.

A third yardstick was "Movement," or the extent to which the person viewing the blot imagined its figures to be in motion. The perception of movement, decided Rorschach, was linked to the richness of one's interior life: it was "nothing other than the ability to create new, individual productions, the capacity for inner creation. In its finest development we call this artistic inspiration [or] religious experience."

As Rorschach had predicted, the inkblots proved useful as a diagnostic device. The asylum staff could "penetrate by way of the test into the world of the mentally ill to an amazing extent," noted a nurse at Herisau. "As time went on, we 'experienced' and 'knew' how, for example, an epileptic, a schizophrenic, or a neurotic responded to the test and therefore to his surroundings, and to life in general." Rorschach himself boasted to a friend that his procedure "provides a diagnosis so accurate that it strikes one with amazement." By now, however, he had caught a glimpse of even grander possibilities.

Rorschach's dream was to pierce the heart of personality itself, and in probing the relationships among his subjects' responses, he believed he'd done it. The ratio of Movement responses to Color responses—the tilt of one's attunement to inner or outer worlds—formed what he called the *Erlebnistypus*, or "experience type." Persons who gave relatively more Movement responses he labeled "introversives"; creative and imaginative, they were often socially awkward or distant. Those who volunteered relatively more Color responses he termed "extratensives"; they were sociable and easygoing though perhaps lacking in depth or emotional stability. "Dilated" types proffered an abundance of both kinds of responses, and their personalities exhibited the best qualities of introversives and extratensives; not so the dull "coarctative" types, who mustered few responses of either sort. According to Rorschach, every human being fell into one of these four categories.

Rorschach was awed by the incisiveness of this tool for exploring human nature. "In all the languages of the world," he asserted, "we would not find words enough to express the numberless nuances of personality originating from the experience type." But he didn't stop there. He imagined administering the inkblots repeatedly to children as they grew to adulthood, creating a detailed map of personality development. He pondered a study of the great paintings of past centuries, predicting that an analysis of form, color, and movement would reveal the mindset of entire epochs. And he proposed employing the test in anthropological work with faraway cultures. "The test itself is technically so simple—it can be done through an interpreter—that it may be done with the most primitive Negro as easily as with a cultured European," he proclaimed excitedly. Rorschach even asked the famous doctor and humanitarian Albert Schweitzer to show his inkblots to natives of the Congo (Schweitzer declined).

As Olga Rorschach put it, for her husband the test was "a key to the knowledge of mankind and his potential, a key to the understanding of culture, the work of the human spirit." His enigmatic inkblots were runes in which a whole life, even a whole era or civilization, could be read. And Rorschach allowed his dream to soar still higher, imagining finally that his creation would lead him to "a method of discovering the possibility of the unification of all men." As his ambitions for the test surged, so did his determination to share it with the world. Working feverishly, like a man with no time to waste, Rorschach began to set his theories down on paper.

Less than two years after he resumed the inkblot experiments, his manuscript was finished, a dense treatise on the method and its interpretation that he titled *Psychodiagnostics: A Diagnostic Test Based on Perception*. Though it borrowed from many sources, this was a singular and rather strange work. High in the Swiss mountains, Rorschach was lifted clear out of the currents of mainstream psychology, including psychoanalysis, then beginning its sweep of European thought. Though Rorschach was intrigued by this bold new perspective, he remained skeptical: "In Vienna they are soon going to explain the rotation of the earth analytically," he commented wryly to a colleague.

Instead, *Psychodiagnostics* reflected nothing so much as Rorschach's own divided nature. By the standards of the time, his studies were highly quantified and data driven. Psychiatric research in the early twentieth century often featured qualitative observations of a single patient; his large sample and precise records were the work of a serious scientist. But it was also the creation of an artist. An associate at Herisau explained: "Although Rorschach tended to stick to the material at hand with its empirical and statistical validity, we had the impression of seeing an artist at work, who made the real person come to life from this material because of his knowledge and his empathy. I often came to think of Michelangelo and his unfinished works, where a limb or an entire figure gradually arises from the raw block."

The book included twenty-eight case studies—vivid illustrations of Rorschach's method, and some of the first examples of personality assessment to appear anywhere. When shown the fourth card in the series, for example, one woman saw "a tiny king from a fairy tale . . . greeting two queens in waving veils who approach from right and left." She also discerned a "swan swimming along the bank of a river," "a bent over old woman standing in front of a tomb," and "two profiles of vagabonds with large, pendant lips." This was an "imaginative individual," Rorschach commented approvingly, with a "great ability to make experiences." Another woman, shown the same blot, replied only that it looked like the "skin of an animal." She was a "pedant," Rorschach noted brusquely, exhibiting "stereotypy, poverty of ideas and lack of originality." (He added: "This is the test of a housewife and such findings are not infrequently seen in this group.") From an individual's responses to a stack of inkblots, Rorschach believed, he could learn everything he needed to know.

Rorschach assumed that the world would be as impressed as he by this breakthrough. An early sign that it would not be so came in December 1918, when Rorschach presented a preliminary report of his work to Herisau's medical association. The event was a flop: a handful of country doctors, more used to setting bones and delivering babies, looked utterly baffled by the young psychiatrist's bold conjectures.

Surely the more sophisticated judges of Europe's scholarly presses would see *Psychodiagnostics* for the revelation it was. In 1919 he sent the manuscript, along with his fifteen favorite blots, to half a dozen publishers. All refused it. Though disappointed, Rorschach remained resolute. Later that year he wrote to a friend, "Unfortunately we are still having difficulties with the publication," adding with caustic humor, "You see, nothing but dark things. Black spots and black souls."

Rorschach revised his manuscript and submitted it again in 1920. It might have failed for a second time to find a publisher if not for the intervention of Walter Morgenthaler, Rorschach's friend and a respected psychiatrist. Morgenthaler persuaded a small Swiss press, the House of Bircher, to print twelve hundred copies, but even so, Bircher balked at the expense of reproducing fifteen blots. Rorschach reluctantly agreed to reduce the number to ten, and the book was issued at last in June 1921. With publication, however, came a new crisis: the printers had turned Rorschach's crisp black-and-white blots into muddles of shaded gray. Surprisingly, the author welcomed the error, deciding that the mottled effect provided new opportunities for interpretation.

Much harder to accept was the yawning indifference and occasional hostility that greeted the book's arrival. Switzerland's only psychiatric review ignored *Psychodiagnostics* completely, and other European journals published only brief summaries. The most sustained attention the book received came at the annual meeting of the German Society of Experimental Psychology, when the prominent psychologist William Stern took the floor to denounce Rorschach's test as contrived and superficial. Almost every copy remained in Bircher's basement, and the publisher made it known that he was sorry he'd ever taken it on. The book was a losing proposition for its author as well: Rorschach's wife estimated that he earned only 25 Swiss francs (about five dollars at the time) for his labors.

Then, suddenly, Rorschach fell ill. On April 1, 1922, he was rushed to Herisau's hospital and diagnosed with peritonitis, an inflammation of the membrane lining the abdominal wall. By ten o'clock the next morning, he was dead at the age of thirty-seven. "Few destinies are more pathetic than that of Hermann Rorschach," laments his biographer, who suggests that his subject actually died from heartbreak over the failure of his cherished dream.

At the time of Rorschach's death, his test was still a work in progress; he considered it already obsolete upon publication, and continued to modify and improve it. Emil Oberholzer, another psychiatrist friend, arranged for the posthumous publication of one of his papers, noting that when Rorschach died, "he was in the midst of his promising elaboration of the numerous problems raised by the experiment. His work approached that of a genius, and heralded a new phase in the study of psychology. The bulk of his experience and conclusions went with him to his unfortunately early grave."

Now it seemed unlikely that the test, which had only a few champions like Morgenthaler and Oberholzer, would survive its creator. "Being permitted to watch Rorschach and share this experience with him was a great gift and an enrichment for us," reflected one Herisau colleague. "But also a deep fate, for when he was no longer among us, there was nobody to turn to who really knew the 'Rorschach.' " As if piling on, Bircher soon went bankrupt, and its stock of *Psychodiagnostics* was sold off at auction.

But confounding all expectations, "the Rorschach" was about to acquire a new lease on life, in the most improbable of places: America.

On July 4, 1934—Independence Day—Bruno Klopfer sailed into the wide-open embrace of New York Harbor. Beckoned by the Statue of

Liberty, Klopfer and his small son, Walter, made it safely to shore, where Walter mistook the holiday festivities for a personal welcome. On his part, Klopfer was able to accept his new nation's hospitality knowing that he had not arrived empty-handed: a set of Rorschach inkblots was packed in his bags.

The Klopfers were German Jews, fleeing the increasingly powerful Nazis. In Berlin, Klopfer had been a successful psychologist, with his own radio program and a position on the staff of the Berlin Information Center for Child Guidance. But once the government began issuing instructions on how Aryan and non-Aryan children were to be treated, Klopfer, though assimilated, could not ignore the threat. At school one day, Walter watched a classmate taunted on the playground, and asked the principal why. "Well, he's a Jew," the principal replied. Puzzled, Walter went home and asked his father, "What's a Jew?" "I'll tell you next week," Klopfer answered. By the next week they were gone, escaped to Switzerland—on their way, ultimately, to America.

While in Zurich, Klopfer learned how to administer the Rorschach, and he brought this expertise with him to the States, where he procured a position as a research associate at Columbia University. Rumors of the Rorschach had preceded him, and were generating more excitement about the test than had ever been seen in its native land. Now word of an expert's arrival spread swiftly among the university's psychology students. Though the students clamored for an official course in the Rorschach, Columbia's professors, suspicious of this European import, would not allow it. So Klopfer began holding informal meetings in his Brooklyn apartment two evenings a week.

The classes did not always go smoothly. For one thing, recalls an early participant, Klopfer "did a little wishful thinking concerning his capacity to use English." More important, students and teacher together discovered how much Rorschach had left undone. His fevered work and early death meant that basic questions of administration and scoring remained unsettled, and the meetings went long and loud into the night as the group thrashed out some answers.

In spite—or partly because—of his exotic accent, Klopfer began to attract a devoted following. Small and bespectacled, he talked softly but radiated an unexpected charisma. "Whenever he walked into a room, everyone stopped speaking," remembers one acquaintance. He had a warm and intimate presence that made those around him feel deeply understood, but he also sported a playful and mischievous side, delighting in jokes and puns. Modest and unpretentious, he preferred cardigans and sandals at a time when academics still wore suits and wingtips.

There was only one subject on which the low-key Klopfer grew impassioned: the Rorschach. It was this fiery zeal, along with his talents as a teacher and organizer, that made Klopfer the center of the growing Rorschach cult in America. Legends sprang up about his almost magical ability to extract detailed information about people—their gender, age, occupation, appearance—from a written record of their test responses. Trying to see what they saw in the inkblots, he would hold the cards inches from his face, giving rise to rumors that he smelled or otherwise uncannily absorbed the essence of Rorschach's forms (in fact, he was simply extremely nearsighted).

Meeting in kitchens and living rooms, debating the Rorschach over home-cooked meals and at impromptu parties, the group around Klopfer felt as if it were forging a new approach to the study of human nature. He and his associates produced a mimeographed newsletter, the *Rorschach Research Exchange*, to share new findings and work out disagreements about the test. Still, the movement retained a furtive air. Though the Rorschach was eagerly adopted by psychology graduate students, their professors were wary, even actively antagonistic. Some adherents had to hide Rorschach materials from their superiors; most continued to convene in private apartments, in coffeehouses, even in an abandoned movie theater rather than in classrooms.

In this covert fashion, the Rorschach made its way across the United States, spread by conversation and debate rather than lectures and textbooks. It met with an enthusiastic reception, at least among younger clinicians, because there was simply nothing else that did what the Rorschach claimed to do: describe the entire individual. Intelligence tests (such as the Stanford-Binet Intelligence Scale) were available, but as a psychologist of the time pointed out, these hardly explained all: "Persons who were intelligent, some at uppermost reaches, behaved very unintelligently." There were a few one-dimensional tests that measured whether someone was "neurotic" or "introverted." But these seemed hopelessly flat next to the richly detailed portraits that "wizards" such as Klopfer could draw from the Rorschach.

Inside this small but spirited circle, Klopfer was honored as an heir to Hermann Rorschach and his intuitive artist's sensibility. He was not alone, however, in claiming the mantle of the Swiss psychiatrist. Another expert was fast making a name for himself within the tight community around the test. The efforts of these two men would both assure the Rorschach's rise in America, and bring about a crisis that threatened to take it down.

Samuel Beck was very different from Bruno Klopfer: reserved and serious, he lacked Klopfer's personal appeal and impish sense of humor. He grew up in Ohio as the son of Romanian immigrants, and his brilliant performance in school won him a fellowship to study at Harvard, where he enrolled in 1912.

At the end of his third year at college, however, his father fell ill and could no longer work. Beck returned home to help support the family, a break in his schooling that was to stretch on for a decade. He got a job as a newspaper reporter, first at the *Plain Dealer* and then at the *Cleveland News*, covering the juvenile and criminal courts. It was an eye-opening experience for the young scholar. "I saw some of the best murderers that a big city has, the best robbers, bootleggers, and embezzlers and people of high ranking who got into trouble," Beck said proudly. He realized that while before he had only understood life "at the surface," now "I was seeing things directly."

In his late twenties, he resolved to return to the university to finish his formal education. He wanted "to find out what it's all about," he said, and decided to study psychology in order to discover "what there is to know by scientific method as to what the human being is like." Proceeding to psychology graduate school at Columbia, he learned about the Rorschach during a research fellowship. To Beck, scientific accuracy was paramount: "I had to have evidence. I had to know what I was talking about," he explained. "Here I saw a test in which I could present the same set of stimuli to any number of people and set up standards . . . [that would meet the] demands of science." He was so impressed with the inkblot test that he traveled to Switzerland to study with Rorschach's friend Emil Oberholzer.

Once there, however, Beck was appalled by the loose, intuitive way European psychologists applied the test. Returning home, Beck wrote the first English-language manual for the Rorschach, laying out precise directions for its administration and scoring. Soon Beck, like Klopfer, attracted a following of his own—one based on the scientific side of Rorschach's divided legacy.

By the late 1930s, Klopfer and Beck were the leading lights of the Rorschach community, a community that was growing larger and livelier by the day. Around the inkblot test, recalled one devotee, "there was feverish activity, unbridled enthusiasm and optimism. We thought we had an instrument which would reveal personality in depth." Proponents reached for metaphors to convey the power of their revered Rorschach: it was "a psychological microscope," "a fluoroscope into the psyche"; it provided a "blueprint of the personality's structure," a "foolproof X-ray of a personality." With their missionary zeal, these "Rorschach workers," as they called themselves, gathered more and more converts to their cause.

Even mainstream psychology began to embrace the test. Before the start of World War II, formal courses on the Rorschach were offered at only two American universities, and an English translation of *Psychodiagnostics* was not published until 1942. In the years following the war, however, the Rorschach would be taught in almost every major psychology program in the country. By 1950, more dissertations and journal articles would be written about the Rorschach than about any other test; between 1955 and 1965, research on the test was streaming forth at the rate of a dozen publications a month. Even William Stern, the German psychologist who had harshly criticized the Rorschach upon its introduction, was led to recant. Aware of the Rorschach's growing success, in 1938 Stern and a student devised their own version, the Cloud Picture Test. It was all but ignored, a pale imitation of the real thing.

So great was the belief in the Rorschach's powers, in fact, that in the war's wrenching aftermath it was called upon for an extraordinary investigation.

In 1934 Bruno Klopfer had fled Germany, bearing the Rorschach as his ticket to a new life in America. Scarcely more than a decade later, a colleague of Klopfer's named Douglas Kelley brought the now-famous inkblots back across the ocean. The Nazis had been vanquished by the Allies, and twenty-two of their most feared and hated leaders were being held in solitary confinement at the Nuremberg jail. The International Military Tribunal would soon try them for war crimes, putting them on trial for their lives. But before the law decided their fates, psychology would pass its own verdict.

During the war, Kelley served as chief of psychiatry for the European Theater of Operations; in civilian life, he was a Rorschach expert who coauthored a book with Klopfer. He and an associate, Columbia University psychologist Gustave Gilbert, were the only people permitted to speak freely with the imprisoned German leaders. Sitting knee to knee with the Nazis in their narrow cells, Kelley and Gilbert showed them Rorschach's inkblots and recorded their often-striking responses. Rudolf Hess, Adolf Hitler's deputy, saw "two men talking about a crime, blood is on their minds." Robert Ley, head of German labor, first saw "a funny bear, fur spread out." When asked to elaborate, he became agitated: "You can see the head and teeth with terrific legs. It has shadows and peculiar arms. It is alive and represents Bolshevism overrunning Europe," he gasped. ("Once started on this point, there was a short intermission until we could get Dr. Ley off the subject of Bolshevism and back to the subject of Rorschach cards," Kelley noted.)

Most compelling among their subjects was the brutal Hermann Göring, mastermind of Germany's concentration camps and commander of its air force, the Luftwaffe. At first Göring was scornful: "Oh, those crazy cards again," he exclaimed as Kelley pulled out the blots. After repeated exposures to the Rorschach, however, he came to admire its acumen, even telling Kelley that he was sorry that the Luftwaffe "had not had available such excellent testing techniques." He grew personally attached to Kelley, as well; the psychiatrist reported that the ruthless Nazi "wept unashamedly when I left Nuremberg for the States."

Once home, Kelley drew on the "Nazi Rorschachs," as the records came to be known, to produce an acid critique of American as well as German culture. "Strong, dominant, aggressive, egocentric personalities like Göring, differing from the normal chiefly in their lack of conscience, are not rare," Kelley insisted in 22 Cells in Nuremberg, published in 1947. "They can be found anywhere in the country—behind big desks deciding big affairs as businessmen, politicians, racketeers." Elsewhere he warned: "There are undoubtedly certain individuals who would willingly climb over the corpses of one half of the people of the

States, if by so doing, they could thereby be given control over the other half."

But perhaps even more remarkable than the content of his analysis was its basis: a personality test that had only recently achieved even grudging acceptance. Kelley and Gilbert had been granted exclusive access to the most infamous malefactors alive, in the hope that a handful of inkblots could provide answers to profound questions. Once reserved for philosophers and moralists, such questions—about good and evil, normality and deviancy—were now to be decided by psychologists. And although the Nazi Rorschachs had no effect on the fates of the German leaders, the same could not be said for the millions of ordinary Americans who would take the inkblot test in years to come. Their responses would help determine whether they kept or lost custody of a child; whether they deserved punishment for their crimes or compensation for their injuries; whether they were fit to do dangerous and important jobs. So while its role at Nuremberg was a symbolic triumph for the Rorschach, it was also a very real challenge: if society was to grant such great authority to a test, it would one day have to prove it was worthy.

Back in America, the Rorschach's phenomenal rise came just as its core group of advocates was riven by a dramatic feud. The question at the heart of the conflict had been there from the beginning: is human nature a subject for art or for science?

Bruno Klopfer was firmly on the art side. His European training, clinical orientation, and empathetic personality inclined him toward a subjective understanding of people and away from what he disdained as the dry formulas of literal-minded psychologists. He refused to sacrifice insight and intuition, he cried, "on the altar of a fetishistic goddess 'Statistic.'" Samuel Beck stood just as resolutely on the side of science, grounded there by his American education, his research focus, and his aloof character. A truly scientific investigation of human nature, he argued, required a precise and uniform approach on the part of every examiner. "It would go far towards clearing up the present state of confusion," he snapped, "if Klopfer and his associates ceased to identify their method by the term 'Rorschach.'"

Their deep differences broke out into the open in the late 1930s with a nasty altercation in the pages of Klopfer's *Rorschach Research Exchange* (intended, ironically, as a forum in which to amicably settle such debates). The two traded blistering criticisms of each other's technique, then lapsed into glowering silence, refusing any further contact. What had been a tight if ragged band of followers split into warring camps. To the loyal Beck and Klopfer supporters were soon added three additional factions, breakaway groups led by disaffected former disciples. Now there was not a single "Rorschach," but five separate systems, each with its own rules for administering and interpreting the test.

The discord among various partisans, as passionate about these small differences as they had once been about the test itself, seemed to mock Rorschach's dream of "the possibility of the unification of all men." His singular vision of a key to human nature had almost faded away after his death. Was it in danger of disappearing again?

———————■———————

This is an ordinary classroom: green chalkboard, flicker of fluorescent lights, merry hum of an overhead projector. But as the students begin to speak, a menagerie of strange and fabulous creatures is set loose: a butterfly lady and a bearded dragon, a rabbit doing a rabbit dance and bugs playing hide-and-seek; girls with feathers in their hair, a frog with its tongue sticking out, a monster wearing a bow tie. A Rorschach expert once called the test "an experimentally induced dream," and indeed these intoxicating images seem to have alighted from some realm beyond wakeful awareness.

It's just before nine on an April morning in 2003, and nineteen students are gathered on the campus of Columbia University to learn about the Rorschach. Seventy years after Bruno Klopfer was forced to hold classes in his apartment, the test is now taught here and in the great majority of other graduate programs across the country. Still, the Rorschach hasn't quite shed its raffish aura: this class is meeting on a Saturday, and it's being taught by an instructor from another institution, since this particular program (at the university's Teachers College) has no resident Rorschach expert of its own.

Barry Ritzler is a professor of psychology at Long Island University and one of the Rorschach's staunchest advocates. Short and stocky, he has a round, pleasant face and a voice that rises often with enthusiasm.

His gray slacks and dress shirt are standard-issue, but his tie is something else: a bright splatter of red and blue. Standing at the front of the room, he has asked the students to tell him about the test results they've been receiving from the patients they work with as part of their training. Interpreting Rorschach responses is a difficult and arcane craft, like building ships inside bottles, and he is guiding them through the process with solicitous care.

"In Card VI, my client saw monsters and a volcano," offers one student, a young woman in jeans and sneakers. "Are the monsters *on* the volcano, or climbing *up* the volcano?" inquires Ritzler. Assured that it is the latter, he replies, "Well then, that's a Movement response." Another student asks what it means when her patient insistently focuses on one small area of the blot. Ritzler tells her that such responses indicate a narrowness of perspective, as contrasted to whole or "W" responses: "W's indicate someone who's ambitious—like you guys," he explains. "You're graduate students at Columbia, living in New York. That kind of ambition takes a lot of W's." Hands raised, brows furrowed, the students pose question after question.

It seems that the Rorschach is still inspiring the kind of confusion that kept Klopfer's followers arguing all night, and that later cleaved the entire community into quarrelsome factions. But today there is a difference. Every one of the students has the same thick book before her, *A Primer for Rorschach Interpretation*. Ritzler, too, has a smaller pocket-sized guide, which he consults often as he parses the fine points of Form, Color, and Movement. Just as frequently, he refers in his remarks to a mysterious figure named "Dr. Exner," always invoked with a certain awe. Dr. Exner appears to be the ultimate authority, the court of final appeal for the disputes that the Rorschach provokes with such regularity.

After a break for lunch, Ritzler places on the overhead projector a Rorschach protocol as interpreted by Dr. Exner and his associates. The score sheet is an intimidating mass of letters and numbers and symbols, dense notations that look as if they might be a formula for rocket fuel. Gently but firmly, Ritzler leads the class step by step through Dr. Exner's analysis of the patient, a troubled fifteen-year-old boy who saw a hissing cat, a squashed ant, and naked wrestlers in the blots.

"So that's that," Ritzler says, stepping momentarily into the projector's glare. He blinks; the *F*s, *C*s, and *M*s of the score sheet are spelled out across his face and across the broad front of his shirt. "Any questions?"

But who is this Dr. Exner? In 1953, John E. Exner Jr. was a psychology graduate student at Cornell University who'd become infatuated with the Rorschach. When he saw the blots for the first time, he recalls, "I was awestruck at the prospect of being permitted into the inner sanctum of clinical psychology." A year later, he had the opportunity to study with Samuel Beck himself. Arriving one day for their lunchtime meeting, Exner saw the older man stiffen. "What's that?" Beck asked suspiciously. Exner showed him the small green volume he was carrying: *The Rorschach Technique*, by Bruno Klopfer. "Where did you get that book?" Beck demanded.

Exner, who knew nothing of the simmering feud between the two men, was intrigued by the depth of feeling Beck betrayed. The following summer, he apprenticed himself to Klopfer. "I fell in love with *both* those guys," he relates. "They were like godfathers to me." Like the child of divorce who imagines he can bring about his parents' reconciliation, Exner set out to heal the rift between his two mentors. "I had hoped that because they were so very nice to me, [I could] get them to sit down in a room with a tape recorder and I would interview them about their differences, and maybe they could come together," he says wistfully.

Beck and Klopfer would have none of it. In the years since their split, the differences between their approaches—indeed, among all five of the Rorschach systems—had only hardened. Each group continued to add its own flourishes and refinements, embellishing an already complex instrument until, some warned, it was becoming too ungainly for routine use. But still the elaborations piled up: there was "Shading," for example, the perception of light and shadow, said to reveal a sense of helplessness, and "Texture," the attribution of a tactile quality to the blot, believed to indicate a need for emotional contact. Then there were lists of "signs," specific responses that were thought to point to whole syndromes or conditions: homosexuality, suicide-proneness, brain damage. Some innovators even introduced content analysis of the kind Rorschach rejected: they viewed the subject matter of individuals' responses as telling, especially in relation to themes evoked by particular blots: Card VII became the "mother card," Card VI the "sex card," and so on.

Since Beck and Klopfer refused to resolve their differences, Exner decided in 1961 to conduct a comparative evaluation of their work, a kind of beauty contest in which he would judge the winner. The two experts consented, each assuming that his own method would prevail. But this appraisal, which took almost a decade and eventually included all five Rorschach systems, did not end in the result anticipated by either. Exner, as one contemporary notes, is "a very, very good politician," and his final decision was prudently diplomatic. Of the five procedures, he wrote that "although each included some highly valuable components, each was also scored by serious liabilities. None was uniformly superior to the others." What was necessary, he concluded, was not the elevation of one of the existing techniques, but the creation of a new system that combined the best, most "empirically defensible" elements of each. Exner, it seems, had a dream of his own.

The Comprehensive System, first published in 1974, was John Exner's answer to Hermann Rorschach's "key to the knowledge of mankind"— Rorschach's dream, updated and improved. Building on the bedrock of the same ten inkblots, Exner constructed a gleaming new edifice, a self-conscious shrine to science. For despite his politic protestations to the contrary, Exner *had* chosen sides, at least philosophically: Beck over Klopfer, science over art.

In truth, he had no choice. American psychology had matured in the years since the Rorschach was introduced, and it had grown overwhelmingly in one direction: toward more precision, more quantification, more standardization. A new class of personality questionnaires—called, perhaps overconfidently, "objective" tests—was overtaking the Rorschach in popularity. And a wave of fresh research, conducted not by Rorschach advocates but by ostensibly impartial psychologists, was casting serious doubt on the now-battered inkblot test. "Until proponents of the Rorschach can produce evidence" to support the usefulness of their test, read one 1965 review, "it seems not unreasonable to recommend that the Rorschach be altogether abandoned in clinical practice and that students of clinical psychology not be required to waste their time learning the technique."

Into this quagmire rode Exner, as if on a white horse. His scientifically minded synthesis, regularly updated, provided welcome reinforcement to the Rorschach faithful and persuasive evidence to those on the fence. The Comprehensive System quickly became the universal standard, taught in universities, applied by researchers, and used by psychologists to this day. In 1998, a grateful American Psychological Association gave him one of its most prestigious awards, declaring, "Exner has almost single-handedly rescued the Rorschach and brought it back to life. The result is the resurrection of perhaps the single most powerful psychometric instrument ever envisioned." The Rorschach had been snatched from oblivion once again.

Today the Rorschach is administered hundreds of thousands of times a year, given to Americans in settings as diverse as schools, workplaces, prisons, and the military—both to detect psychological problems and to delineate general personality characteristics. Among mental health professionals, it is the second most popular personality test available; in a recent survey, eight out of ten clinical psychologists said they included it in their test batteries at least "occasionally," and four out of ten reported that they "frequently" or "always" used it. Psychology students like those in Barry Ritzler's class are routinely trained in the Rorschach: 93 percent of all graduate programs approved by the American Psychological Association teach the test, and 90 percent of clinical practitioners in the field believe that psychology students should be skilled in Rorschach assessment.

But just when it looked like the Rorschach's place in psychology was secure for some time to come, its star-crossed fate stepped in again. Twenty years after John Exner "resurrected" the Rorschach, it was due for one more near-death experience.

The first blow to the reinvented Rorschach was struck in January 1996. That was the month that James Wood, a University of Texas psychology professor who would soon emerge as the Rorschach's leading detractor, and two coauthors published a highly critical article in the respected journal *Psychological Science*. "Basic issues regarding the reliability and validity of the Comprehensive System have not been resolved," they alleged. Judgments made about people who take the test are often based on insufficient evidence or are simply wrong, they said, and Exner's supporting studies are frequently flawed or inadequate. These problems, they contended, "are so fundamental as to raise questions about the Comprehensive System as a whole."

Other critics soon joined Wood in his attack: "There is currently no scientific basis for justifying the use of Rorschach scales," wrote a pair of scientists in *Psychological Assessment*, concluding that decades of research had managed to give the Rorschach only "meager support" as a useful and effective test. A psychologist at the University of Pittsburgh called for an immediate moratorium on the administration of the Rorschach outside the lab, warning that clinicians would continue to draw inaccurate inferences about people if use of the test was not halted. Another group of critics, writing in *Psychology, Public Policy, and Law*, pointed out that the Rorschach's popularity was no assurance of its value: after all, they noted, at one time "phrenology was in vogue."

Some Rorschach adherents reacted angrily to this barrage: on an e-mail discussion list devoted to the test, one furious correspondent denounced Wood and his associates as "terrorists" and "assassins." But most of them, secure in their belief in the test, remained casually dismissive. Barry Ritzler calls the criticisms "a bunch of hooey," adding, "I tell my students who've had half a semester of Rorschach instruction that they know more about the test than these guys." Irving Weiner, president of the International Rorschach Society, brushes off "this so-called controversy," saying airily, "The Rorschach is a wonderful old test, it's been around for eighty years or so now, used by generations of psychologists, all around the world, who have found it pretty useful."

But perhaps they should be more concerned. For once, most of the passion seems to be on the side of those who would do away with the Rorschach. James Wood is an amiable man, with owlish glasses and chipmunk cheeks. When he talks about the inkblot test, however, he is unsparingly harsh. "If psychologists used tea leaves instead of the Rorschach, we'd probably be better off, because then, at least, no one else would take the results seriously," he says.

The test's potential defects first came to Wood's attention when he was asked to consult on a custody case involving allegations of child abuse. He was troubled to learn that although the mother in the case was described by several trustworthy sources as honest, caring, and sensible, her Rorschach test labeled her seriously disturbed, prone to pathological lying, and unable to express affection to her children. "I didn't know then that the Rorschach was a hoax," says Wood. "I started digging into the research." The result was a series of articles beginning with his 1996 publication in *Psychological Science*, and eventually a book, *What's Wrong With the Rorschach?*, written with M. Teresa Nezworski, Scott Lilienfeld, and Howard Garb and released in 2003.

Wood and his coauthors' numerous criticisms of the Comprehensive System come down to three very serious charges. First, many of its scores have "essentially zero validity"—that is, when the Rorschach reports that a test taker is depressive, or narcissistic, or overly dependent, that person is quite likely not to exhibit those traits at all. In part that's because the Rorschach makes claims about a large number of human qualities, often based on scant evidence. For example: under the Comprehensive System, if a test taker reports seeing just one "Reflection"—a mirrored image in what are, after all, symmetrical blots—he or she is deemed egocentric, with "a marked tendency to overvalue personal worth." If the test taker discerns a single item of food, that individual "can be expected to manifest many more dependency behaviors than usually expected," according to Exner. Only a handful of the more than one hundred variables in the Comprehensive System, says Wood, have stood up under investigation. (His contention is supported by a study published in the *Journal of Clinical Psychology*, which found that only 20 percent of Comprehensive System scales examined by the article's authors could identify a statistically significant difference between groups of normal people and groups of people with serious mental illness.)

The second of the group's criticisms concerns the "norms" provided by the Comprehensive System, or the standards of normality against which test takers are judged. The Rorschach routinely "overpathologizes" healthy people, Wood and the others maintain, making them seem much more dysfunctional than they really are. "If Rorschach scores for a normal adult are interpreted according to Exner's norms," they write, that person will appear "self-focused and narcissistic," "unconventional with impaired judgment and distorted perceptions of reality," "depressed, anxious, tense, and constrained in emotional expression," "insecure and fearful of involvement," "vacillating and inefficient," with "low empathy," "a tendency to withdraw from emotions," and "poor emotional control." The Comprehensive System's model of normality, they say, doesn't actually represent normal people.

Their third point of contention takes aim at the very foundations of Exner's method. In the edition of the Comprehensive System published in 1993, Exner cites mostly his own research to support his claims for the Rorschach's usefulness. Less than a quarter of these works, however, take the form of science's gold standard: articles published in peer-reviewed journals. More than half are unpublished studies from the Rorschach Workshops, a series of seminars organized by Exner (Barry Ritzler has often led them).

Since 1968, the Rorschach Workshops have produced more than a thousand studies, but many of these have never been published—and some of them have not even been *written*, existing only as raw data. "I make no apology" for relying on such loosely compiled data, insists Exner. Many of these investigations, he says, were conducted at the workshops by graduate or post-doctoral students who "really didn't want to take the time to sit down and write a fifteen- or twenty-page paper and submit it" to a professional journal.

When Wood and others asked to see some of this research, which forms the empirical underpinnings of the vaunted Comprehensive System, they encountered resistance from Exner and his staff at the Rorschach Workshops. The psychologists were told that some of the studies were not in the workshops' files, and that others could not be released. They could get raw data related to specific questions, but they might have to pay for the cost of retrieving it from the organization's antiquated computer system. On at least one occasion, Exner refused outright to show research to Wood and his colleagues.

In a field that relies on the scientific method of peer review, open debate, and the free exchange of information, such practices are, to put it mildly, unusual. "It's outrageous," declares Scott Lilienfeld. "I think it's a scandal. They say that these studies support their claims about the Rorschach's effectiveness, but then they won't share those data with other people. They can't have it both ways."

Wood et al.'s claims about the Rorschach's lack of validity, skewed norms, and questionable scientific support might seem like yet another bitter internal battle, of interest only to its bloodied combatants—except for one thing: the Rorschach's regular appearance in our nation's courts.

■ ■ ■

Today the Rorschach inkblot test is used in a great variety of ways: to diagnose the mentally ill, to evaluate troubled children, to select candidates for high-risk jobs, even to check out professional athletes and
Catholic priests. (The screening process for applicants to Roman
Catholic seminaries and religious orders, in fact, includes the Rorschach
almost half the time.) But one of its most common, and most controversial, uses is as evidence in criminal and civil legal cases. Along with interviews and other tests, the Rorschach is often employed to determine
whether accused criminals should be held fully responsible for their actions. In a recent survey, 32 percent of psychologists reported using the
Rorschach in criminal forensic evaluations; in another poll, the test
ranked third among forty instruments administered by forensic psychologists. The Rorschach has been given to a number of notorious criminals, including John Hinckley Jr. (who saw skulls, bones, empty eye
sockets, and shrunken heads) and Jeffrey Dahmer (whose responses, a
psychologist testified at his murder trial, "were normal to the point of
being mundane"). Rorschach test results also contribute to decisions
about sentencing and parole.

When plaintiffs in civil cases avow emotional distress, the Rorschach
is often brought in to help validate their claims: a 1999 survey of forensic psychologists found that the test was used in almost a third of
emotional-injury assessments. Damages in the hundreds of thousands or
even millions of dollars can hang on the results of the inkblot test. Recently, psychologists have warned that crucial information about the
Rorschach—including, in some cases, the blots themselves—has begun
appearing on Internet sites intended to help test takers manipulate their
results. Estimates of the rate of deliberate deception on tests taken in a
legal context run as high as 60 percent. Indeed, a survey of lawyers who
frequently handle cases requiring psychological evaluations found that
42 percent believe that "an attorney should provide a client with as
much specific information as possible about psychological testing," including the kind of information most likely to facilitate cheating.

Finally, the Rorschach frequently plays a role in custody cases, used
to determine whether mothers and fathers are fit parents and whether
children have suffered abuse or neglect. A 2001 survey of psychologists

who conduct child custody evaluations found that 44 percent of them used the Rorschach, making it the second most frequently used test for this purpose. In this context, too, advice on exploiting the test is showing up on the Web. "It's not fair to be separated from your family because you saw a wolf instead of a butterfly," explains the operator of one such site, a Seattle-area divorced father who asked to be identified only by his first name, Waylon. Waylon's criticisms of the Rorschach, though more forcefully expressed, echo those of Wood and other scientific critics. "If you research the Rorschach and find out where it came from, you will laugh yourself silly," he confides. "It was created as a parlor game."

The Rorschach, then, is used to make enormously important decisions that affect the lives of millions of Americans. Yet an increasing number of experts are convinced that it shouldn't be allowed into court at all. Two of these critics, psychologist William Grove and lawyer R. Christopher Barden, have argued strenuously that the Rorschach "clearly fails to meet the standards for admissibility" set out in recent Supreme Court decisions. These standards should bar the inkblot test as evidence, they believe, because it's simply too flawed: "In our opinion, the adjudicated rights of citizens should not turn on such an error-prone way of obtaining diagnoses and personality descriptions." Their contention is seconded by Robyn Dawes, a psychologist at Carnegie Mellon University and a former member of the American Psychological Association Ethics Committee. "The use of Rorschach interpretations in establishing an individual's legal status and child custody is the single most unethical practice of my colleagues," he declares. Having such momentous decisions ride on the outcome of a Rorschach test, he says, "amounts to losing one's civil rights on an essentially random basis."

Science—including psychological science—does and should play a role in the courtroom. But it must be sound science, and mounting evidence demonstrates that the Rorschach doesn't qualify.

There are signs that the skeptics' offensive against the Rorschach is having an effect. A survey of forensic psychologists published in 2003 found that a majority rated the Rorschach "unacceptable" for use in many of the tasks they perform for the court, including evaluating an individual's risk of violence and competency to stand trial. Some lawyers and expert witnesses say that they now avoid reference to the test in court, if only because it's so readily ridiculed by the other side's attorneys. Thomas Grisso is an authority on psychological assessment who tests litigants and offers testimony in courts around the country. "I use the Rorschach a lot less than I used to because I don't want to put up with the kind of cross-examination I get," he says. "It's very easy for an attorney to make you look silly—to say, 'I see a butterfly here—does that mean I'm crazy?' I'll stand back and ask myself, Is the information I'm going to get from the Rorschach worth the aggravation and the damage to the credibility of my other testimony? Typically, the answer is no."

The Rorschach has also become a casualty of managed care's crusade to cut costs. In 2000, a work group convened by the American Psychological Association to examine the status of psychological assessment reported that the practice is "under assault" by insurance companies and health-maintenance organizations, which increasingly refuse to pay for time-consuming or scientifically dubious tests. Besieged by questions about its validity, and taking several hours to administer and interpret, the Rorschach is an inviting target. John Hunsley, a University of Ottawa psychologist and Comprehensive System critic, notes wryly: "The changing of hearts and minds among Rorschach diehards is a long-term prospect, but not getting reimbursed for giving the test may have a more immediate impact."

The row over the Rorschach has even grown loud enough to reach the public's ears. In an article reprinted in newspapers across the country, *The New York Times* asked in February 2001, "What's in an Inkblot?" and answered, "Some Say, Not Much." It spotlighted Wood, Lilienfeld, and Garb and their contention, as the *Times* reporter wrote, that the Rorschach is "seriously flawed and should not be used in court or the consulting room." More attention to their claims followed the March 2003 publication of *What's Wrong With the Rorschach?*.

Rorschach expert Irving Weiner shrugs off this popular coverage, remarking jovially that "I wouldn't have had my picture in *The New York Times* if this thing hadn't happened." He and other advocates may be genuinely unworried, but there are hints that a shift in their strategy is underway. In 1994 Weiner declared in the *Journal of Personality Assessment* that the Rorschach test "is not a test" at all, but rather a "method," and that users should forthwith refer to it as the RIM (Rorschach Inkblot Method). Skeptics suggest that Weiner, aware that the

Rorschach could not meet the strict standards psychology applies to instruments calling themselves "tests," elected simply to remove the Rorschach from that category.

In the same vein, perhaps, are the comments offered by Gregory Meyer, assistant professor of psychology at the University of Toledo in Ohio. Meyer is a rising star in the Rorschach world, in line to become what Barry Ritzler calls the next great "guru" of the Rorschach. The controversy around the inkblot test "has to do with different views of human nature and different views of what it means to be a psychologist," says Meyer. "Those who find the Rorschach useful are people who are really interested in understanding clients in complex ways, who attempt to see them in three dimensions, who believe that people are put together in complicated ways." Those who reject the Rorschach, on the other hand, are "opposed to, or at least ambivalent about" seeing individuals in all their manifold glory.

The argument has a familiar ring: it's the old art-versus-science debate, revived by a movement that tried, and failed, to make science its ally. Should it prove necessary, the ever-resourceful Rorschachers still have one more trick up their sleeves.

Given its repeated death-defying recoveries, the Rorschach should never be counted out entirely (one exasperated psychologist calls it "the Dracula of psychological tests, because no one has been able to drive a stake through the cursed thing's heart"). This time, however, the inkblot test may have met its match. James Wood and his fellow critics have made a persuasive case that the Rorschach is bad science: invalid, unreliable, imprecise. These failings are especially dangerous in settings like the courts, where validity, reliability, and precision are indispensable attributes of any evidence used to make life-changing decisions.

But the Rorschach, at least as it's used today, is also bad art. We need art—literature, music, Hermann Rorschach's beloved drawing and painting—as well as science to make sense of human nature, and we value it for just those qualities that science can't provide: its suppleness, its subjectivity, its intimacy. Today's Rorschach, with its rigid dictates and picayune rules, can't provide them either. There is one way, however, in which the Rorschach is indisputably vital, and likely to remain so no matter what the outcome of the psychologists' debates: as an idea.

Hermann Rorschach contributed to the culture two seminal concepts, and the culture has reciprocated by making his name and his images ubiquitous: in everyday speech, in journalism, in advertisements, even in cultural totems like Andy Warhol paintings and *New Yorker* cartoons.

The first is that people seek to find meaning where there is none. As John Exner himself has pointed out, the only logical answer to Rorschach's famous query "What might this be?" is "It's an inkblot"— but generally, only the severely mentally ill give it. The rest of us see flamingos, fairies, beetles, butterflies: evidence of an adaptive, and entirely human, need to make the world make sense. Rorschach's second inspiration is that the ways we create meaning are highly individual and idiosyncratic. What we attend to and what we ignore, what draws our eye or rouses our imagination—these are telling facts from which we can learn much about ourselves and each other.

These ideas offer a profound insight into human nature, even if they don't quite constitute "a key to the knowledge of mankind." But such a key was Rorschach's grandiose dream, shared by his successors and by almost all those who would test personality. Nearly a century later, it's a dream from which they have not yet awakened.

THREE

Minnesota Normals

A bicycle, a radio, an electric circuit: there seemed to be nothing that Starke Hathaway couldn't put together with his own hands. As a boy growing up in Marysville, Ohio, in the early decades of the twentieth century, Hathaway loved to tinker, to take things apart and see how they worked. When he was eight years old his family let him set up a workshop inside a big crate in the backyard. In high school, Hathaway founded a group called the Boys' Science Club, whose members read a textbook titled *Electricity and Magnetism* and met once a week to discuss it.

Hathaway simply assumed he would become an engineer. When he arrived at Ohio University in 1923, however, he found to his surprise that he was more interested in the delicate machinery of the human mind. He began studying psychology, but he didn't relinquish his role as a tinkerer. He saw, in fact, that the disjointed discipline of psychology could use some tweaking and tightening: "This is the unknown field," he said to himself. "This is the field with room." After graduation he proceeded to the University of Minnesota, where he acquired a PhD in psychology and then a position at the school's mental hospital.

Lank and angular, Hathaway had a long, narrow face crowned by a Strangelovian fluff of hair. His expression was usually somber, and he blinked frequently behind his thick-lensed glasses. He spoke slowly, with long pauses and with a flat Midwestern accent: *dee*-vice, auto-*mo*-bile. He seemed permanently distracted. To talk with Hathaway "one first had to get his attention, which was often engaged elsewhere," notes an acquaintance. He forgot the names of his students and colleagues, even of the leaders in his own field, and would refer to "that man who wrote the book about psychopaths," or "that woman with the book about psychological theories." He often went coatless in Minnesota's frigid winters; he sometimes wore shoes that didn't match.

But beneath his apparent fogginess he was fiercely intelligent and keenly observant. "You had to watch your language around him, because he was very quick to pick up on slips of the tongue," says a former research assistant. It was rumored that Hathaway had an uncanny talent for "mind reading," and he became known as a particularly insightful therapist, to whom colleagues would refer puzzling or difficult cases. Staff members in Hathaway's office were regularly obliged to avert their eyes as one or another august figure from the campus or the community arrived for an appointment.

Hathaway was also stubbornly independent, skeptical of authority, and unimpressed by precedent. In college and graduate school he was introduced to the grand theories of human nature proposed by psychology's early eminences. "I took little interest in them because I considered the systems to be premature," Hathaway later remarked. "Data for their rigorous validation were not available, and one merely wasted time on them because they would not be enduring; in the meantime, they tended to distract one from more profitable studies." Such studies, in his view, involved not airy speculations but practical, efficient interventions.

Even while working as a psychologist, Hathaway kept on building things. He designed devices that marked off short intervals of time, that delivered pulses of electrical stimulation, and that monitored the electroconductivity of the skin. The earnings from these assorted contraptions yielded enough money for Hathaway to marry his wife, Jinny, and to buy a house in Minneapolis. Once a homeowner, he equipped his garage door to respond to a signal from his car (long before such gadgets were commercially available), and he rigged a canvas awning to roll out over a patio at the first drops of rain. It was not uncommon for Hathaway to show up for class with fresh grease stains on his trousers.

But Hathaway's most famous invention by far was an entirely different kind of machine: a test that gauged human nature itself. Pragmatist that he was, Hathaway never indulged the notion that he was creating some comprehensive key to personality. Step by logical step, however, he was nonetheless constructing a scale on which millions of people would one day be measured.

At the time Hathaway was hired, the University of Minnesota was modernizing its mental hospital, and its newest employee brought his ingenuity to bear on the unusual needs of such a facility. "We had many devices to keep patients from hanging themselves and rounded corners to keep patients with epilepsy from falling and knocking holes in their head, and that sort of thing," said Hathaway. He laid sound-carrying conduit throughout the hospital so that conversations could be recorded "from anywhere we wished," and he set up an elaborate system of buzzers. "If you were in one of our new rooms and a girl patient began to be too forward with you or a male patient began to be too strong with you, in two corners of the room there were buttons and you could go push these and help would come running, theoretically." He harrumphed. "Practically, there was enough accidental pushing of buttons that help didn't usually come, but that was the idea."

Hathaway could make or fix just about anything the new building required. The patients, however, were another matter. He often evaluated them alongside a team of psychiatrists and physicians. "As we went on grand rounds, I with my white coat and newly developing sense of role, expected that the medical staff would want the data and insights of a psychologist," he recalled. "I still remember one day when I was thinking this and suddenly asked myself: Suppose they did turn to me for aid in understanding the patients' psychology? What substantive information did I have that wasn't obvious on the face of the case?" Armed only with intelligence tests and a few crude personality tests, Hathaway was forced to acknowledge that he had little enlightenment to offer.

An opportunity to show that psychology could make a genuine contribution soon appeared, emerging, he said, out of "sheer frustration." At the time, neither psychiatry nor psychology had many effective treatments for severe mental illness. One promising new possibility was insulin coma therapy (ICT), an admittedly brutal procedure that entailed placing a patient in a temporary state of unconsciousness with a high dose of insulin. It had been discovered that such comas sometimes brought about improvements in schizophrenia. Along with electroshock therapy, introduced around the same time, it offered the only hope for many of those suffering from the grim disease.

The difficulty was that ICT was dangerous, with a mortality rate as high as 10 percent, and psychologists could not tell in advance who would benefit from the treatment. There was simply no way to know if the wards at one clinic were like those given ICT at others, because there was no universally accepted way to classify the mentally ill. Hathaway saw a problem he could fix: what if he devised a pencil-and-paper questionnaire that sorted patients cleanly into categories? Such a test, he realized, would have uses far beyond its application to candidates for ICT.

Something similar (though more limited) had been tried during World War I, after American military commanders in Europe had cabled home an urgent message. The horrors of a new kind of warfare—powerful explosives, poison gas, trench fighting—were breaking down their men's minds and bodies. Soldiers were suddenly blinded, or lost the ability to smell or taste. Whole chunks of their memories went missing. They forgot how to walk. Some stared mutely, unable to speak. Others seemed to become entirely different people: silent men turned garrulous, prudent ones turned careless; polite men became coarse, aggressive ones became meek. Doctors diagnosed these as cases of "lost personality."

Robert Woodworth, a professor of psychology at Columbia University, volunteered to produce a test that would pick out vulnerable recruits before they reached the battlefield. Working quickly, he composed a list of 116 questions: "Does the sight of blood make you sick or dizzy?" "Do you nearly always feel that you have strength or energy enough for your work?" "Are you often frightened in the middle of the night?" A quick count of no's and yes's provided an index of "neuroticism," thought to be a crucial predictor of shell shock. Early tryouts on new conscripts and returning veterans were promising, but peace intervened before it could be put to wider use. And though the test—called the Personal Data Sheet to those who took the test, the Psychoneurotic Inventory among those who gave it—was employed after the war in a civilian version, its true significance was as a template for a much more important test to come.

The Personal Data Sheet was perhaps the world's first "personality inventory": a written test on which individuals were asked to respond to questions about their psychological state. Others soon followed: tests for maladjustment, for introversion, for dominance. They formed a starting point for Starke Hathaway's efforts at the Minnesota mental hospital, but he soon saw that they were hopelessly inadequate. "No existing personality test was worth anything at all," he scoffed. To begin with, most of them focused on just one dimension, while he intended to survey the whole spectrum of disorders.

For another thing, their questions were laughably transparent. The Personal Data Sheet, for example, made inquiries like "Do you usually feel well and strong?" and "Are you happy most of the time?" The test had worked well enough in wartime, when, as Hathaway noted, "men who were afraid and who considered themselves unfit for war were offered symptoms that permitted them to admit the fact." But when peace returned, so did the vanity, self-consciousness, and shame that made test takers reluctant to confess such weaknesses. Without imminent combat to coerce honesty, something more subtle was called for.

But perhaps the most puzzling deficiency of these tests was how often they were simply wrong. Most had been developed in the same straightforward fashion: a psychologist had decided which questions to ask and which answers indicated abnormality. Such decisions were really no more than educated guesses, and not infrequently, these guesses were mistaken. Robert Bernreuter was a Pennsylvania State University psychologist who designed one of the era's most popular tests, the Bernreuter Personality Inventory. In it he posed the question "Are you critical of others?" surmising that a positive response suggested psychological difficulties. As it turned out, more than two-thirds of normal people taking the test answered "yes," a reply given much less frequently by neurotics and psychotics. Likewise, the query "Do you daydream frequently?"—assumed by Bernreuter to be a sign of psychological instability—was endorsed more often by healthy individuals than by the mentally ill.

People, it seemed, had the inconvenient habit of contradicting psychologists' expectations. Hathaway wanted an instrument that didn't let ideas about human nature get in the way of its reality, and since he couldn't find the tool he needed, he set out to make it himself. His test would be a machine fueled by solid facts, not by the thin vapors of theory and conjecture.

In this project, Hathaway had a partner: University of Minnesota neuropsychiatrist J. Charnley McKinley. McKinley was, if possible, more hard-nosed than Hathaway on the subject of scientific rigor, and just barely forgave his protégé for not being a psychiatrist. "Psychology was not a reality with him," Hathaway said of his collaborator. "But I was a reality with him." Hathaway's knowledge of anatomy and physiology made him a helpful adjunct to McKinley, and the younger man often assisted at brain surgeries as students looked on in the medical school's great amphitheater. Hathaway had his own reasons for allying with McKinley: the psychiatrist's involvement gave him access to the extensive resources of the university's hospital and medical school.

The pair began by collecting as many symptoms of mental illness as they could find. They trawled psychiatric textbooks. They pored over case studies. They quizzed their colleagues. And they borrowed items from other personality tests, lifting several straight from the Personal Data Sheet. In a move that would cost them much trouble later on, McKinley insisted that they also include questions of a strictly medical nature. "McKinley was not wholly an advantage to me at that time," Hathaway noted tactfully. "Most of those items I would have kept out if I could have. But being diplomatic I could not, because McKinley felt that no proper, meaningful group of items could leave these out." As a mere psychologist, Hathaway acquiesced.

Before long the two men had amassed over a thousand potential questions for their test; by eliminating redundant items, they pared the list to about half that. But then Hathaway and McKinley did something revolutionary. Instead of assuming that they already knew how normal and abnormal individuals would answer their queries, they let the people decide. In this republic of the insane, citizens were allowed to vote—with their fears, their neuroses, and their obsessions. As Hathaway put it: "We permitted the patients to design their own test."

Using large groups of subjects in psychological research was itself a relatively new phenomenon. In the discipline's early days, experiments frequently involved just one participant: the investigator himself. His method was that of introspection, or observing and recording his own mental processes. Even after individual differences among people became a point of interest, research was usually conducted with only a handful of subjects, often individually identified by name or initials. Introspection remained the method of choice, and many scientists believed that participants had to be highly trained (generally, psychologists themselves). In 1893 Edward Bradford Titchener, a leading experimental psychologist, insisted it was folly to believe that "since we are all using our minds, in some way or another, everyone is qualified to take part in psychological experimentation. As well maintain, that because we all eat bread, we are all qualified to bake it."

This approach began to change early in the twentieth century, when advances in statistical procedures—and the need to sort and manage large numbers of people—led to the notion of a comparative norm. Now an individual's performance was of interest only in relation to the averaged scores of others, a generalized standard one could match or fail to meet. Information was gathered not through introspection but objective measurement, and the subjects of experiments need not be sophisticated self-observers, only naïvely natural. In 1904, the American psychologist James McKeen Cattell delivered a cheeky retort to Titchener: "It is usually no more necessary for the subject to be a psychologist," he said, "than it is for the vivisected frog to be a physiologist."

For Starke Hathaway, of course, abnormal subjects were easy to come by. Relying on his own diagnostic judgment, he selected groups of patients with "pure," uncomplicated cases of particular disorders: first hypochondriacs, later depressives, psychasthenics, hysterics, psychopathic deviates, hypomanics, paranoiacs, and schizophrenics. (Some of these classifications are no longer in use or go by other names.) But where to find a sufficient number of normal people?

As it turned out, they too were right under the psychologist's nose: pacing the corridors, fidgeting in the waiting rooms, downing another cup of coffee in the cafeteria. Hathaway hit upon the idea of using the friends and family members of patients at the university's regular hospital as a control group, and soon he and McKinley were "testing visitors and anybody else we could get hold of who came into the hospital and said he was not under a doctor's care." By trolling hallways and lobbies, Hathaway found 724 presumably sane subjects for his research.

The members of his scavenged comparison group had a few things in common with each other: They were all Minnesotans. They were all white. Almost all were Protestant, and many were of Scandinavian descent. They ranged in age from sixteen to fifty-five, with an average age of thirty-five. Almost all were married, and many were parents. The majority were rural people, employed as farmers, blue-collar workers, and housewives. They had an average educational level of eighth grade. This rather small and provincial group soon came to be called the "Minnesota Normals," and though no one could have guessed it at the time, they were to form psychology's major benchmark of normality for the next fifty years.

Now Hathaway had his subjects, normal and abnormal, and he had his long list of symptoms. All that remained was to put the latter to the former and find out which items "discriminated": which questions effectively distinguished the Normals from the psychiatric patients. The answer ("true" or "false") given by the majority of Normals to a particular question became, ipso facto, the normal answer; the answer offered by the majority of, say, depressives became, ipso facto, a sign of depression. The items that discriminated best—that produced the cleanest divisions between normal and abnormal—were the ones included in the questionnaire.

This was a radically new way of creating a test, and its results were often confounding. Early personality tests like the Bernreuter Personality Inventory and the Personal Data Sheet were "face-valid," meaning the intent of the questions was clear on their face. Test givers, and more importantly test takers, understood what was being asked and why. Not so with this test. Even its creators were often at a loss to understand why the normal answer to one question should be "false" instead of "true," or why a second question seemed to tap one form of mental illness rather than another. "Frequently the authors can see no possible rationale to an item in a given scale," Hathaway and McKinley noted in an early paper, adding stoically, "it is nevertheless accepted if it appears to differentiate."

This aspect of the test developed at Minnesota was to inspire much controversy in coming years, not only among the public but among Hathaway and McKinley's professional colleagues. One critic assailed their "who-gives-a-damn-why-it-works attitude"; another, the prominent psychologist Gordon Allport, denounced what he called "galloping empiricism," which "dashes forth like a headless horseman." Such an approach, he protested, "has no rational objective; uses no rational method other than mathematical; reaches no rational conclusion. It lets the discordant data sing for themselves."

To Hathaway, however, the "discordant data" sounded sweeter than any mellifluous strains of theory. His test was the epitome of "dustbowl empiricism," the just-the-facts style of science practiced in the nation's sturdy Midwest. Let the New York psychoanalysts have their tortuous theories about Oedipal complexes and death drives; Hathaway just wanted something that worked.

But for all the plain pragmatism that went into its development, the test Hathaway and McKinley ultimately produced was without a doubt one of the weirdest creations in the history of man's attempts to understand himself. One observer has puckishly, though accurately, described it as "a Joycean soliloquy in Whitmanic rhythms, the interior monologue of a neurotic modern Everyman."

There was the content of the items (written as bald statements, to be countered "true," "false," or "cannot say"). McKinley's insistence on the inclusion of medical topics meant there were lines like "I have never had any black, tarry-looking bowel movements" and "I have had no difficulty starting or holding my urine." There were questions about sex: "I have never indulged in any unusual sexual practices," "There is something wrong with my sex organs." There were questions about religion: "I believe there is a Devil and a Hell in the afterlife," "Everything is turning out just like the prophets of the Bible said it would." And there were questions that were simply odd: "I think I would like to belong to a motorcycle club," "Often I feel as if there were a tight band around my head."

Even stranger than the content were the items' flat, affectless tone and their careless alternation of the weightiest subjects with the most banal. "I loved my father." "I like to flirt." "I believe my sins are unpardonable." "I have a good appetite." The items seemed stripped of context, as though one were overhearing a conversation on Mars: "I think Lincoln was greater than Washington." "Women should not be allowed to drink in cocktail bars." Some statements sounded pious and prim: "A large number of people are guilty of bad sexual conduct." Others sounded almost frisky. "If the money were right, I would like to work for a circus or carnival." Altogether, the test—504 items long—presented its takers with an often distasteful, often tedious, always bewildering experience.

At the time, no one worried much about how peculiar and potentially offensive the test might be. This was a minor venture, designed specifically for mental patients, intended for use at a thirty-eight-bed hospital in snow-swept Minnesota. But that was all about to change.

■ ■ ■

Admittedly, the test's formal introduction to the world was not auspicious. Hathaway and McKinley gave it a long, awkward name: "Minnesota," because that's where it was made, "Multiphasic," because it measured a number of different dimensions. ("I remember being in McKinley's office one day," trying to come up with a term to describe this feature of the test, said Hathaway. "We scrounged around and finally came up with this name, 'multiphasic,' which is a Greek-Latin bastard, and that satisfied us for the moment.") Lastly, "Personality Inventory," because it was meant to catalogue all relevant aspects of abnormal personality. The resulting mouthful—the Minnesota Multiphasic Personality Inventory—was almost immediately shortened to MMPI.

The MMPI had to overcome obstacles other than its name. Hathaway had chosen an unconventional format for the test: instead of listing the items on a sheet of paper, he had typed each one on a three-by-five-inch slip, creating something like a deck of cards. Test takers were instructed to sort the deck into three piles according to their answers: "true," "false," or "cannot say." Hathaway had speculated that people would be more willing to admit to embarrassing thoughts or practices if they didn't have to put it in writing, but many users found the card format confusing and cumbersome.

Perhaps most discouraging for the test's prospects, the country was still emerging from the Great Depression, and few companies had the resources or the inclination to reproduce Hathaway's strange invention. He and McKinley approached three major test-publishing firms about distributing the MMPI. All three declined ("unduly awkward and impractical," demurred one). Finally, the University of Minnesota Press agreed to take it on, if its authors would put up half the money. Hathaway and McKinley found a patron to contribute the requisite sum, and in 1942 the presses started to roll—at the university printing shop. "We were beggars, not choosers," Hathaway wryly observed.

But their test—what Hathaway and McKinley called "an easily applicable measuring device"—soon piqued the interest of psychologists and psychiatrists around the country. There were a number of reasons for its unexpected appeal. As had been true for the Rorschach, there were few other options available to test givers who wished to survey the entire personality. But the MMPI also had distinct advantages over the Rorschach and over existing personality questionnaires. Its relentless emphasis on quantification avoided the taint of unscientific artistry that still clung to the inkblot test. And its scrupulously empirical construction made it more valid and reliable than tests based on clinicians' best guesses.

The MMPI's major innovation, however, were the clever devices Hathaway had built into the test to detect false or careless responses. A common charge made against self-report questionnaires (especially by Rorschach proponents) was that these tests were easily faked. After all, the critics demanded, would we trust an intelligence test that asked people how smart they were? In response, Hathaway designed special scales—sets of questions with separate scoring keys—that would alert the test giver to a possibly duplicitous subject.

Actually, Hathaway had long had an interest in uncovering deception. As a senior in college, he devised a rudimentary lie detector and "got a little notoriety," he recalled, when he used his machine to help find a thief who'd stolen a diamond ring. He became a consultant to the police in Athens, Ohio, assisting them on a murder case, and later worked with law enforcement in Minneapolis and St. Paul to develop psychological profiles of at-large criminals.

The first of the traps Hathaway laid in the MMPI was the Feeble-mindedness Scale, meant to identify test takers who could not read the items or who were responding randomly. Individuals who offered answers different from an overwhelming majority—at least 90 percent—of the Minnesota Normals could be identified by an elevated score on this measure. Answering "true" to "Evil spirits possess me at times," for example, would raise a red flag (but so would responding "false" to "I believe in law enforcement").

Even more ingenious was the Lie Scale, intended to foil those who would deliberately place themselves in a flattering light. Hathaway included in the test a number of items like "I do not always tell the truth," and "I gossip a little at times." A truly conscientious person might honestly answer "false" to a higher-than-average number of these items, noted Hathaway and an associate, "but for a person to have six or eight of them seemed almost impossibly good." (Interestingly, high scores on the Lie Scale are not infrequently obtained by members of the clergy—who might really be saintly, or who might feel the need to present themselves that way.)

Most sophisticated of all was the Correction Scale, which came about after Hathaway noticed that obviously disturbed patients occasionally generated perfectly normal results. With a student, Paul Meehl, he developed a scale to detect "defensive" responding by mentally ill people wily enough to answer as if they were sane.

With such fine tuning, Hathaway succeeded in building a better test than any other available. Though he largely declined to promote it, his graduate students were not so modest. As they departed the university to take teaching jobs all over the country, they carried with them their faith in the "Minnesota Way": quantified, empirical, objective. If the "Multers," as they called themselves, lacked the cultish fervor of the Rorschachers, they did have an unshakable confidence that science was on their side.

Early on, the test also received midcentury America's ultimate salute: a story in *Time* magazine. "By using the inventory, a physician may know a new patient, in an hour or two, as well as his family doctor does," exclaimed the article, which also featured a photograph of Hathaway and his trademark fluff of hair. ("This picture aroused a certain amount of amusement among my colleagues around here," Hathaway remarked dryly. "Those who knew me best said, 'Why did he slick his hair down so?' and those who didn't know me at all said, 'Why didn't he comb his hair?' ") The newsmagazine noted that the MMPI "is already the most widely popular test for its purposes . . . in use in universities, penitentiaries, corporations, [and] clinics."

Three years later, in 1946, a medical journal reported that the MMPI "is used routinely by hundreds of private clinics and individual doctors; it is part of the personnel procedure in some of our largest corporations; it was used by individual medical and psychological personnel in all theaters of war . . . [and] it is used today in all veterans' administration medical clinics." Demand for the test soon grew so intense that Minnesota's press couldn't keep up. "The university printing office was doing nothing but Multiphasics. The whole doggone place was covered with them," Hathaway marveled. "A new producer had to be found." In 1947, just five years after Hathaway and McKinley had gone begging, the distribution of the MMPI was assumed by The Psychological Corporation, one of the country's largest test-publishing companies. By then, Hathaway noted with some satisfaction, "the Corporation was glad to get what they had turned down earlier." Within fifteen years, the MMPI would become the world's most widely used objective personality test.

Unhappily, Charnley McKinley didn't live to see the success of the test he'd had a hand in creating. Already in failing health by middle age, McKinley made Hathaway promise to help him kill himself if he ever became seriously disabled. In 1945, when he was fifty-three, McKinley suffered a cerebral hemorrhage, which had the odd and awful effect of destroying his ability to express emotion. Hathaway, hoping he might recover, could not bring himself to assist his friend's suicide. McKinley slashed his own throat but failed to cut his main artery. Hathaway recounted quietly: "Later that evening I sat in the big medical amphitheater, watching our best surgeon put McKinley's neck back together." McKinley died five years later.

In a sense, however, the MMPI that achieved such popularity was not the same test that McKinley had helped to design. In the years following its initial publication, a subtle but important transformation took place, a shrewd shift that obscured a simple fact: judged on its own terms, the MMPI was a failure.

The original purpose of the MMPI, of course, was to sort a group of mental patients into diagnostic categories. A high score on the Depression scale would indicate the presence of depression; a high score on the Schizophrenia scale would point directly to schizophrenia. If a test taker's responses were plotted on a graph, Hathaway expected to see a large spike on a single dimension. But that's not what happened. As the MMPI became more widely used, psychologists began reporting that their patients showed such elevations on several scales at once, and that normal people were often elevated as well. Hathaway's sleek machine was looking more like a lemon.

By now, however, the MMPI had a core of committed users—many of them Hathaway's former students—and they were determined to get their test up and running again. Perhaps there was meaning, they suggested, in the *patterns* of scores that test takers produced. Such patterns would describe not simple categories but complex syndromes, and would therefore be more accurate than Hathaway's original groupings. A test taker who rated high on both the Psychopathic Deviate and the Hypomania scales, for example, was a very specific sort of person: aggressive and impulsive, with a careless conscience and an inclination to bend the rules. Likewise, the individual who achieved elevations on the Depression and the Hysteria scales was something more than the sum of these two conditions: she was likely to be moody, insecure, and dependent, with a sensitivity to criticism and a tendency to play the martyr. This new use of the old MMPI provided not an elementary diagnosis but a comprehensive profile.

As the approach gained ground, an even grander possibility came into view: What if the MMPI could be used to describe *normal* personality types? The scores of normal test takers, though less elevated, also fell into distinctive patterns. By this measure, every one of us was an assemblage of ailments, mild or severe—some composite of tendencies toward mania, hysteria, paranoia, depression. A test that had been designed to spot pathological extremes of behavior was now expected to sort out the much subtler differences among normal people.

Soon MMPI users abandoned the original names of the scales, replacing them with numbers: the Hypochondriasis scale became Scale 1, the Depression scale became Scale 2, and so on. A neat shorthand was thereby created: a person could now be referred to as a "4-9" or a "2-3," the numbers summing up the personality with brisk economy. Minnesota graduate students and others trained to think in terms of the MMPI found its abbreviations becoming a reflex, a language to describe not only patients but acquaintances, friends, and family. Guides to these numerical sequences and what they meant, called "codebooks" or "cookbooks," began to be compiled. Paul Meehl, once Hathaway's student and now his colleague, applauded the fact that at last personality description could become "an automatic, mechanical, clerical kind of task." Each person was a lock, and the MMPI held the precise combination.

Profile coding, as the method came to be called, was a brilliant stroke, for it didn't just preserve the MMPI as a test for the psychologically troubled. It expanded its use exponentially, to spheres far beyond the mental ward: business suites, army barracks, courtrooms, high schools, doctors' offices. By the early 1960s, the MMPI was given at least as often to normal people as to psychiatric patients, used to screen job applicants, offer vocational advice, settle custody disputes, and determine legal status. The MMPI had expanded in a philosophical sense as well: from a utilitarian tool designed to solve a specific problem, the test had become a key to personality, a code breaker that would decipher at last the enigma of human nature.

So sweeping were the test's claims, and so heavy-handed were its methods, that the MMPI was bound to inspire a backlash. In the middle of the 1960s, it arrived.

"I have never seen anything to equal the outrage and indignation from government employees, their families and their friends," thundered Senator Sam J. Ervin Jr. The date was September 24, 1966, and the setting was a hearing on Capitol Hill. Ervin, a Democrat from North Carolina and chairman of the Senate Constitutional Rights Subcommittee, had called the hearing to address complaints that the government's use of personality inventories was invading its workers' privacy. Ervin had been an early critic of the communist-hunting tactics of Senator Joseph McCarthy, and of wiretapping and eavesdropping by government and industry. He saw similar dangers in personality testing. "Clearly, the government should not send out an investigator to peer through an employee's or an applicant's bedroom window," he had declared before the hearing. "Neither should the government ask, through subtle psychological questioning, what a person does and thinks after he draws the curtains."

Unease about the increasingly prevalent use of personality tests like the MMPI had been growing for more than a decade. In 1956's *The Organization Man*, William Whyte sounded a warning about the stifling conformity such tests imposed on American executives. Whyte even included a half-serious guide to giving the boss the answers he wants: "I loved my father and my mother, but my father a little bit more. I like things pretty much the way they are. I never worry much about anything. I don't care for books or music much. I love my wife and children. I don't let them get in the way of company work." More explicit critiques, with titles like *The Brain Watchers* and *The Tyranny of Testing*, appeared in the early 1960s. Newspapers and magazines ran investigative exposés under such headlines as "The Snoops" and "The 'I Love My Mother' Tests." There were even reports of public burning of test data by parents angry that their children were given the questionnaires at school.

In 1965 and 1966, a series of congressional hearings compelled the testers to respond to their critics. For decades, psychologists were the ones asking the questions; now they would be interrogated about their own motives and methods. They knew the stakes were high: Ervin had introduced a bill, cosponsored by thirty-five senators, that would severely limit or even eliminate personality testing in government. This "barrage," wrote one psychologist, "is the most serious attack that has ever been launched by citizen groups or by government against any part of psychological research or services."

The testers mounted an impassioned self-defense, both at the hearings and in the pages of professional journals and popular magazines. They began by insisting that their intentions were pure. Hathaway himself published a long "Letter to Mr. R," replying to a correspondent's questions about the MMPI: "I hope you will see," he implored, "that its origins were motivated toward virtue." They were no "peeping toms," the psychologists protested, but serious scientists doing worthy work. Many people are made nervous by doctor's visits, noted Hathaway's former student W. Grant Dahlstrom, "but there is no corresponding legislative pressure now to outlaw the use of needles and scalpels in the practice of medicine." The apparent intrusiveness of personality tests was all for your own good, the testers told the public, and with a little education you'd see that, too.

"To change even a comma in an item may change its meaning," Hathaway explained, adding that though he would alter some MMPI items "if I could," the value of decades' worth of research depended on the test remaining exactly the same. Besides, shrugged another psychologist, "as one cannot make an omelet without breaking eggs, so one cannot find out anything important about personality without some pointed questions." Growing confident, the testers turned the tables on their critics, insinuating that their opposition to the MMPI was evidence of prudishness or irrationality. They even hinted that it grew out of the accusers' own (presumably warped) personalities.

Their tactics worked. Senator Ervin's law failed to pass, the media frenzy died down, and the picketers outside the American Psychological Association ("Help stop psychological sex tests. Write your Congressman") packed up their signs and went home. Lost in the hoopla over the supposed immorality of using the MMPI to test workers was "the real issue," noted psychologist Malcolm Gynther a few years later, "which is that the test wasn't devised for this purpose and isn't effective for predicting who will be a good employee." The gears of Hathaway's personality-measurement machine kept on clicking.

———■———

Walt Disney World was already a curious choice for the 1998 meeting of Rent-A-Center managers. The giddy whirl of theme park rides and the melting heat of a Florida September made an odd setting for talk about the rent-to-own couches and coffee tables that were the company's stock in trade.

Things got even stranger early one morning when the managers were herded into a chilly conference room. They had been scheduled to participate in a budgeting workshop, but company leaders instead announced an abrupt change in plans. Employees would immediately begin taking the Management Test, a five-hour battery of nine separate examinations.

"We thought, 'Uh-oh, this must be that test we've been hearing about,' " recalls Art Staples, then a manager of several San Francisco-area stores. Rent-A-Center had been bought by another firm just a month before, and word had gotten out that the new company required all employees to take a long and demanding test. "There was nothing we could really do except refuse to take it, walk out of the room—and find our own transportation back to California," Staples says.

The managers knew, too, that their score on the test could determine the course of their careers at Rent-A-Center—or even whether they had a job at all. "We had been told that if you did not pass the test, then you would not be allowed to work in management," says Scott Hadley, another store supervisor from the Bay Area. "We were afraid that if we failed, we would be let go."

An anxious hush fell over the room as the exams were passed out. Within minutes, however, the silence was breached by a stir of astonishment. "People were looking around at each other with this expression of, 'You've *got* to be kidding me,' " Staples recalls. The questions in front of them had nothing to do with renting furniture, or managing employees, or keeping the books.

"My sex life is satisfactory." "I have diarrhea once a month or more."

"I would like to be a florist." "Everything tastes the same." "My mother was a good woman." "I am a special agent of God." Arriving at the question, "I liked *Alice in Wonderland*, by Lewis Carroll," the managers might well have felt that they had slipped down the rabbit hole. The test, of course, was the MMPI.

Hadley and Staples were offended and angered by the personal nature of the items. "These questions had no relation to what we did for a living, to whether we were good managers or not," Hadley says. "Our employer just didn't need to have all that information." He was particularly struck by an item that read, "I like tall women." "How was I supposed to answer that?" he asks. "My wife is five foot three."

Things only got worse when the test's results were returned. Rent-A-Center hired an outfit in Kansas, Associated Personnel Technicians, to produce an extensive personality description of each manager: how self-sufficient, self-confident, and dominant he or she was, how fearful, depressive, and impetuous. Most needed work in one or more of these areas, APT advised, and so each profile included a specific plan for improvement. Employees who were "restless and impatient" should lay off nicotine and caffeine, they counseled; workers with the "tendency to retreat from reality" should drink lots of water.

APT prescribed reading material, too: managers who were found to be "independent and hard-headed" should take in *How to Read a Person Like a Book*, while those "resistant to rules and codes" should review *Your Erroneous Zones* and *Codependent No More*. These self-help books, the anonymous sages at APT directed, should be read "one chapter at a time, with a significant person in his life. After reading and discussing each chapter, he needs to write down what he has learned that is new to him and what he is actually doing differently, then submit these two sentences per chapter to his training supervisor for further discussion."

Of Scott Hadley, APT concluded: "He makes assumptions without checking them out. We suggest he learn to ask more of the 'how' type questions to validate his assumptions and expectations and avoid the 'why' type questions." Hadley was also instructed to read *I Ain't Much, Baby—But I'm All I've Got*. "Stupid pop psychology," says Hadley, who declined to do his required reading. "If I actually needed help I would go to a professional, not read some book I could buy at Wal-Mart."

For his part, Art Staples was admonished to write out daily "self-affirmations" to build his self-confidence. He rather confidently refused. "I thought I was a pretty good person and had been pretty successful," he says, "and if they felt that they could somehow improve me—you know what, thank you, but I like the way I am."

Like Scott Hadley and Art Staples, an increasing number of American workers are finding that an intrusive personality test is the price of getting or keeping a job. Today the MMPI (in an updated version) is employed by 86 percent of clinical psychologists and administered, by one estimate, to 15 million Americans each year. Some of these are mental patients like those for whom Hathaway originally designed the test. But many others are perfectly sane individuals: people who want to become doctors, psychologists, firefighters, airplane pilots, paramedics, nuclear power plant operators, law enforcement agents. The MMPI is used by 60 percent of police departments evaluating prospective officers, for example, and by 91 percent of psychologists screening applicants to Roman Catholic seminaries and religious orders. Personality tests featuring MMPI-like items are given to even more people, mostly job applicants in industries from retail to banking to security services.

But there are no congressional hearings, no newspaper headlines, no protesters with picket signs; whatever redress workers have received in recent years has come through the courts. That was the case for Scott Hadley and Art Staples, who filed a class-action suit against Rent-A-Center in 1999. The company agreed to a $2-million settlement, distributed among the employees forced to take the test. More important than the money, say the two men, was that Rent-A-Center promised to destroy all test records in California and to cease administering the test nationwide.

A small number of other cases have yielded similar results. The one that paved the way for the rest was *Soroka v. Dayton Hudson Corporation*, settled in 1993. A security guard named Sibi Soroka had applied for a job at a Target store in California, and was asked to take an exam called the PsychScreen—a combination of the MMPI and another test. "These are questions you wouldn't even answer for your own mother if she asked you, let alone some personnel director at some company you're not even sure you want to work for," said Soroka. "It doesn't take Einstein to figure out that these questions really don't have any bearing

on our world and life today, or certainly on a job walking around looking for shoplifters." Soroka's case was taken on by Berkeley lawyer Brad
Seligman, who likens Target's use of the MMPI in a workplace setting to
"killing a gnat with an atomic bomb." He presented to the court evidence indicating that the PsychScreen had a 61 percent false-positive
rate, rejecting as unfit six out of ten psychologically healthy applicants.

Seligman wrested a $1.3-million settlement from the company, the
first of several he would win from organizations accused of misusing personality tests. In 1995, he filed suit against Contra Costa County, a local
government in California that had administered an MMPI-like test to
welfare applicants. The questionnaire, which included items like "I believe everything is turning out just the way the Bible said it would" and
"Pornography and obscenity have become serious problems and must be
curbed," was intended to pick out substance abusers. Anyone who failed
it was labeled "chemically dependent," obligated to sign statements ad-
mitting to addiction, and required to participate in a six-month rehab
program (if they refused, they were denied welfare). The problem was
that—according to a study jointly commissioned by plaintiff and defen-
dant—the test incorrectly classified 44 percent of all applicants as addicts. The county agreed to pay $1.2 million to the mislabeled test
takers, and it stopped using the test.

Most recently, Seligman and three other lawyers initiated a lawsuit
against Burns International Security Services, part of the nation's largest
security guard company, on behalf of a job applicant named Mel
Thompson. Thompson was given a personality test that included
pointed questions about his political beliefs, including items like
"Workers usually come last as far as most companies are concerned,"
"Most companies make too much profit," "The drinking age should be
lowered," and "Marijuana should be legalized." The test amounted to "a
true-or-false pledge of allegiance to corporate America," says Seligman.
"Anyone who believes that employers are not perfect, or who believes
drug and alcohol laws should be modified in some way, flunks this test."
Burns agreed to pay up to $2.1 million to the eight thousand people
who'd answered the questionnaire.

Seligman has had some success fighting intrusive personality tests
with a handful of applicable laws: a California constitutional provision
that limits the invasion of privacy, a section of the California labor code

that bars discrimination against employees based on their political beliefs, and the Americans with Disabilities Act (ADA), which restricts employers' ability to make a medical examination a condition of employment. But this legal patchwork, different in every state, is hardly an impermeable defense against the spread of personality testing in the American workplace, and a few out-of-court settlements are no match for what has become a vast and growing industry.

As successful as the MMPI has been, its origins in the mental ward have imposed certain limits on its use: it must be administered by a psychologist, for example, and it is bound by the ADA's restrictions on medical examinations. (These restrictions may be waived, however, in the case of workers charged with public safety—such as airplane pilots, police officers, and firefighters—and indeed many of these workers are required to take the MMPI.) But no such caveats apply to the hundreds of MMPI imitators now on the market: tests that borrow its format, its language, even the unusual way it was constructed.

Though these tests are cheaper, shorter, and more readily available than the MMPI, all of the quirks of the original are preserved intact. There is the MMPI's smug piety: "This country needs higher moral standards." There are its opportunities for guilty confession: "I guess I know some pretty undesirable types." There are its muddled propositions: "Illegal use of marijuana is worse than drinking liquor." There are its suspiciously scrupulous assertions: "I have never wanted to buy things I couldn't afford." And there are its sweeping, context-free statements: "Most people would lie to get what they want." Anyone familiar with the MMPI will recognize the provenance of these items: Starke Hathaway's peculiar test, as reflected in the funhouse mirror of American capitalism.

Instead of measuring depression or mania or hypochondria, these personality tests set out to identify qualities of interest to employers: dependability, honesty, friendliness, and the "desire to follow rules, policies, and procedures," as well as the appropriate "customer service attitude." More important, such tests promise to screen out those who will be chronically late or absent, who will engage in theft or "computer abuse" (e-mailing and Internet surfing on company time), who will have "personal and/or transportation problems" and who will indulge in "counterproductive behavior" or "alienated attitudes." Still more ambitiously, these questionnaires purport to predict whether employees will be injured in a job-related accident, will file a fraudulent workers' comp claim, will abuse drugs or alcohol, or will engage in workplace violence. (One workplace personality test alerts employers to applicants who fit a "Litigious Profile" or a "Corporate Stalker Profile.")

The MMPI mimics even have their own versions of mental-patient groupings and Minnesota Normals. As promotional materials for one such test, the Step One Survey, explain, it "compares the applicant's responses with those of two distinctly different groups—recently released ex-convicts and long-term retail store employees with excellent work histories. The ex-convicts' crimes were predominantly offenses dealing with theft and drug use. Test items for the Step One Survey consist of questions in which there were statistically significant differences between the two groups." As another test purveyor puts it, their questionnaire will tell you "whether job applicants think like trusted employees or convicted felons."

Aggressively marketed to managers and business owners, these tests are often promoted with a dose of alarmism. One test provider's Web site features a photograph of smiling people dressed in business attire, over which flashes the message: "Which one physically hurt an employee? Which one faked an injury? Which one uses illegal drugs? Which one will be late for work? Which one stole $500 from their employer? We can tell you!" The terrorist attack of September 11, 2001, gave the personality-testing industry an additional boost. In a speech given five months after the tragedy, David Arnold, general counsel of the Association of Test Publishers, told an audience that "invasion of privacy—or rather, what the courts deem to be an invasion of privacy—may be a whole new ball game since September 11." Increased fears of terrorism, Arnold predicted, would both induce employers to do more testing and put them on safer legal ground when they did so. Indeed, testing companies around the country reported increased interest in personality tests following 9/11.

The test publishers' hard sell seems to be working: a 2003 survey by Management Recruiters International showed that 30 percent of companies now administer personality tests. But, as always, the tests' popularity is no guarantee of their value. To begin with, many of the characteristics they claim to measure are broad, fuzzy categories covering many kinds of behavior. For example, "the construct of honesty or integrity remains vague and ill-defined after more than 50 years of research," note two experts writing in the journal *American Psychologist* in 1995. Nevertheless, so-called honesty tests or integrity tests are administered by an estimated five thousand to six thousand U.S. organizations and taken by as many as five million Americans each year. These tests are scattershot in their attempts to target liars, cheats, and thieves. According to a review conducted by the federal government's Office of Technology Assessment, 95.6 percent of people who fail integrity tests are incorrectly classified as dishonest—an error rate far worse than that of the notoriously unreliable polygraph machine.

These "false positives" may be turned away from jobs and other opportunities before they've had a chance to demonstrate their probity. One test provider recommends that its questionnaire be administered in advance of an interview. "After all," goes the sales pitch, "if a candidate's integrity, reliability, work ethic, and attitudes toward substance abuse are below your requirements, why waste your valuable time even talking to them?" Full information about integrity tests (and about most other workplace personality tests) is often unavailable, since these are proprietary instruments of profit-making companies disinclined to submit their products to scientific scrutiny. For some integrity tests, "almost no evidence at all is available beyond assurances that evidence exists," reported a task force appointed by the American Psychological Association. The task force also found that more than half of integrity-test publishers do not require any training or other qualifications of people who administer their tests.

Less obvious, though perhaps more troubling, are several other aspects of workplace personality screens. First, the reflexive testing of job applicants may reduce employers' incentive to provide a constructive workplace. If emphasis is placed from the beginning on an employee's supposedly inherent, unchanging qualities, it's likely that little energy will go into on-the-job training, mentoring, or development. Second, the intrusiveness of the tests' items may itself carry a message. As social critic Barbara Ehrenreich, author of *Nickel and Dimed*, has observed:

"Maybe the real function of the tests is not to convey information to the employer but to the potential employee, and the information being conveyed is, You will have no secrets from us. We don't just want your time and your effort, we want your entire self." And lastly, recent financial scandals at Enron, WorldCom, Tyco, Adelphia, and other American companies should clue many employers that they're testing the wrong people. The billions of dollars allegedly looted by these firms' high-ranking executives make tardiness or "computer abuse" look like small change. A true test of integrity would be holding boss and worker to the same ethical standard.

Even as it absorbed the blows of grandstanding senators, crusading journalists, and angry citizens, even as it inspired the creation of dozens of shameless knockoffs, the MMPI itself stayed exactly the same. The test that Starke Hathaway and J. Charnley McKinley invented in 1942 persisted in asking the same eccentric questions, even as their language and subject matter—"I used to like to play drop-the-handkerchief," "Horses who don't pull should be kicked or beaten"—grew antique.

Just as outdated were the MMPI's norms. In the decades following the test's publication, Americans experienced extraordinary political and social change: a second World War, the civil rights and women's liberation movements, the Vietnam War, Watergate, the beginning, middle, and end of the Cold War. During this period the country also absorbed millions of immigrants from all over the globe, and saw its economy shift from agriculture to industry to service. But psychology's standard for normality remained those 724 white Minnesotans dragooned into Hathaway's experiment in the late 1930s. As the test was given to succeeding generations and to an ever-broader slice of the population, the MMPI's norms showed themselves to be increasingly outmoded.

The item "I am an important person," for instance, was endorsed by only 9 percent of the Depression-era farmers in Hathaway's normal sample, and so was scored as a sign of grandiosity and narcissism. After decades of human-potential and self-esteem movements, however, an affirmative response was an indicator not of mental illness, but of relative psychological health; in more recent samples, as many as eight out of ten test takers answered "true." Another example: when the MMPI was administered to a group of Alabama residents, the item "I think Lincoln was greater than Washington" divulged little about test takers' personalities, but it revealed with unerring accuracy which were black and which were white.

Clearly, an update was sorely needed—a fact brought home to one testing expert in 1977, when he asked a taxi driver in Tampa, Florida, to drive him from the airport to the annual MMPI symposium. "Are they *ever* going to restandardize that thing?" the cabbie demanded. (He was a transplant from Minnesota, where the homegrown test was almost famous.) Actually, the idea had been raised at the 1969 symposium, but it would take two decades and a Herculean effort to change what the MMPI's publisher calls "almost a sacred text." Just as believers don't want the Bible or the Koran to be altered, says Beverly Kaemmer, devotees of the test "don't want the MMPI to be tampered with." They also didn't want to lose the value of decades of research on the MMPI, contained in articles and books currently numbering around fourteen thousand. And the test's distributor (now Pearson Assessments) presumably didn't want to give up what had become a very lucrative franchise.

For these reasons, the revision proceeded with great caution. New "Normals" were chosen, drawn from mail and newspaper-ad solicitations. This control group numbered 2,600 people, more than three times as many as the Minnesota Normals, and its members were more representative of America's demographic makeup. The committee charged with revising the MMPI also took this opportunity to remove some of the items that had offended countless test takers over the years, such as the infamous "I have never had any black, tarry-looking bowel movements." "It never really did tell us anything," confesses James Butcher, a former colleague of Hathaway's who served on the committee.

The four psychologists directing the update also incorporated new scales, a list that reads like a litany of modern ailments: Anxiety, Fears, Obsessiveness, Anger, Cynicism, Antisocial Practices, Type A Behavior, Low Self-Esteem, Social Discomfort, and Family Problems, among others. But when the long-awaited MMPI-2 was finally unveiled in 1989, little about the test had really changed. Eighty-four percent of the items in the MMPI showed up again in the MMPI-2; it was, as Butcher proclaimed, the original "in but slightly altered form."

Even so, some diehards refused to make the transition; one fanatic pre-

dicted that "the MMPI-2 will go the way of 'New Coke,' and consumers
will say they prefer the Classic." A number of organizations (including
Rent-A-Center, Art Staples and Scott Hadley's employer) continued administering the old test even after the new one became available. And so,
on September 1, 1999—fifty-seven years after it was first published—the
original MMPI was officially "withdrawn from service."

Today the MMPI-2 is a familiar presence in America's human resources
departments and in its courts of law (more than 90 percent of psychologists conducting evaluations in child custody and emotional-injury cases
use the MMPI). By far the world's most frequently used clinical personality test, it is now not only a national phenomenon but a global one.
The original was translated into 115 languages (and the MMPI-2 is fast
catching up, with about 50), including Arabic, Chinese, Russian, and
even sign language. One can now respond to the statement "I loved my
mother" in Hmong, Norwegian, and Turkish. James Butcher, who was
involved in many of these conversions, was told by a Pakistani linguist
that translating the MMPI was "like translating poetry." Butcher notes
that even countries hostile to the United States have embraced this particular export: "They may hate Americans and the U.S., but they still
like the MMPI!" he exclaims.

Proponents maintain that the test has received such a wide welcome
because it taps into a shared human nature. Says publisher Beverly
Kaemmer: "There are some things about humans that are universal, so
although there are cultural differences, still, humans are humans. And
the MMPI I think does a very good job of finding out what humans are
about." Butcher is more blunt in his explanation of the test's overwhelming success: "The damn thing works," he declares. He and others
promote an image of the MMPI as straightforward and sincere, an instrument as modest and matter-of-fact as its creator, Starke Hathaway.
But the reality is far more ambiguous.

Take, for example, the assertion that the MMPI operates on a beauti-
fully simple principle: as Butcher puts it, "if you want to know what's
wrong with somebody, you ask them." It's true that the MMPI confronts
test takers with direct—sometimes disconcertingly direct—questions
about their mental and physical state. But then it does something utterly
unexpected with their replies. More than any other reason, perhaps, the

MMPI has stirred controversy in its six decades of existence because it violates a basic tenet of human communication: if you ask someone a question, it's because you're interested in the content of the answer. The MMPI displays a heartless indifference to content, concerning itself only with how a given response "discriminates." Its defenders become impatient when test takers object to this indifference, but in fact it's their test that has broken one of the rules by which we all live.

Or consider a second assertion, part of the MMPI's instructions to test takers from the very beginning: "There are no right or wrong answers." Again, in the most literal sense this is true; the MMPI is not a test of reasoning with factually correct or incorrect replies. But in a real-life sense, with important outcomes—the custody of a child, the sentencing of a criminal, the offer of a job—riding on the results, this statement is not only inaccurate but dangerously disingenuous. In testing's terms, "right" and "wrong," "normal" and "deviant" are not logical propositions or moral prescriptions. They are statistical artifacts: what most people do or don't do. The MMPI helped to create, and continues to reinforce, a culture in which our unique and varied personalities are subject to the petty tyranny of the average.

Finally, MMPI buffs often assert that the test offers a comprehensive, definitive reading of personality. But it can do no such thing. The test doesn't owe its huge popularity to its profound insight into human nature; quite the opposite. The MMPI deliberately skims the surface, and that is the secret of its success. It asks questions, analyzes answers, and doesn't bother itself with what's in between. But what is in between is the person herself, and she is as much a mystery as she ever was. The danger lies in thinking that because we have labeled personality, we have understood it. Louise Douce is a Minnesota-trained psychologist who is now director of student counseling at Ohio State University. "It's really crazy when you start thinking that the test is what's true and the person is a reflection of its categories," she says, "as opposed to the test being a reflection of what's going on within the person."

But like it or not, the MMPI machine will almost certainly remain a juggernaut. Its dozens of translations, thousands of research studies, and legions of faithful adherents mean that the MMPI has become an inexorably self-perpetuating phenomenon. This fact would have displeased one person above all: Starke Hathaway.

■ ■ ■

From the start, Hathaway was self-effacing in his role as creator of the MMPI. He refused to teach or give speeches about the test, and declined invitations to MMPI meetings and symposia. Even to get him to talk about it, says Butcher, "was like pulling teeth." Unlike the leaders of the Rorschach community, Hathaway actively discouraged the development of what he called "a personal cult." Soon after the test's original publication, his professional concerns shifted to psychotherapy and juvenile delinquency, and he regretted that this research did not receive more attention. "At times I have become impatient, wishing that my connection with the MMPI could be forgotten in favor of my other work and interests," he remarked. There was little chance of that: Hathaway would always be known first and foremost as the author of the MMPI. Decades after his death in 1984, Butcher reports, "people still write and try to telephone Hathaway to discuss his test."

During his lifetime, as the MMPI grew increasingly popular, Hathaway's initial modesty seemed to deepen into something more like dissatisfaction. He began referring to the test, once so cutting edge, as a "Stone Age ax," and lamented that psychologists had so few alternatives. "I fear that the aged MMPI will be tolerated for some time by those concerned with practical problems in psychological evaluation," he said in 1972, expressing dismay that "we are stuck" with the MMPI "for a dreary while longer." Puzzling over what he called "the mystery of the missing progress," he wondered: "With so many competent efforts over so many years, why have we not yet developed better personality tests?" Rather astonishingly, he concluded that progress could only come from iconoclasts, from "those students who think differently and who stage sit-ins against worn-out designs and tactics." The man whose test defined normality for a generation seemed to be ruing the conformity it helped enforce.

Unlike other creators of important personality tests, Hathaway did not entertain high-flown ideas of creating a key to human nature. "I have never had the conviction that I had real insight into a patient's problems," he confessed. Though admirers like James Butcher may call him "a true visionary" and "a great pioneer," Hathaway's own highest hope was to apply a useful tweak, a well-timed nudge toward greater health and happiness. The humbleness of his aims is suggested by his favorite analogy: many of us are like "a bug in a cup," he liked to say, circling endlessly around the circumference of life, lacking the perspective to climb out of our worries and preoccupations.

As he grew older, Hathaway began to question whether the assessment of personality was possible at all. "Everyone knows the word 'ghost' and we can use it for communication; but most of us would not seriously expect to devise a ghost-measuring or analyzing test," he mused. "By analogy I often have serious doubts about whether it is meaningful to expect that we can develop tests to measure or analyze personality." Perhaps the essence of who we are will always elude capture; perhaps, he concluded, "personality is a ghost!"

Early in his career Hathaway had tried to break down human nature, to take it apart and see how it worked. Once he'd done so, he found that the thing he was looking for was no longer there.

FOUR

Deep Diving

Henry Murray had a secret, and he'd come here, to the shores of Switzerland's Lake Zurich, to tell it.

On its surface, the life of Henry Alexander Murray Jr.—Harry to his friends—seemed as perfectly placid as the lake itself. He was the handsome oldest son of a wealthy and prominent New York family, raised among a houseful of servants on the city's East Side. (Some whispered that the posh Manhattan neighborhood of Murray Hill was named after the family, and though it wasn't true, Murray relished the rumor.) The clan summered in a Long Island mansion so grand that when it was sold it was turned into a country club. Murray was an indifferent student at his New England prep school but proceeded to Harvard anyway, where, he said, he "majored in the three R's—Rum, Rowing, and Romanticism." Something of a playboy in his youth, he straightened out, went to medical school, and married an heiress named Josephine Rantoul, with whom he had a daughter, Josie.

But now, in the spring of 1925, he'd left wife and child behind to make an expedition on his own. For despite the shining future laid out before him, Murray had lately been drawn to another, darker side of life. While an intern at New York's Presbyterian Hospital (just a few miles but worlds away from where he grew up), he "spent more time than was considered proper" talking to his patients, trying to figure out what made these unusual individuals tick. "Whatever I succeeded in doing for some of them—the dope fiend, the sword-swallower, the prostitute, the gangster—was more than repaid when, after leaving the hospital, they took me through their haunts in the underworld," Murray related. "This was psychology in the rough, but at least it prepared me to recognize the similarity between downtown doings and uptown dreams."

Such exploits also drew him down into his own churning depths.

Murray had always been conscious that beneath his "sanguine surplus," as he called his abundance of expansive energy, there was a contrasting "marrow of misery and melancholy," a streak of sadness and even despair. His life-changing journey to Lake Zurich would lead him to create a most unusual personality test, one intended to plumb the depths of his and others' secret selves.

Though Murray was dimly aware of a stirring below the surface, he had no map to this realm as he'd had guides to the city's underworld. Then, browsing in the medical school bookstore on an evening in 1923, he found one. *Psychological Types*, by Swiss psychiatrist Carl Jung, had just been published in an English translation. Murray read it all night and through the next day, skipping his rounds at the hospital. The book opened the unconscious to deep and probing exploration; it was, he said later, "a gratuitous answer to an unspoken prayer."

Less than a month later, Murray encountered another important guide. At a dinner party he was seated next to a beautiful young woman named Christiana Morgan. Twenty-six years old, Christiana was the well-bred daughter of a Boston family who was in New York studying drawing at the Art Students League. By way of small talk she asked him, "Do you favor Freud or Jung?" Murray was enthralled to discover that she was intimately familiar with both men's work. Learning of his new-found interest in Jung, Christiana suggested that he go to Zurich to meet the "Old Man" face to face.

Two years later, Murray got his chance. He was granted a fellowship at Cambridge University, as was Christiana's husband, an anthropologist named William Morgan. The two couples, now friends, took up residence in neighboring houses near the university. While in England, Murray was studying for a doctorate in biochemistry—back in the States, he'd spent several years researching the development of chicken embryos—but he was growing increasingly impatient with the subject. He resolved to travel to Switzerland over his Easter break to consult with Carl Jung about a career in psychology.

As it turned out, their meeting was no cool, formal interview, but an intense encounter lasting three weeks. Each day, Murray would join Jung in Küsnacht, the town on Lake Zurich where Jung lived with his wife, Emma. Some days Jung would take his guest to his tower across the water, a place he'd built to think and write. "We talked for hours, sailing down the lake and smoking before the hearth of his Faustian retreat," Murray recalled. Their conversation bobbed on the surface only briefly before darting into the depths, and to his surprise Murray found himself confessing his darkest secret: he was desperately in love with Christiana. Though his wife, Jo, was a kind and loving woman, she "had few intellectual interests, almost nil," he said. By contrast, he and Christiana "talked alike and thought alike." She was moody, intense, volatile—drawn, like Murray, to the shadowy side of life. Together the two went "deep diving," as they called it, plunging into their own psyches and into the art, literature, and philosophy that fed their understanding of the mind's hidden currents. Their emotional and intellectual bond was intensified by a powerful sexual attraction, one they had not acted upon—yet.

If Murray wondered at his own candor, he was even more astonished by his confidant's response: Jung revealed that he had once faced the same dilemma. In the "dark years" following his painful break with his mentor, Sigmund Freud, Jung had found solace with a former analysand named Antonia Wolff. Unwilling to give up either his wife or his mistress, he persuaded the women to allow him both. As if to show Murray how the arrangement worked, Jung took him back to the house in Küsnacht. There, calmly serving tea together, were Toni Wolff and Emma Jung. "He must have seen that the way to treat me was not to hide," Murray later remarked.

Witnessing the cozy scene, Murray was agog—but also inspired. During his turbulent weeks with Jung, he wrote, "I saw things that my philosophy had never dreamt of," both out in the world and deep within himself. "I had experienced the unconscious, something not to be drawn out of books." He returned to England a different man, one determined to make two great changes in his life. First, he told Jo and Christiana of his intention to be involved with them both, and after much coaxing secured their reluctant acceptance. (Jo had suspected that her husband was in love with Christiana, but she blamed Jung—"dirty old man," she called him—for giving Murray ideas.) And second, he abandoned biochemistry for psychology. Murray had discovered that he had a natural "bent of empathy" for human beings, and "when it came to chicken embryos, lovely as they were, the opportunities for empathy were critically curtailed."

In the space of a few weeks, Murray had turned his seemingly perfect world upside down. It was anyone's guess what he would do next.

As if to confirm the wisdom of his rash choices, a position in psychology was waiting for Murray when he returned to the United States in 1926. A psychiatrist named Morton Prince had founded a clinic at Harvard University to study hypnosis and abnormal psychology. Prince needed an assistant, and Murray got the job; soon after, he was appointed an assistant professor of psychology as well. It's no exaggeration to say that he was completely unqualified. His formal education in psychology consisted of a single lecture he attended during college—a lecture that bored him so much he walked out. That was the last time he was in a psychology class, he liked to say, until he taught one himself.

By virtue of his Harvard connections (and his convenient lack of concern about the position's paltry $1,800 salary), Murray had landed in the perfect spot. Almost immediately, however, he began to make trouble. What was researched and taught at Harvard, Murray soon learned, bore no relation to the penetrating explorations of Jung and Freud. "At first I was taken aback, having vaguely expected that most academic psychologists would be interested in Man functioning in his environment," he commented dryly. "But not at all: almost everyone was nailed down to some piece of apparatus, measuring a small segment of the nervous system as if it were isolated from the entrails." From the Harvard Psychological Clinic, which was housed in its own small building separate from the psychology department, Murray began launching his attacks.

"Academic psychology has contributed practically nothing to the knowledge of human nature," he charged in a caustic journal article that the department head warned him not to publish. It has "not only failed to bring light to the great, hauntingly recurrent problems but it has no intention, one is shocked to realize, of attempting to investigate them." Undeterred by his inexperience in the field, Murray assailed its reliance on narrow laboratory experiments, deplored its cramped intellectual scope, and mocked its pretensions to being a "real" science. "Nowadays it is the mounting ambition of these theorists to build, so far as possible, a psychology in the image of physics," he scoffed, "their scientific standards forever unattainable by anyone who is genuinely interested in human nature." Murray quickly acquired a reputation as the defiant "id" of psychology at Harvard. "I was a very obnoxious person," he admitted, "because I didn't have any respect for the psychology that was taught and for the people who taught it."

Murray reveled in the hostility he provoked among Harvard's academic psychologists, an antagonism that only intensified when he was named director of the clinic in 1928. "Things have come in so fast during the last two years," Murray marveled in a letter to a friend. His dramatic change of course seemed to have been vindicated: "I am so happy and serene that I am ashamed to acknowledge it." His "sanguine surplus" would stand him in good stead as he prepared to make his deepest dive yet.

In taking control of the clinic, Murray had a single aim, breathtaking in its ambition: "to understand man and human nature in all its phases." No studies of startle time or muscle reflexes here; at the clinic he would act on his conviction that psychology must address the most profound questions of existence. And he would do it with Christiana at his side.

Murray's fierce ardor for Christiana was undimmed, though he was unable to manage the affair with Jung's cool aplomb. He gave Christiana an office at the clinic, but he hid the extent of their relationship from Jo—still dismayed by his infidelity—and his colleagues by renting a suite of rooms near Harvard Yard. The two met there often, their encounters obscured by the traffic of customers at the tobacco shop downstairs. (Or so they thought: the building's janitor knew the cook at the Rantouls' country house, and through this link Jo was kept apprised of the lovers' frequent trysts.)

But it was at the clinic that Murray and Christiana's intellectual romance reached full bloom. Located at 64 Plympton Road, the clinic was a homey clapboard house, painted yellow, with purple wisteria growing above the front door ("wisteria outside, hysteria inside," quipped one wag). Inside was "a world of small rooms" hung with fine engravings, carpeted with Oriental rugs, and appointed with Murray's family antiques. Walls were painted in rich colors, chosen by Christiana; vases were filled with fresh flowers; cats twined around banisters and slouched across seminar tables.

If the setting was as different as possible from the psychology department's brass-instrument labs, the activity at the clinic was just as exceptional. Murray created a kind of salon, hosting lavish teas and luncheons at which the conversation flowed freely. (As did the wine: the clinic's cellar was stocked with a supply of the Chilean white Murray preferred.) Christiana poured the tea and even, at first, made the sandwiches; later a professional cook was hired. To these luxurious meals came an impressively eclectic group of artists and intellectuals, including Paul Robeson, Bertrand Russell, Erik Erikson, Conrad Aiken, Archibald MacLeish, Aldous Huxley, Paul Tillich, and Wallace Stevens.

Even in this illustrious company, one of the main attractions of the clinic was Murray himself. From the confused and divided young man who had visited Jung in 1925, he had grown into a confident, dynamic, and magnetic figure. One former student describes him as "redolent with charisma"; another admirer speaks of his "almost shattering vitality," adding that "when he enters a room, electrons crackle." The brightest young professors and graduate students were drawn to Murray and to his expansive vision for the clinic.

Soon he had assembled a brilliant and varied crew: psychologists, psychiatrists, psychoanalysts, physicians, an anthropologist, a sociologist, an artist, a poet. Those who agreed to collaborate with Murray had the sense that they had signed on for a great adventure; he made them feel, said one associate, "like bold explorers." They were energized by Murray's "infectious zest" and inspired by his goal of capturing human nature: "It was a tall order for science," acknowledged another student, "but anything less now seemed like nibbling around the edges of personality."

In line with Murray's rebel reputation, the work at the clinic was unusual in several respects. It was not limited by the confines of a particular school—"I have never called myself a Freudian, a Jungian, or any other -ian," Murray declared—or even by the boundaries of psychology. Murray believed that mythology, anthropology, medicine, and especially literature all deserved a place in the study of personality. He revered the novel *Moby-Dick* and regarded its author, Herman Melville, as "the greatest depth psychologist America ever produced." So fervid was his enthusiasm for the book, in fact, that he filled the clinic with maritime memorabilia and adorned his stationery with a whale; he referred to the building as "the Baleen" and smiled when his students called him "the Skipper."

A second point of departure: Murray was interested in normal personality, not the deviations introduced by disease. Like Hermann Rorschach and Starke Hathaway, Murray drew his subjects from the population most accessible to him—but in his case, that meant gifted Harvard students rather than mental ward patients. His plan was to study fifty undergraduates in depth, understanding each as a whole, integrated individual and not as a collection of traits or ailments. Because he was convinced that "a person is different in different contexts and with different people at different times," these young men would be examined by a diverse group of judges, whose observations would ultimately be synthesized into a single report. More than one personality test would be used, as well, in order to cover every facet of character.

But which tests to use? Self-report instruments like the precursors of the MMPI were too clumsy for the sensitive probing Murray had in mind: "Armed with questionnaires, rating scales, pop-guns, quizzes, pegboards and numberless other mechanical contraptions, the testers have borne down on their subjects—so heavily, in fact, that the souls of their subjects have been forced to shelter," he shuddered. These tests confronted head-on the very subjects "which we should be creeping up on gradually and craftily." But the Rorschach, then gaining a foothold in the United States, was not right, either. Murray often quoted the philosopher George Santayana to the effect that "in the human being, imagination is more fundamental than perception." Interior fancies and inventions—what Murray liked to call "apperception"—were more revealing of personality, he felt, than reactions to the exterior world. To find what he was looking for, he would have to go deeper.

The English gentleman scientist Francis Galton had gone there first. In 1879 he disclosed the startling results of his "word-association experiment": "No one can have a just idea, before he has carefully experimented upon himself, of the crowd of unheeded half-thoughts and faint imagery that flits through his brain, and of the influence they exert upon his conscious life." Galton had made the discovery after writing down seventy-five words on slips of paper, then drawing the slips in random order and noting the thoughts stimulated by each. This simple task revealed his inner self so starkly it was almost embarrassing: such responses, he reported, "lay bare the foundations of a man's thoughts with a curious distinctness and exhibit his mental anatomy with more vividness and truth than he would probably care to publish to the world."

Following Galton's lead, Carl Jung added several refinements to the procedure, developing a list of one hundred words that seemed to evoke especially rich associations ("mother," "death," "to kiss," "to sin") and recording the length of time his subjects took to reply. The two scientists were united in their conviction that unconscious forces drive much of our behavior (those who deny it, Jung wrote, "do not see the spectacles which they wear on their noses"), and in their confidence that associative methods provide a peek at such hidden forces. "Experiments such as these allow an unexpected amount of illumination to enter into the deepest recesses of the character," Galton announced, "which are opened and bared by them like the anatomy of an animal under the scalpel of a dissector in broad daylight."

Murray, too, believed that the "real facts" of human nature "are to be found not on the surface of the body nor in the full light of consciousness, but in the darker, blinder recesses of the psyche." In particular, he predicted that the key to personality would be found in fantasies: our private daydreams, laden with longing and desire. Word-association tests hinted at such preoccupations, but he suspected that other catalysts—literature, music, art—could expose them still further. To find out, he devised a number of inventive tests for use at the clinic.

There was the "musical reverie test" in which subjects were seated in a comfortable chair, played a classical composition (Tchaikovsky's Symphony no. 4, Mozart's Quintet in G Minor), and instructed to "allow your mind to drift." There was the "literary composition test," in which students were given a synopsis of the Nathaniel Hawthorne tale "The Minister's Black Veil" and told to "take this idea as a nucleus for a story of your own." And there was the "odor imagination test," in which participants were blindfolded and asked to sniff a variety of substances, among them whiskey, violet perfume, aftershave lotion, art gum eraser, and Worcestershire sauce. They were then requested to "invent a short anecdote or episode" suggested by each smell.

Murray developed dozens of other procedures. But from this crowd, only one emerged to take a place among psychology's most widely used personality tests. At the clinic, "the experimenters came to regard this test as the one which could be most certainly relied upon to supply the necessary clues" to the subject's inner self, Murray noted. He himself had a special fondness for the test: he and Christiana had created it together.

All this time, the relationship between Murray and Christiana was growing deeper. She was a constant presence at the clinic: analyzing patients, advising students, presiding over its convivial mealtime meetings. Research associate Cleome Wadsworth remembers her as the "handsome lady who always wore fantastic Indian jewelry and usually a red dress." On Wadsworth's first day at the clinic, she recalls, "I saw Harry look around the room. I got that gesture and I said, 'Ah, there is something over there in the corner.'" Turning around, she spotted Christiana, and thought, "Ah, that's it, that's the other part of this little house; that's what makes things run."

Murray and Christiana maintained their elaborate subterfuge, retreating almost daily to their rented rooms; afterward, Christiana confided in her diary, she would return to the clinic "aflame" with an awareness of their intimacy. She invented a system by which she could telegraph her feelings without saying a word: A red bracelet meant "I want your body." A sapphire pendant meant "I have something to tell you." And a string of red beads meant "I love you very much but do not need you." Despite their involved precautions, the affair was common knowledge among denizens of the clinic. It was a "secret from nobody," says one.

Their passion spilled over into their intellectual partnership. With Christiana, Murray rhapsodized, it all came together, "being in love with your work and your lover and the theories." He went so far as to claim that "a developing and enduring love affair is the best model for psychology." The peak of their personal and professional collaboration came in the creation of one particular personality test, what they called a "method for investigating fantasies." The concept was simple: show people pictures and have them tell stories about what they saw.

Just as Murray used experimental subjects that were close at hand—Harvard students—he selected pictures from a readily obtainable source. He, Christiana, and other members of the clinic staff got to work paging through stacks of popular periodicals: women's magazines like *Woman's Home Companion*, newsmagazines like *Life* and *Time*, general interest magazines like *Collier's* and *The Saturday Evening Post*, hobbyist magazines like *Camera Craft* and *The Sportsman*. Soon the building's closets were crammed with the glossies, and the team had collected about two thousand photographs and illustrations.

The pictures were shown to colleagues, students, and family members (including Murray's and Christiana's children) in order to judge their "stimulating power"—their ability to evoke complex and deeply felt fantasies. Through such casual experimentation, Murray and the others determined the qualities that each picture needed to exhibit. It had to feature a "hero," a figure with whom the viewer could identify. It had to touch on some recognizable and even universal human dilemma. But it also had to be sufficiently ambiguous to allow room for individual interpretation. Gradually the heap of pictures was reduced to a set of thirty-one, which Christiana (an erstwhile art student) then redrew and mounted on cardboard. Only one of these was sketched from life rather than from a magazine clipping: it depicted a man lying supine on a couch, with another man standing over him. A graduate student studying at the clinic posed for the drawing.

The other illustrations were similarly unsettling, as Murray's own descriptions suggest: "A woman has her hands squeezed around the throat of another woman whom she appears to be pushing backwards across the banister of a stairway." "On the floor against a couch is the huddled form of a boy with his head bowed on his right arm. Beside him on the floor is a revolver." "A woman is clutching the shoulders of a man whose face and body are averted as if he were trying to pull away from her." One of the cards was the ultimate in disconcerting ambiguity: it was completely blank.

Each test taker was shown twenty such images (the particular group of cards was determined by the subject's age and gender) and given these instructions: "I am going to show you some pictures, one at a time, and your task will be to make up as dramatic a story as you can for each. Tell what has led up to the event shown in the picture, describe what is happening at the moment, what the characters are feeling and thinking, and then give the outcome." Certain cards were thought to "pull" for specific topics: Card 1, for example, featuring a young boy looking at a violin, often inspired fantasies about competition and achievement. (The boy in the picture was a real-life prodigy, violinist Yehudi Menuhin.)

The test giver wrote down all responses to the cards, but did not compare these to some statistical norm. Rather, when analyzing the results the psychologist immersed himself in the subject's stories as in an absorbing novel, looking for theme, character, and plot. He paid particular attention to what Murray called "needs" (internal forces driving the stories' actors) and "presses" (external forces acting on those figures), and the way the two combined to create "thema," or meaningful motifs.

Murray and Christiana named their creation the Thematic Apperception Test—"Thematic" because it elicited the animating themes of a person's life, "Apperception" because it drew on the internal imaginative process that Murray prized. At the clinic, the test (which soon came to be known as the TAT) was subject to a final step, the integration of its results with those of other tests and with the observations of several different examiners. Arriving at a consensus about the personality of the individual under discussion was a long and contentious process, one often "surrounded by a halo of frayed tempers," said a participant. But Murray, speaking last, made it look easy. "Harry's enthusiastic interpretation of the TAT was the climax, the Grand Finale, of each case presentation meeting at the Clinic," remembers a former graduate student. "Harry could astonish us by giving an interpretation of the subject's TAT that was always brilliant—and sometimes may even have been right." As another student put it, Murray "knew where to find the skeletons."

The test seemed to prove its mettle at the clinic—"We found out things in two hours that didn't come out for six or seven months in psychoanalysis," Murray claimed—but its value was confirmed for him when he gave it to his own mother. He visited her in 1934, just after his father died. Always reserved, she appeared as poised as ever, but her TAT responses told a different story. Studying one of the pictures, she pointed to a female figure and said, "This woman has lost her husband," proceeding to describe the character's feelings of grief and desolation. Murray was flabbergasted. "I would have thought, 'She's teasing me,' but that's the last thing she'd have done," he recounted. Without his mother's awareness, the test had directly tapped her deepest thoughts and feelings. The time had come to share this wondrous instrument with the world.

The TAT's introduction to society was not quite as charmed as Henry Murray's had been, however. An article presenting the test, coauthored by Murray and Christiana, was rejected by the *International Journal of Psychoanalysis* before appearing in the *Archives of Neurology and Psychiatry* in 1935. Even then, the test itself would exist for the next eight years only as a mimeographed manuscript distributed by the clinic.

But in 1939, psychology started to catch up to Murray. That year, an influential paper by psychologist Lawrence Frank gave a name to tests like the TAT: "projective methods." In 1894, Sigmund Freud had introduced his theory of "projection," the idea that when we experience an unacceptable thought or feeling, we cast it outward onto objects or other people. Frank cleverly adapted this concept to testing: if test givers could provide a target for projection, they could deliberately elicit from test takers information of which the individuals themselves were unaware. Projective techniques, Frank wrote, are intended "to obtain from the subject 'what he can or will not say,' frequently because he does not know himself and is not aware of what he is revealing about himself through his projections."

When the TAT was finally produced by Harvard University Press in 1943, it was the first projective technique published in the United States. It was far from the last: a veritable flood of such tests followed. Many shared the TAT's method of prodding the imagination and waiting to see what emerged. The Tautophone, for example, developed by two American psychologists, played a phonograph record of a not-quite-intelligible voice. "You will have to listen carefully," the test administrator would announce. "As soon as you have an idea of what he is saying, tell me at once." In fact the voice was spouting nonsense words, but the imagined speech was thought to reveal much about the hearer.

Other projective techniques added a twist to the formula, proposing to find meaning in what we embrace and what we reject. The Szondi Test, imported from Hungary, presented the subject with photographs of human faces. Each person depicted was a mental patient with a different diagnosis (including "sadistic murderer" and "practicing male homosexual"). Test takers were asked to select which faces they liked and which they didn't; their choices were presumed to reveal aspects of their own personalities. The dozens of new projective techniques that now appeared incorporated an almost boundless array of objects, from knotty pieces of wood to plastic shapes purchased at a hobby shop.

So intemperate was the enthusiasm they generated among psychologists that in 1948 a testing newsletter chided, "The flowering of the projective technique of studying personality has brought to clinical psychology a somewhat dandelion-like broadcasting of seed." Murray himself complained of "anarchy" in "the realm of projective techniques." But their popularity continued to grow—linked, in part, to the rise of psychoanalysis in America. The relationship was a loose one, to be sure: Freud himself never used the tests, and when Murray showed him the TAT he would grant only that "it can do no harm." But the emphasis psychoanalysis placed on unconscious motivations fit neatly into the premise of projective techniques, and the tests soon acquired some of psychoanalysis's mysterious glamour.

During this time, "objective tests" like the MMPI were also gaining users, but a significant number of psychologists found them unsatisfactory. The questionnaires measured only conformity to social norms, they argued, and allowed little room for distinctive self-expression. As personality inventories became ever more dominant, these psychologists began promoting projective techniques as a "protest movement" upholding the dignity and uniqueness of the individual. Perhaps their own self-regard was involved as well: the TAT, commented one psychologist, offers "the 'aha' experience of seeing things hang together—fulfilling a need to understand things that probably is a basic motivation in all clinicians. One does not get this from the MMPI." Compared to the thin descriptions yielded by objective tests, said another, the rich portraits provided by projective techniques were like "heady wine."

But as projective testing was put forth as a comparatively humane and compassionate endeavor, its more disturbing aspects went unmentioned and even unrecognized.

The first lesson of projective techniques is that we are not as we seem. According to Murray, "The patterns of the imagination and the patterns of public conduct are more apt to be related by contrast than by conformity"—that is, when we appear to be one thing on the surface, we are likely to be its opposite underneath.

This was true of no one more than Murray himself. An observer beholding him in 1936, the year after the first TAT article was published, would have seen a patrician Harvard professor, living in a graceful house in Cambridge with his beloved daughter and devoted wife of twenty years. Such were Murray's "patterns of public conduct"—but his "patterns of the imagination" were another matter. That same year also found him in a secret tower he and his mistress had constructed in emulation of Jung's, wearing a green Hindu shirt and a black velvet skirt, whipping Christiana before they had sex. Clearly, Murray himself knew something of contrasts.

Projective testing's second claim is that we are just as unfamiliar with our inner selves as are our unsuspecting friends and neighbors. Murray regarded his sexual game playing with Christiana as part of his "deep diving," a conscious exploration and acting out of fantasies that are usually repressed. But he acknowledged that few people would be willing to go so far: for most, he wrote, such introspection "is as distressing as the reopening of an old wound." So we remain strangers to ourselves; our self-awareness, he lamented, "is like a tiny coral isle growing in a sea of dreams."

An elegant demonstration of this phenomenon was offered by the work of German psychologist Werner Wolff, who began one experiment by photographing the hands of a group of people who knew each other well. When he presented the images to the participants, many competently matched pictures to subjects while failing to recognize their own body parts. Likewise, when Wolff recorded them as they spoke and then played back the recordings interspersed with the speech of strangers, people were frequently unable to identify their own voices. Projective testers contended that we are equally oblivious of our emotional selves and that only their instruments could penetrate such determined ignorance. As one expert proclaimed, the tests are "no less than a magic set of optics without which psychologists have only partial psychological vision." (Projective techniques were said to have the additional benefit of foiling fakers, since one can hardly hide a truth of which one isn't aware.)

With this "magic set of optics," psychologists granted themselves exclusive access to their patients' hidden selves, access they often didn't extend to the patient herself. The professional wisdom of the time was that sharing the results of projective tests was ill advised and even dangerous, since most people could not handle the truth about themselves. Murray occasionally expressed guilt about the deeply personal information he obtained by administering the TAT, remarking that the test "exposes so much to a discerning experimenter that the latter can hardly escape the feeling that he is prying." But even these confessions could not disguise his pickpocket's glee at pilfering a subject's secrets without his knowledge: "Usually, he comes in, talks about a few pictures, and leaves, without the slightest realization that he has provided the experimenter with a fluoroscopic screen for apperceiving his emotional skeleton."

The alleged power of projective techniques, combined with the high-handed way they were used, created a queasy ethical dilemma to which psychologists themselves remained largely oblivious or indifferent. Their claim to possess intimate knowledge of an individual, and their refusal to share that knowledge with the person herself, was distastefully condescending at best. At worst, it opened opportunities for manipulation and exploitation of vulnerable clients cowed by the doctor's supposedly superior insight. Such hazards increased as the TAT and other projective tests moved from research labs to hospitals, courtrooms, and the workplace. Decisions that should be transparent—diagnoses of mental illness, determinations of legal status, judgments about employability—were instead swathed in self-serving mystery.

Psychologists also seemed not to notice that they applied the central insight of projective testing selectively. While laypeople were hopelessly blinded and benighted ("The individual rarely has any understanding of himself or awareness of what his activities signify," Lawrence Frank had asserted), psychologists, apparently, always saw themselves and others clearly.

Even while conducting his research at the clinic, Murray engaged in practices that demonstrated his own brand of blinkered consciousness. He deceived his young subjects, for example, about the purpose of his experiments, insisting that each participant "should certainly not be enlightened as to the real purpose of the tests" but should be given "a plausible but fictitious objective," usually that they were measures of intelligence or creativity. He recorded the students without their knowledge via a microphone hidden in a lamp; his associates secretly observed them through a one-way screen. In Murray's view, such expedients merely served a larger purpose, his aim "to understand man and human nature in all its phases." The first part of that grand project was completed in 1938, with the publication of *Explorations in Personality*.

This book, a collaboration of the clinic staff, was an account of their energetic efforts to beat a path through personality, which Murray called a "jungle without boundaries." Like their leader, it was bold, expansive, and endlessly ambitious. (While struggling to edit the unwieldy manuscript, Murray showed a TAT card featuring an angry figure to his young daughter, Josie. "This man is trying to write a book," she responded brightly.) Its contents were a clear reflection of Murray's professional priorities: it included a ninety-eight-page case study of a single individual, and when the publisher complained the manuscript was too long, Murray gleefully lopped off a chapter on statistics. Upon its release, *Explorations* was hailed as an instant classic.

Despite the book's success, Murray regarded it as a preliminary effort, an early report from a wide-ranging expedition. There was still so much about human nature to discover: "There is no end to it," he exulted. He couldn't have known that the end of his ambitious undertaking was far closer than he imagined.

The bombs dropped on Pearl Harbor on December 7, 1941, landed more than five thousand miles from the Harvard Psychological Clinic, but the blast seemed to send a shudder through the yellow house on Plympton Road, rattling china cups and jarring picture frames askew.

With the entry of the United States into World War II, the exuberant atmosphere at the clinic turned suddenly sober, and work on the project to map personality all but ceased. The close-knit crew began to disperse; by summer less than half of the original group remained. "Too soon the season came when the aging center could not hold," declaimed Murray in grandiloquent elegy for the glory days of the clinic. In truth, however, he was eager to transfer his knowledge of human nature to the nation's fight. While still at Harvard, he coauthored a journal article about combat officer selection, began collecting pictures for a potential military version of the TAT, and even, at the government's request, generated a personality profile of Adolf Hitler. (The Führer, Murray concluded, was a "paranoid type with delusions of persecution and of grandeur.")

Then he was offered the opportunity he'd been waiting for: an invitation to join a top-secret mission at the heart of the war effort. A newly created agency called the Office of Strategic Services (the forerunner of the CIA) had been charged with selecting and training spies, but it was botching the job. A report from the field admonished: "The organization has been recruiting too many men who have intelligence and the necessary mechanical training but who lack common sense, know nothing about working with men or how to look after the welfare and the morale of men under them. We simply must have men who can shoulder responsibility and use initiative with common sense." The OSS needed help—and who was better equipped to select spies than a man who'd spent a decade studying "covert mental processes"?

Murray jumped at the chance. "I must leave—cutting everything off in the middle," he wrote to a friend. By December 1943 he had relocated to Station S, a secret training camp on a 186-acre estate outside Washington, D.C. He brought with him several young associates from Harvard, one of whom, James Grier Miller, recalls a cryptic phone call from Murray. "Would you like to work with me?" Murray asked. I'd love to, Miller replied. Where? "Well, I can't tell you." What will we be doing? "I can't tell you that either." You'll enjoy it, Murray assured him, and Miller signed on.

Murray and his team faced a daunting task. They had to determine, quickly and accurately, whether candidates were capable of duties like leading resistance groups, "disintegrating" enemy morale, conducting sabotage operations, and withstanding physical torture. About 10 percent of the recruits were female, and each woman was asked if she "would be willing to use sexual means to obtain information." (The staff was "somewhat surprised," commented Miller, when every one of them said yes.) This was not the spirited intellectual play of the Harvard clinic but urgent, serious work.

Independent-minded iconoclast that he was, Murray had a rather bumpy adjustment to military life. He was given a snappy uniform and the rank of captain, but he made "a very strange soldier," as one of his colleagues at Station S noted. "He simply disregarded regulations, not

because he opposed them, but because he considered them unimportant.
I had to remind him constantly to sign out before he left his post." Pay-
checks piled up, uncashed, on Murray's desk because he didn't need the
money. But he threw himself with characteristic zeal into the work, gal-
vanized by a genuine hatred for America's enemies. Hitler's regime, he
wrote in a letter to the now-teenaged Josie, "is the destruction of free inquiry, free speech, free thinking, art, science & everything that is mature
& humane."

Despite the radically different setting and circumstances, Murray was
determined to apply what he'd learned at the clinic to the selection of
spies. Once again he decided that multiple tests were necessary, and
once again he devised his own procedures when he could find no suitable ones available. There was the "belongings test," intended to assess
recruits' powers of observation, in which they were given four minutes
to look at an array of personal effects and then describe the person who
owned them. (The items actually belonged to Murray himself.) There
was the "interrogation test," in which candidates had to come up with a
plausible alibi for their activities, then defend it against sharp questioning while sweating under a spotlight and seated in "an unstable chair
which rocked with any nervous movement." And there were the "leaderless group situations," in which a gaggle of people had to cross a road
sown with imaginary mines, scale a wall while lugging a "king-sized
bazooka" (actually an eight-foot-long log), and complete other collabo-
rative tasks while working out the group's power dynamics.

Perhaps Murray's most infernally ingenious scheme was the "construction test," in which an individual was asked to build a small structure with the aid of two assistants, "Buster" and "Kippy." Unbeknownst
to the subject, these "helpers" were actually there to thwart and frustrate
him as much as possible. This exchange was recorded during the testing
of one hapless candidate: "Hey there, you, be careful. You knocked that
pole out deliberately," the recruit exclaims. Retorts Kippy: "Who, me?
Now listen to me, you son of a bitch. If this damn thing had been built
right from the beginning, the poles wouldn't come out. For Christ's sake,
they send a boy out here to do a man's job and when he can't do it he
starts blaming the helpers. Jesus, they must really be scraping the bottom of the barrel now." (With this exercise, Murray may have outwitted
himself. "No candidate ever completed this task," he admitted, "and

there were those who became either markedly upset or enraged by the humiliations they suffered.")

After three days of such trials—including a party held on the last night at which the aspirants were plied with liquor and then closely observed—a group of psychologists gathered, as they had at the clinic, to evaluate each hopeful. By the time the fighting ended almost two years later, more than five thousand people had been assessed at Station S and at similar camps Murray helped establish in the United States, China, and India. Awarded the Legion of Merit and the rank of lieutenant colonel, he returned to Harvard aglow with his triumphs. His method of personality assessment, Murray believed, had helped win the war.

When the thrill of victory faded, however, Murray's accomplishment began to lose some of its luster. Although a book he later compiled with his staff, *Assessment of Men*, claimed that "for researches into normal personality, the OSS system of assessment, or something comparable to it, is essential," in truth they didn't know if the system had worked or not. Given the highly classified nature of the spies' work abroad, evidence of their success or failure was hard to come by, and the authors ultimately acknowledged that "the final validity is a question mark." Some critics were far harsher, with one calling the venture "a total flop": "Obviously the test of cruel war proved more challenging than the psychological cover games played on the rolling Virginia estate."

A more positive take, however—a review of *Assessment of Men* published in a popular magazine—pointed to the program's actual destiny. The book would be useful, the review's author predicted, "to any organization employing large numbers of people which seeks to select fewer square pegs for round holes." And in fact Murray's OSS process, which soon went by the name "assessment center," was seized upon by the country's prospering postwar corporations. Instead of undercover agents, they needed savvy strategists. Instead of saboteurs, they needed ruthless competitors. Instead of propagandists, they needed cagey advertising men. Personality testing had helped America win the war, its advocates claimed; now it would help America profit from the peace.

When *Assessment of Men* was published in 1948, one of its most avid readers was a young psychologist named Douglas Bray. About to receive his PhD from Yale University, Bray was inspired by the confident account: "I couldn't wait to try it!" he recalls. He did have to wait—almost eight years, in fact—but in 1956 he was hired by the American Telephone and Telegraph Company to set up a similar program, first for research purposes and then to select promising AT&T managers. Just as Murray had, Bray devised a series of exercises to test aspirants' personalities and abilities and then convened a group of judges to arrive at a consensus opinion on each candidate. AT&T found Bray's evaluations so useful—they were 50 percent more accurate than predictions made by other methods, according to one report—that it eventually established seventy such centers all over the United States.

Soon the trend spread to other companies. Bray helped another psychologist, William Byham, create an assessment center for J.C. Penney. As department stores moved from small towns to the nation's modern malls, Penney's used the assessment center to identify managers who would be effective in the new setting. Byham was so impressed with the results that in 1970 he penned an effusive article in the *Harvard Business Review*. "The assessment center technique has shown itself a better indicator of future success than any other tool management has yet devised," he declared. While "previously developed yardsticks have not really been worth their salt," he said, this method was far more scientific: "Under the controlled conditions that obtain in the assessment center, managers can observe promising young men in action and evaluate them objectively."

Byham's enthusiastic advocacy had its desired effect: "Suddenly, big companies—Ford, Shell—called and said, 'We'd like to have one of these,'" he recounts. Byham, who teamed up with Bray to create the consulting firm Development Dimensions International, was happy to oblige. Among the corporations that early on employed DDI to create an assessment center or developed their own were General Electric, Standard Oil, IBM, and Sears Roebuck. Also in the 1970s, the public sector became aware of the advantages of an ostensibly objective system for assessing job applicants and current employees. By 1981, 44 percent of federal, state, and local governments were using assessment centers.

Henry Murray played no part in this efflorescence; he didn't even meet Douglas Bray until 1983, when Murray was ninety years old. "He was completely unaware that his example had spawned hundreds of assessment centers in the United States and abroad," Bray marvels. Indeed, in their broad outlines the centers are essentially civilian versions of Station S: simulated situations, observed by a group of judges, who pool their ratings to produce a collective evaluation of each candidate. The average assessment center conducts seven exercises over the course of two days; rather than taking place in special facilities, the centers usually occupy a given space only temporarily, though the backdrop is more apt to be a hotel conference room than a bucolic estate.

Today, the assessment center process is used by thousands of American companies (DDI, Byham and Bray's Pittsburgh-based firm, has annual revenues of $100 million and is credited with assessing more than fifteen million people in seventy countries). The approach has proven even more popular with government, thanks largely to legal concerns about fairness in hiring and promotion. A recent survey of police and fire chiefs and public-sector human resources professionals found that 62 percent of them used assessment centers. Only academia, it seems, remains resistant to their appeal: few psychologists unaffiliated with assessment centers have bothered to evaluate their effectiveness. With so little objective evidence to go on, it may be safest to assume that the centers are valuable mostly for the semblance of impartial selection they provide. Compared to questionnaires that base sweeping judgments about personality on the answers to inane or invasive questions, assessment centers—with their relatively detailed and substantive evaluations, drawn from people's performances on tasks similar to actual jobs—seem positively humane. Too bad this extensive (and expensive) process is usually reserved for executives and others of high rank, leaving their employees to check boxes, fill bubbles, and choose answer (A) or (B).

So what did the future hold for Murray's other brainchild, the Thematic Apperception Test? As was his habit, Murray kept working at it, elaborating on the original. Toward the end of his stint with the OSS, he created TAT cards depicting Chinese citizens, to be used to select paratroopers for the Chinese Army. After the war, he helped develop a set especially for the U.S. Navy. Given to five thousand soldiers, including some who served in the country's first nuclear-powered submarine, the cards featured scenarios like "Sailor and Officer With Girl." (Great significance was attached to whether an enlisted man taking the test

claimed the girl for himself or allowed the officer to have her.) And
Murray and Christiana collaborated on another, highly personal set of
TAT pictures.

The TAT-II, as it was called, drew not from popular magazines but
from Jungian archetypes and the lovers' own intimate history. One card,
for example, portrayed a tower like the one they built as a monument to
their union. In the upper right corner was the face of a bearded man re-
sembling Carl Jung; in the opposite corner was the visage of a dark-eyed,
dark-haired woman who looked like Christiana. Murray intended to use
these images to test Jung's theory that such archetypes are universally
shared, but this was one of his many projects that never became more
than an intriguing idea.

Almost three decades after they met, Murray and Christiana were
still carrying on their affair. They spent days and nights at the tower
they built thirty miles outside Cambridge, and vacationed together on a
Caribbean island. But the relationship had grown rancid. Christiana,
whose husband died in 1934, became needy and difficult; she drank too
much and suffered from serious health problems. Their professional
partnership foundered as well. In the course of revising the TAT, Murray
directed another artist to redraw some of Christiana's illustrations.
Though it was originally called the Morgan-Murray Thematic Apperception Test, eventually Christiana's name was dropped and Murray was
designated its lead author. Whether she requested or resisted this
change, it was clear that Christiana was receding into the shadows even
as Murray became more prominent and esteemed.

By mid-century the TAT was firmly established as one of psychology's
most frequently used personality tests, administered by a majority of
clinicians. Employed in all the usual ways—with mental patients, job
applicants, juvenile delinquents—the TAT also lent itself to more inventive applications. Following Murray's lead, psychologists developed
myriad variations on the original cards, eventually bringing out special
sets for children, teenagers, the elderly, African-Americans, South
Africans, American Indians, Pacific Islanders, North Korean prisoners
of war, amputees, the disabled, blue-collar and white-collar workers,
pro-communists and anti-communists. The test was used to estimate
various societies' "need for achievement" (seconding the German sociologist Max Weber, this motivation was found to be higher in Protestant

countries) and to correlate "power motive imagery" in inaugural addresses with measures of "presidential greatness."

It was even embraced by researchers from other branches of social science: in 1955, anthropologist S. F. Nadel noted that "a new kind of routine seems to be emerging whereby anthropologists, before setting out for the field, pack into their kitbag a set of Rorschach cards and a TAT much as they do cameras [and] a compass." As one psychologist observed, the TAT "very early became everybody's favorite adopted baby to change and raise as he wished." Although such improvisation was very much in Murray's freewheeling spirit, it created problems for the TAT as a test. Within a few years of its publication, there was no agreed-upon way to administer, score, or interpret the procedure. There are as many TATs, it's been said, as there are TAT users.

Today the test retains both its popularity and its slippery mutability. Sixty percent of clinical psychologists use the TAT, according to a recent survey, and more than three-quarters of accredited clinical psychology doctoral programs still require their students to learn about it. Over the past four decades it has stayed among the top ten most frequently used psychological tests, and along with the Rorschach and the MMPI it continues to be (according to a recent book on the TAT) "a reigning member of psychology's personality assessment triumvirate." At the same time, it's difficult to speak of "the TAT" when most clinicians who use it select their own subset of cards, compose their own instructions to test takers, and evaluate the stories they hear according to their own idiosyncratic standards. (Murray, of course, never created norms for the TAT, and the most recent ones developed by others date from the 1950s.) A 1993 survey of psychologists practicing in juvenile and family courts found that only 3 percent used a standardized system when scoring the TAT, with the rest relying on their individual judgment.

Even when used in a uniform manner, the TAT has dubious validity and reliability, falling "woefully short of professional and scientific test standards," wrote University of Ottawa psychologist John Hunsley and two coauthors in 2003. It is not an effective way to diagnose mental illness, and its results may be affected by transitory moods and states (people who are hungry, for example, tell more TAT stories about food). So indeterminate is the TAT that some argue it does not qualify as a test at all. Yet still it has passionate defenders. Declares eminent psychiatrist

Leopold Bellak: "If I could have one device only [to assess personality], I would want it to be TAT Card 1," the picture of a young boy with a violin. The TAT, he says, has "a unique ability to stimulate rich and useful responses." Psychologist Morris Stein echoes the Harvard clinic's original "explorers": when using the TAT, he writes, "one feels as if one is a discoverer in an uncharted land," forced "to draw on all that one knows about human behavior."

But clinicians are not the only ones drawn to the TAT. Like Murray's assessment center, his test has been embraced by industry in a way its creator could never have imagined.

———————■———————

"What might be happening here?" Dr. Glenn Livingston hands a picture to Monica, who studies it closely.

"This is a happy family," she says slowly. "The parents are watching their only son, with approving love in their eyes."

"I see," Livingston murmurs. He has steel-rimmed glasses and a neat salt-and-pepper beard. "And what might have happened just before?"

"The little boy was running around and woke the parents up," Monica says with more certainty. "They came downstairs and turned on the TV. They don't want him to watch cartoons, so they've put on *Animal Planet*, something educational."

"Mm-hm," Livingston responds. "And what might happen next?"

Monica replies without hesitation. "The mom is going to go into the kitchen and make Pop-Tarts."

Her story is a long way from Henry Murray's deep dives into the unconscious—but then, this is a long way from Harvard's Baleen. The exchange takes place not in a clinic but in an office park in Syosset, New York, a white concrete slab beached before a sea of cars. And Livingston, despite his genial manner and sympathetic murmur, is not Monica's therapist. Along with his wife, Sharon, also a psychologist, he owns and directs Executive Solutions Inc., a firm that conducts market research for such corporations as Procter & Gamble, Johnson & Johnson, Colgate-Palmolive, and Nabisco. The Livingstons specialize in "qualitative techniques": intensive research methods, many of them borrowed from psychology, that give companies information on how consumers feel about their products.

One of the pair's most useful tools is a procedure they call a "modified TAT." On this day in March 2003, Glenn Livingston is demonstrating its use for a gathering of professional market researchers, including Monica, who directs such studies for a large insurance company. The way it works, he explains, is that a researcher shows an advertisement to a group of consumers and asks them to tell stories about what's going on in the ad. By analyzing these stories as a psychologist would, the researcher can explore the fantasies and emotions the image evokes (or fails to evoke) in potential customers. "Although personality tests were developed in a clinical setting to assess people's personalities, we don't use them that way," Livingston tells his audience. "We use them to get information about how people behave in the market." He adds, "We're looking for the soul of a person's relationship with a product."

Almost as soon as projective techniques were introduced to psychology, in fact, they were commandeered for use in marketing and advertising. The leading appropriator was a Viennese-born psychoanalyst named Ernest Dichter. After studying psychology at the Sorbonne in Paris (and living across the street from Sigmund Freud in Vienna), Dichter emigrated to the United States in 1938. Confident, colorful, even flamboyant, he quickly established a niche for himself by applying psychological tools and theories to the selling of goods. One of his earliest campaigns—"Be smart, get a new start with Ivory soap"—followed from his sense that women desire to wash away their sexual sins before a date. In Dichter's view, cars were vehicles for men's aggressive urges, so he advised Exxon to "put a tiger in your tank." Mothers were jealous of their daughters' curvaceous Barbies, so he counseled Mattel that playing with dolls is how "a little girl becomes a lovely lady."

Central to Dichter's approach was his conviction that people didn't know or didn't want to acknowledge why they bought things, so it was useless to question them directly. "Don't ask the murderer if he committed the crime," he said coyly, for "he'll always deny it." Under his influence, qualitative techniques became the busiest area of consumer research in the 1950s, before declining in popularity for several decades. Now, however, such psychologically informed methods are enjoying a resurgence. In recent years, projective techniques have been used to sell everything from Oreo cookies to Campbell's soup to Playtex bras; they helped create slogans like General Electric's "We

Bring Good Things to Life" and Visa's "Everywhere You Want to Be."

Companies might apply a version of the TAT to probe reactions to an embarrassing product, as one advertising agency did when developing a campaign for Clearasil. A group of adolescents was asked to tell stories about pictures of people with acne. "We got a very clear image that a blemish meant social isolation and differentness and all those things that a teenager fears most," reports an agency executive. He and his coworkers designed ads around the promise of speedily rejoining the social scene.

Corporations also use the TAT technique to evaluate the effectiveness of an image they've already produced. Sharon Livingston, the president of Executive Solutions, recalls showing consumers a picture to be used in a campaign for Budweiser beer. "The print ad featured a beat-up jalopy in the desert, with a woman's legs sticking out from underneath. She had on short-shorts and high heels, and off to the side you saw a man from the chest down, wearing jeans and cowboy boots," she says. "Some people thought it was very sexy, very fun. But some men who had guilty feelings about their sexuality had a very different response. More than one person imagined that the woman was a kind of monster—that she had the legs of a human but the head of a serpent. More than one person!"

Finally, firms may employ projective techniques to uncover the real reasons why a particular product isn't selling. The McCann-Erickson advertising agency, for example, set out to discover why sales of Combat insecticide disks lagged behind those of Raid roach spray in some markets, even though the disks were easier to use. They asked a group of a hundred low-income Southern women (all frequent users of roach spray) to draw pictures of the bugs they were trying to eradicate. Every one of them depicted roaches as men. "A lot of their feelings about the roach were very similar to the feelings that they had about the men in their lives," said Paula Drillman, executive vice president at McCann-Erickson. Like a no-good boyfriend, the women said, a roach "only comes around when he wants food." For these consumers, the insecticide disks were *too* easy to use, Drillman concluded: "They used the spray because it allowed them to participate in the kill."

Marketers use projective techniques (in this case, a drawing task) for the same reason clinicians do: people often don't care to admit, or aren't even aware of, the motives behind their actions. Using the tools of personality psychology, these sellers strive to make contact with our uncensored inner shopper. So profound is the "strange life of objects," Ernest Dichter once mused, that the effort to understand why we buy "is possibly a very direct and new and revolutionary way of discovering the soul of man."

Perhaps the use of Henry Murray's imaginative instrument to sell roach spray and pimple cream shouldn't be surprising; perhaps it's even, in a sense, fitting. After all, the TAT was itself distilled from the effluvium of commercial culture: soapy serials in women's magazines, how-to guides for hobbyists and amateurs, ads for Fleischmann's Yeast and for Veedol, "the Aristocrat of Motor Oils." The great difference, of course, is that Murray was concerned not with creating slick surfaces but with peering beneath them. And under these banal images he found another world: one enchanted by fantasies, roiled by nightmares, driven by forceful needs and desires. The marketers' use of the TAT throws Murray's astonishing revelation into reverse, squeezing our expansive imaginations back into the toothpaste tube, the detergent bottle, the beer can.

Murray might have expected as much. His early attacks on the triviality of academic psychology eventually expanded to include his entire society. "Americans have fashioned a cosmetic culture, in which a pleasing appearance at quick contacts is the thing that counts," he noted caustically in 1940. "A successful personality can be bought (and paid for). Our civilization is skin-deep, and the best epidermis triumphs. This is all part and parcel of the race for goods, comfort, and social recognition. It is the ideology of big business." His fellow citizens, he accused, had traded "surfaces for depths, gadgets for great ideas, behaviorisms for feeling, craft for faith, skill for wisdom, ostensible success for inward joy."

In the hands of literal-minded psychologists, even his inspired TAT had become just another way to package people in boxes. "In this country, we're so interested in gadgetry," he griped. Like Starke Hathaway, Murray retreated from his invention as it grew more popular. The test he created to sound the depths of personality had become just a "better mousetrap"; it was, he said dismissively, "an inert question for me now."

As Murray's long life wore on, the "marrow of misery and melancholy" that was always in him seemed to dilate. The wartime hawk became a fervent convert to pacifism, committed to world government and antinuclear activism. Still, inward-looking as always, he feared that such efforts couldn't touch the heart of the conflict. "Human personality," he warned in 1959, has become "the problem of our time—a hive of conflicts, lonely, half-hollow, half-faithless, half-lost, half-neurotic, half-delinquent, not equal to the problems that confront it, not very far from proving itself an evolutionary failure." His personal life was no more cheerful. In 1962, his dependable Jo died, and he was consumed with guilt for the hurt his affair had inflicted. Five years later, Christiana also died, and in an appalling way: while the two were on one of their jaunts to the Caribbean, she drowned in shallow waters as Murray slept on the beach nearby.

His work, once an absorbing pleasure, now gave him nothing but trouble. Murray held fast to his youthful aim of creating a key to personality, but he was hindered by his fading powers and his excessive ambition. The closest he came was a chapter published in 1959, "Preparations for the Scaffold of a Comprehensive System," but the scaffold, let alone the comprehensive system, was never built. He picked up projects only to put them aside: a novel of ideas, a biography of Herman Melville, a follow-up to the great *Explorations in Personality*—in all, almost a dozen books that were "unfinished and unfinishable," as he lamented to a friend.

Even as Murray became well known outside the university—he did a star turn as an expert witness, for example, in the Alger Hiss trial of 1950—academia continued to rebuff him. Harvard did not make him a full professor until twenty-four years after he arrived at the Psychological Clinic, when he was almost sixty years old. Murray did his best to live up to his ignominious reputation. In 1961 he tried the hallucinogen psilocybin, then presented a paper about his drug trip at an international psychology congress. (The experience was underwhelming, he reported, to someone already well acquainted with the unconscious.) At another professional conference, he analyzed in detail the personality of Satan. Suggesting that the rigid PhD system is "one of the Devil's cunningest contrivances," he jested that academic psychology is "obviously in league with the objectives of the nihilist Satanic spirit."

Throughout his career, Murray stood apart from most others who shared his goal of mapping human nature. He found himself "disquieted by the once-born, unripe confidence, the peculiar callousness of these testers—men who talk as though they had never been sensitized by a moving grief or joy." That could certainly not be said of Murray, who'd felt more than his share of both. And for him there was always another adventure. Late in life he fell in love with Caroline Fish, a tall, elegant professor of education, and married her in 1975 at the age of eighty-two. "I am a species of Pagan," he once twinkled, "who can't bear to think of a male-monopolized heaven." He lived contentedly with his new wife until he died, in 1988.

For Murray's ideas, too, there will probably always be another hearing. Though the test for which he became famous is best left as an intriguing experiment, its spirit is well worth preserving. The trends that Murray railed against—the surrender of uniqueness to standardization, the preference for predictability over dynamic change, the impulse to simplify what is irreducibly complex—have gained even greater momentum in recent years. Out of the mainstream during his own lifetime, his work has grown only more remote from the concerns of today's psychology. But on the fringes, where he was always most comfortable, the student of personality can still find Henry Murray's devotion to depth, to nuance, to uncompromised humanity. "Await the unforeknown. Expect the unforeseeable. Welcome the improbable," he urged. "Dive. Dive until you find."

FIVE

First Love

Mr. and Mrs. Briggs were anxious to learn more about the boy who was courting their daughter. In 1915 they had seen her off to college in Pennsylvania, more than a hundred miles from their home in Washington, D.C. Two years later, she was bringing the man she planned to marry home for Christmas.

This was no small occasion, for Isabel was a cherished only child. Now just past her twentieth birthday, she had been educated mostly at home by her mother, Katharine. "I went to school very little until I went to Swarthmore College," Isabel later recounted. "I grew all the way up to college with the idea that you can do things without having formally studied them." Katharine herself had been home-schooled, and enrolled in Michigan State University when she was only fourteen (at a time when it was unusual for women to go at all). After she married and started a family, Katharine focused her prodigious energies on her daughter, keeping elaborate records of her development.

Isabel amply rewarded her mother's effort. A soft-featured girl with thick, dark hair and a radiant smile, she laughed so often that her nickname was "Joy." Ferociously smart and ambitious, she became a published author at the age of fourteen with the appearance of "A Little Girl's Letter" in *Ladies' Home Journal*. In her book-length chronicle of Isabel's childhood, Katharine wrote that since her daughter was a toddler, she had been called "gifted," "a genius," "a little Shakespeare." The last line of the volume noted that Katharine's headstrong child had announced her intention to attend Swarthmore College, and "knowing her as I do, I have no doubt she will."

Isabel's father, Lyman, was a respected physicist who later headed the National Bureau of Standards, the federal agency in charge of establishing uniform rules of measurement. Isabel learned from him, too: "Research was what he cared about most, and so I grew up thinking that the greatest fun in the world was to find out something that nobody knew yet." Together, Lyman, Katharine, and Isabel made a snug family of three. Mother and daughter were especially close: "Katharine did everything but breathe for Isabel," a relative once quipped. Even when Isabel went off to college, they wrote each other almost every day.

And then along came Chief.

Clarence "Chief" Myers was a tall, handsome Swarthmore student, an Iowa native. (His college nickname, from a popular baseball player of the time, followed him through life.) Isabel met him early in her first year. "I wasn't having a very good time at the Junior-Fresh reception," she wrote in her diary that November—until she met "the nicest part of the evening." Chief Myers was six foot four, a good dancer, and a worthy sparring partner. Isabel immediately engaged him in a debate about "whether women were fickle." (Though Isabel may have been meeting Chief for the first time, he was already aware of her—as the woman in the front row in Astronomy 262 who had her hand up for every question.) When the moment arrived to change partners, they kept dancing.

Tightly knit as they were, the Briggs family shared certain qualities: they were imaginative and intuitive, big-picture thinkers. Chief was different. An aspiring lawyer, he tended to be practical and logical, focused on details. On that Christmas visit in 1917, both Lyman and Katharine found Chief an admirable young man, but Katharine was also perplexed by him, and intrigued. She wanted to understand just *how* he differed from others she knew. When the blissful young couple returned to Swarthmore, Katharine retreated to her study, intent on "figuring out Chief." Her curiosity would lead her, and the daughter she doted on, to create one of the world's most popular personality tests.

Katharine started with the notion that the world is populated by people of different types. She sought to identify these groups by reading stacks of biographies and by combing through works of psychology and philosophy. In time she settled on four categories: "meditative," "spontaneous," "executive," and "sociable." She was still developing her system when, in 1923, it was swept completely aside. This was the year (as

Henry Murray knew) in which an English translation of Carl Jung's *Psychological Types* appeared.

Like Katharine, Jung had begun pondering the differences among people for, he said, "a very personal reason." As he had confessed to Murray, his break with Sigmund Freud had plunged him into a deep depression. For months he ruminated on the conflicts between him and his mentor: how was it possible that they saw things so differently? "In attempting to answer this question, I came across the problem of types," Jung related, "for it is one's psychological type which from the outset determines and limits a person's judgment." This budding theory of personality type helped the psychiatrist "to find my own bearings," as he went on to conclude that Freud was an extrovert who liked and needed people, while he himself was an introvert who craved solitude.

Another, more ordinary experience led him to a second crucial distinction. After a party, his wife told him he had been rude to the guests. Jung, cerebral and aloof, had been unaware of his tactlessness, but now he directed his attention to the difference between Emma and himself. "It took me quite a long time to discover that there is another type than the thinking type, as I thought my type to be," commented Jung. "There are other people who decide the same problems I have to decide, but in an entirely different way. They look at things in an entirely different light, they have entirely different values." These, he decided, are the feeling types.

To these introverted-extroverted and thinking-feeling dimensions Jung added one that, for Katharine, made sense of the mysterious Chief. Some people encounter the world through their imaginations, Jung wrote, acting on intuitive hunches; others rely on their senses, collecting concrete information about their environment. "This is it!" Katharine exclaimed to Isabel. In a dramatic display of conviction she burned all her own research and adopted Jung's book as her "Bible," as she gushed in a letter to the man himself. His system explained it all: Lyman, Katharine, Isabel, and Chief were introverts; the two men were thinkers, while the women were feelers; and of course the Briggses were intuitives, while Chief was a senser.

Chief's practical and deliberate disposition was apparent in a letter he wrote to Katharine early in his courtship of her daughter: "Isabel seems to stand the test of all the uncomplimentary criticism I can mass, in my own mind, against her," he reported. After weighing her "in the most brutal of scales," he had concluded that she was the woman for him.

Isabel and Chief returned to the Briggs household six months after their Christmastime visit. On June 17, 1918, at the end of Isabel's junior year, they were wed in her parents' parlor. "Mother Briggs," as Chief now called Katharine, welcomed her intriguing son-in-law into the family.

The new Isabel Myers finished first in her class at Swarthmore, but in the years following graduation she devoted herself to being a wife and mother. The couple bought a small house in the Philadelphia suburbs, near their alma mater; Chief joined a local law firm; they welcomed two children, Peter and Ann. Still, Myers's energetic ambition could not be contained for long. In August 1928, she was leafing through an issue of *New McClure's* magazine when she came across an exciting announcement: a contest to write the best mystery novel, for which the winner would receive $7,500 and publication of the book. The deadline was December 31, less than five months away. Of course, she decided to enter.

By now, Katharine had thoroughly imbued her daughter with the idea of psychological type, and Myers's novel—*Murder Yet to Come*—made liberal use of the theory. The convoluted plot, involving a creaky mansion, poison darts, and a missing will, turns on the murder of a rich old miser, Malachi Trent. When he is found dead at the start of the book, a houseful of potential suspects must figure out who done it, and each goes about the investigation in his own distinctive way. Playwright Peter Jerningham employs his quick, intuitive flashes of insight. His old friend, detective Carl Nilsson, relies on his "slow, plodding logic." Jerningham's secretary, Mac, makes use of his detail-oriented memory. In the end, only the intuitive Jerningham is able to put together all the scattered clues to solve the crime and finger the culprit.

Myers won the contest, beating out a young Ellery Queen to take the prize. Her novel became a best seller, was translated into five languages, and went through seven printings. Reviews of *Murder Yet to Come* were generally glowing, but its author did not accept her negative press with equanimity. When a *Philadelphia Inquirer* critic deemed it "perfectly impossible" for Malachi Trent to have been murdered in the manner Myers devised, she wrote him an outraged rebuttal. Couldn't *you* kill someone with a marble statue by "whanging them over the back of the neck"? she demanded, adding pointedly, "I know I could—given sufficient provocation."

After a few more ventures into novel- and play-writing, Myers went back to raising her children. She would remain a homemaker for eight years, until another irresistible temptation came along.

Once again, the mailman delivered opportunity right to Isabel Myers's front door. In January 1942, she read an article in *Reader's Digest* titled "Fitting the Worker to the Job." It extolled a "people-sorting instrument" called the Humm-Wadsworth Temperament Scale, described as "a device to place the worker in the proper niche, keep him happy, and increase production." Myers immediately saw the "extraordinarily interesting potentialities" of such an instrument—and sat down to write her mother a letter.

People-sorters were early personality tests designed to meet the needs of business. First appearing in the 1910s, the exams were used by many of the nation's leading companies—Metropolitan Life, Western Electric, American Tobacco—to hire and promote employees. The tests became even more popular in the boom years of the 1920s, when their widespread use led to some questionable applications. At times they were employed to screen out political liberals and union sympathizers; the Humm-Wadsworth itself was administered at Lockheed Aircraft to eliminate "potential troublemakers." Another company used a personality test to select henpecked husbands, presuming that a man dominated by his wife could be controlled by a boss as well.

The whole selection industry, in fact, was riddled with frauds and shams. "Character analysis," for example, was a widely used technique based on physical attributes like hair color (blonds, its practitioners claimed, were more aggressive than brunets) and facial profile (great importance was attached to whether an applicant's features were "convex" or "concave"). Some methods were nothing more than simple prejudice. In a 1919 speech to the American Psychological Association, a selection expert declared that "the laborer's attitude toward industrial relations is determined by his nationality more than any other single factor": Swedes and Germans were "placid," Italians were "sullen and moody," and Jews were "keen-witted" and "radical." Even the more legitimate procedures rarely lived up to the extravagant promises made by their promoters, and the entire enterprise crashed just a few years before the economy itself did.

The need for such tests did not abate, however, and in fact grew only more pressing as the country geared up to fight World War II. By the time Myers learned of it in 1942, the Humm-Wadsworth Temperament Scale (known by the jaunty nickname "the Humm") was just one of many selection tests on the market. For Myers, their resurgence came at a propitious moment. These were "the darkest days of World War II," she wrote with typical dramatic flair, "when the Germans were rolling irresistibly along and my shoulders ached with trying to hold them back and a horrible sinking feeling lived in the pit of my stomach." In the Humm she saw a spark of hope, a way to help Americans—especially the women entering factories and offices for the first time—find the jobs from which they could make the greatest contribution.

After writing excitedly to Katharine about her discovery, Myers set about learning as much as she could about this marvelous tool. Through the father of one of her children's classmates, she found a local bank where the employees had taken the Humm and began analyzing their scores. To her surprise, however, the test turned out to be disappointingly ineffective in predicting performance. She reported this discouraging development to her mother, who responded with a lively suggestion: why not create your own test, one based on Jung's psychological types?

Myers was never one to back down from a challenge. If she wanted a people-sorter that worked, she would have to create it herself.

Isabel Myers was about as likely a candidate for personality-test creator as she had been for best-selling novelist. At the time she discovered the Humm, she was a forty-four-year-old housewife with two teenage children. She had no training in psychology, no knowledge of test construction, no lab, no funding, not even a university affiliation.

None of this deterred her in the least. Myers had always taught herself what she needed to know, and she headed now to the public library, returning home with piles of books on statistics and psychometrics. Her next step was to draw up some preliminary questions, items she thought would reveal aspects of an individual's personality type. She employed a "forced-choice" format that required test takers to select one of two responses—for example: "Do you prefer to (a) eat to live, or (b) live to eat?" The idea was to find "straws in the wind," seemingly mundane preferences that would point to deep underlying differences. She wrote out these questions on index cards and then posed them to family members, friends, and acquaintances—anyone who came through the door.

Myers soon moved on to larger samples of people, distributing her questions to her son's classmates at Swarthmore High. She cajoled local school principals into giving the items to their students and convinced a platoon of Navy recruits training on the Swarthmore College campus to try them out. An additional advance came through Lyman Briggs, who mentioned his daughter's work to the dean of the George Washington University School of Medicine. Intrigued, the administrator allowed Myers to question his first-year class of doctors-in-training. At night Myers spent long hours scoring and tabulating the results, scratching away with a pencil while seated in an armchair in her living room.

Peter Myers remembers that this sudden infatuation with personality testing "brought on an observable social change" in his mother. "Her tremendous enthusiasm for anything that was happening in our family, or that could be made to happen, was gradually withdrawn from the people around her and became increasingly focused" on the questionnaire she was developing. Many evenings, his mother was still at work on her test when he went to sleep. "If I happened to wake up, I would hear her typewriter going far into the night," he recalls. "Not only that, but no matter how early I came down the next morning, I would find her at work in her corner of the living room. I often asked her if she had been to bed at all."

From her labors at last emerged a test. Though it was indeed inspired by what she called Jung's "magnificent idea," Myers had not hesitated to change that idea in her effort to bring it "down to everyday life." Jung had proposed three pairs of opposites: introverted-extroverted, sensing-intuiting, and thinking-feeling. To these, Myers added a fourth axis: judging-perceiving. Every test taker was thus assigned a four-part type, determined by his or her standing on each of the dimensions. Chief, for example, was classified as an introverted-sensing-thinking-judging sort of person; Myers herself was introverted-intuitive-feeling-perceiving. Early on, a shorthand was developed whereby the first letter of each preference formed a snappy acronym: Chief was an ISTJ, while his wife was an INFP ("intuitive" was represented by the letter "N"). All told, there were sixteen possible combinations in Myers's system.

Another departure from Jung was Myers's deliberate focus on healthy, high-functioning individuals, rather than persons whose problems had driven them into psychoanalysis. Although Jung's musings on type arose "from a critique of my own psychological peculiarity," the psychiatrist also incorporated insights gained from his work with patients. Myers, by contrast, intended her personality profiles "to apply to each type at its best, as exemplified by normal, well-balanced, well-adjusted, happy, and effective people." Her aim was accompanied by an insistent belief that no one type was better than another, that everyone had a different set of "gifts" to contribute to the world.

This conviction was reflected in the descriptions Myers developed for each type. Extroverts "like to focus on the outer world of people and activity," she wrote, while introverts "like to focus on their own inner world of ideas and experiences." Sensers "like to take in information that is real and tangible—what is actually happening," while intuitives "like to take in information by seeing the big picture, focusing on relationships and connections between facts." Thinkers "like to look at the logical consequences of a choice or action," while feelers "like to consider what is important to them and to others involved." Judgers "like to live in a planned, orderly way, seeking to regulate and manage their lives," while perceivers "like to live in a flexible, spontaneous way, seeking to experience and understand life, rather than control it." Each description was carefully crafted to avoid hurt feelings and injured vanity.

In any case, it was not Carl Jung but Katharine Briggs who exerted the greatest influence on the instrument, and in honor of her mother's contribution Myers named it the Briggs-Myers Type Indicator Test. Chief helped her copyright it, and on May 5, 1943, "the Indicator," as she and Katharine called it, was born.

Of course, Isabel Myers and Carl Jung were not the first to sort humanity into separate categories. Perhaps the earliest such system was the theory of the humors and their corresponding temperaments, proposed by the ancient physician Galen: sanguine, melancholy, bilious, and choleric. But modern psychology dabbled in types, too: William James divided people into the tough-minded and the tender-minded; Sigmund Freud set out the oral, genital, and anal paths of development; Freud's followers (including Jung) offered their own groupings, such as Erich Fromm's exploitative, hoarding, receptive, productive, and marketing types.

Like Galen, some twentieth-century researchers tied psychological type to physical type. In 1921, the German psychiatrist Ernst Kretschmer introduced an influential theory linking body build and vulnerability to particular mental illnesses. There was the slender, frail "asthenic," susceptible to schizophrenia; the round, stocky "pyknic," predisposed to manic depression; and the muscular "athletic" type, usually normal. His classifications were employed by the Third Reich to select military officers—used to indicate, for example, which members of the Luftwaffe should become fighter pilots and which should fly transport planes.

Kretschmer's notions found an American home in the work of psychologist William Sheldon, who developed his own set of anatomical-psychological connections: ectomorphy (thin and irritable), endomorphy (fat and jolly), and mesomorphy (muscular and even-tempered). Every individual belonged to one of these biologically determined categories, Sheldon declared, and it was his aim "to tell them apart, not as Jim and Joe but as kinds and types of animals."

Sheldon's system, reminiscent of the pecking order at a boys' boarding school, was welcomed by the public (*Life* magazine ran a cover story in 1951) and even by academia. During the 1940s and 1950s, the psychologist persuaded the administrators of Ivy League and Seven Sisters colleges to allow him to photograph their freshman students, naked, in order to pursue his research. Sheldon took nude pictures of tens of thousands of collegians—pictures that caused a scandal when they resurfaced half a century later.

Sensitive and excitable, restrained and unrestrained, subjective and objective, herbivorous and carnivorous: for centuries, even millennia, types exerted an irresistible appeal, especially for laypeople. They reduced the exhausting variety and complexity of human beings to a small number of well-defined groups, each possessing a reassuring solidity and stability. (An ectomorph will no more turn into a mesomorph or an endomorph than a "mastiff will change into a spaniel or a collie," Sheldon maintained.)

But in the wake of World War II, type theories began to fall out of favor, at least within mainstream psychology. Adolf Hitler's insistence on the unvarying qualities of Aryans and Jews made types politically unpalatable, and a maturing science of personality found them intellectually suspect as well. Types could never be more than crude simplifications, contended most academic psychologists, who preferred to understand personality as an agglomeration of various traits. William Sheldon's work, once so popular, vanished from sight, and theories of psychological types more generally were dispatched to the disreputable realm of astrology, phrenology, and fortune-telling.

This skeptical, even scornful, attitude toward type formed one formidable strike against Isabel Myers's new test. Another obstacle to its acceptance was its origins in Jungian psychology. Though Carl Jung enjoyed an ardent following, his excursions into mythology, alchemy, and the occult had aroused wariness among many American psychologists, who found his system of psychological types both too vague and too complicated to be useful. A third barrier thrown up before Myers and her test was the hostility toward amateurs long present in psychology. Responding to the testing abuses of the 1910s and 1920s, the profession had instituted a crackdown on what it regarded as dangerous chicanery. In 1915 the American Psychological Association passed a resolution denouncing "the use of mental tests for practical psychological diagnosis by individuals psychologically unqualified for this work." (Much of their outrage was likely motivated by the fact that these freelancers were stealing their business. One of the nation's largest test-publishing companies was The Psychological Corporation, a firm whose original stakeholders were all psychologists. It compiled "a blacklist of charlatans and ignoramuses" who threatened to siphon off its lucrative trade in testing.)

Given these conditions, it's no surprise that the Indicator encountered a chilly reception. Even with her by-now well-honed talent for persuasion, Myers had trouble finding a psychologist or publisher willing to take her seriously. Even Carl Jung reacted with only tepid enthusiasm to her adaptation of his ideas. Myers, who had picked up her mother's correspondence with the psychiatrist, mailed him a copy of the Indicator in

1950. Jung thanked her "for kindly sending me your interesting questionnaire," but declined her request for a visit, explaining that a "tedious illness" would keep him on holiday for several months.

Myers's only real encouragement came from her own family, and their support—emotional and financial—was crucial. Katharine provided firm guidance, and Lyman supplied his statistical and mathematical expertise. Their generous gifts also constituted the test's major source of funding. When Myers turned fifty-two, her birthday gift from her parents was a check intended for the Indicator. "A thousand Thanks!" she effused in a letter to her father. "You and Mother have been so wonderful in backing it up." On another occasion, she spent their present on file cabinets large enough to hold five thousand test cases—and "someday," she vowed to her parents, "I am going to have five thousand cases."

Chief, too, supported his wife's efforts, though he didn't quite share her zeal. He was too busy being a lawyer "to really get interested in type," he explained to a relative, adding that his role was simply to drive Isabel wherever she wanted to go. Chief contributed his legal skills to Isabel's testing enterprise, and also his talents around the house: he scrubbed the floors that his wife was too busy to clean, and built a fireproof room below the basement to store her precious data.

Myers was buoyed by her family's faith in her, and by the enthusiastic response the test elicited from her friends and neighbors in Swarthmore. But the true source of her drive was a passionate belief in the importance of her work. From her original intention of helping wartime Americans find suitable jobs, her ambition for the Indicator had expanded enormously: it became nothing less than a way to change the world. On an individual level, the awareness of psychological type it provided made life "more amusing, more interesting and more of a daily adventure," she declared. On a societal level, the test could do even more: "It is not too much to hope that wider and deeper understanding of the gifts of diversity may eventually reduce the misuse and nonuse of those gifts," Myers asserted. "It should lessen the waste of potential, the loss of opportunity, and the number of dropouts and delinquents. It may even help with the prevention of mental illness."

And on a global level, the insights afforded by the Indicator could work wonders of diplomacy. If President Woodrow Wilson had not been so wrapped up in his own introversion, she confidently explained, he would have negotiated more effectively at Versailles, and World War II might have been averted. Almost any event or circumstance, in fact, could be viewed through the prism of type—for example, the United States's character as a nation. "In the early days of colonial America, the appeal of the New World's possibilities were probably felt so much more strongly by intuitives than by sensing types that it introduced a potent factor of selection," Myers professed. "Commonly attributed national characteristics" could be explained by the fact that the American colonies "drew off a disproportionate share of the intuitives and left an unusually large majority of sensing types in England."

The housewife from Swarthmore, Pennsylvania, had devised a key to human nature and history the world over. Psychologists of the day may have scoffed, but Myers's hard-driving history suggested that she should not be underestimated.

Isabel Myers's aspirations for her test may appear grandiose, but in fact this was one way in which she was firmly in psychology's mainstream. In midcentury America, science seemed close to solving most of man's pressing problems, including those created by man himself.

Earlier in the century, psychologists in the employ of industry had focused mainly on the factory and on the work being done there. Scientific management experts like Frederick "Speedy Fred" Taylor dedicated themselves to finding the "one best way" to perform a specific task, then set each employee on the assembly line to doing it in just that fashion. In the name of efficiency, jobs were restructured, machines rejiggered, and plants reorganized; the worker himself was expected to simply go along with these changes. A popular philosophy of the time was summed up by the motto of the 1933 World's Fair: "Science Finds, Industry Adopts, Man Conforms."

In the postwar era, however, the limits of this approach became evident. Even as America's factories were pumping away at full capacity, the nation's other organizations—schools and universities, corporate bureaucracies, government agencies—were also rapidly expanding. Within these institutions, it was people themselves who required sorting and shaping. These were not mass-produced products, however, but irregular and idiosyncratic individuals, and there was no "one best way" that could be imposed on all. Personality psychology provided a solution to this puzzle, permitting individual variation among employees but placing it under the control of the employer. A worker was allowed to have a distinct personality so long as it was defined and limited by his boss; his boss could then use that label to assign him to a particular niche.

Personality tests, of course, would assist in this process. The Humm-Wadsworth Temperament Scale, for example, detected in test takers tendencies ranging from "cycloid" (emotional) to "schizoid" (withdrawn) to "autistic" (compulsive). "Normal-cycloid" individuals made good salesmen and truck drivers, the Humm's authors advised, while "normal-autistic" people were better suited to being bookkeepers and night watchmen. Every position, from machinist to secretary to chairman of the board, had an ideal personality to fill it, and the only remaining problem was finding the right "fit." Unpredictability was eliminated, uncertainty banished, complexity and changeability reduced to a notation in a personnel file. Each human cog would fit smoothly in its predetermined place.

There were a few protests raised against this tidy system. "It will not do to assume that certain jobs can be successfully handled only by a narrowly limited range of character types: that we need 'extrovert' or 'oral' salesmen and administrators, and 'introvert' or 'anal' chemists and accountants," demurred sociologist David Riesman in *The Lonely Crowd*, published in 1950. "Actually, people of radically different types can adapt themselves to perform, adequately enough, a wide variety of complex tasks." In *The Organization Man*, appearing six years later, author William Whyte asked: "Is the individual's innermost self any business of the organization's? In return for the salary that The Organization gives the individual, it can ask for superlative work from him, but it should not ask for his psyche as well."

Workers themselves, of course, often had little choice but to hand over their psyches at their superiors' request. But many seemed persuaded by the psychologists' vision of a rationalized workplace, and so willing to accept and even embrace the identities provided by their employers. No one was more infatuated with this orderly ideal than Isabel Myers. She viewed her test, and its potential to organize human affairs, with something like awe. Writing to her father, she reflected that the Indicator seemed to have assumed an independent existence, "with a future and rights of its own to growth and fame and fulfillment," and with

Myers herself in "the role of its general manager." In another letter to Lyman, written in 1954, she was even more reverential. The Indicator, she declared, "is clearly my destiny."

The first sign from the outside world that Myers's passionate conviction might be justified came in 1956, fourteen years after she began to develop her test. Henry Chauncey, head of the Educational Testing Service, was interested in the Indicator.

ETS, as it's known, is the publisher of the SAT, the standardized test taken by almost every college-bound high school student in the nation. Now a $700-million giant employing more than two thousand people, it was then a small, clubby firm run largely at Chauncey's whim. For years he'd looked for an effective personality test to add to ETS's aptitude and achievement exams, so he listened closely when Harold Wiggers of Albany Medical College told him about the Briggs-Myers Type Indicator. (Wiggers was one of the many medical school deans whom Myers had inveigled into administering the test.) Chauncey was immediately intrigued, and directed a staff member to send a letter to this Mrs. Myers, inviting her to visit ETS's offices in Princeton.

Myers was thrilled: at last, the Indicator was receiving the attention she felt it richly deserved. On May 22, she marched into an ETS meeting room full of young, male PhD's, whose jaws dropped at the sight of her: a middle-aged woman, frumpily dressed, her graying hair pulled into a bun. Myers launched into an enthusiastic explanation of her test, employing her own improvised vocabulary and statistical methods. Chauncey was sufficiently impressed with the large amounts of data Myers had collected that he signed her to a contract. Six years later, in 1962, her long-cherished dream became a reality with the publication of the Myers-Briggs Type Indicator. (ETS had persuaded her to change its name to reflect her own leading role in its creation.) Even at this point, the test was intended only for research applications, having been judged too crude for consumer use—a caveat that did not dim Myers's delight at being taken seriously by a mainstream publisher.

The employees of that publisher were hardly united in their support for the Indicator, however. Out of Chauncey's earshot, many ETS psychologists derided it as unscientific rubbish. An early internal evaluation of the test hints at their disapproval: "A veil of suspicion hangs

about it. It had an unorthodox origin, it is wedded to a somewhat un-
fashionable theory, and the enthusiasm it has aroused in some people
has provoked sterner opposition in others," read the report. Even the
manual for the Indicator, produced for ETS by a young staffer named
Lawrence Stricker, read more like a harsh critique of the test than a
helpful guide to its use. (Myers told a friend that after reading the manual, she felt "like I sent for the Marines, and they came over the hill
shooting at *me!*") She did not, of course, meekly accept such criticism
but fired off a letter to Chauncey, her chief ally at ETS, decrying
Stricker's "misinterpretations, distortions, and omissions." She filed the
manual in a folder labeled "Larry Stricker, Damn Him." And she wrote a
scolding missive to Stricker himself, admonishing him that his commentary would be more useful if it adopted a neutral tone, rather than a
barely concealed contempt that sought to "cut off the dog's tail behind
its ears." She closed with a self-assured flourish: "The dog," she announced, "just might turn out to be a champion."

The episode vividly demonstrated Myers's transformation from an ardent young woman to a formidable matron, convinced of her correctness and determined to have her way. The complaints of the ETS
personnel, in fact, quickly shifted from the test to its creator. Staffers referred to her as "the little old lady in tennis shoes" or simply "that horrible woman," and some asked for a day off or a place to hide when she
came to their office. Another internal document alludes to the problem:
"Mrs. Myers has dedicated her life and that of her family to the concept
of type; she believes it to be a profound and extremely important social
discovery," it noted. She sees herself as "a kind of modern Joan of Arc,"
and for her, "anything that may further the development and promulga-
tion of the Indicator and its acceptance by the professional public tran-
scends any other code of behavior."

At home and on her regular visits to ETS, Myers continued to work
tirelessly on behalf of the test, sustained by an ever-present Thermos of
"Tiger's Milk," a concoction of brewer's yeast, milk, and Hershey bars
that she deemed the "perfect high-energy diet." She liked to roam her
publisher's office late at night, a habit that allowed her free access to files
that wary staffers kept off-limits during working hours. Such liberties,
along with her incessant requests for more research assistance from the
firm, led some at ETS to recommend that its relationship with Myers be

terminated. She lost her most enthusiastic champion at the company when Henry Chauncey retired in 1970. Meanwhile, sales of the SAT were topping two million as the baby boomers entered college; by comparison the Myers-Briggs was "a very small fly on the wall," says one ETS executive. Lacking internal support for the test, the company let it languish, investing little in its development or promotion.

In 1975, ETS notified Myers that it was dropping the Indicator altogether. Her embrace by psychology's establishment had been temporary and equivocal; now, once again, Myers was on her own.

Her association with ETS, begun with such high expectations, had ended in crushing disappointment. But the indomitable Myers refused to give up, and she was rewarded with a new reason for optimism. In spite of ETS's neglect, interest in the Indicator had been growing steadily, spread by a small group of committed users. The first to discover the test were counselors working with college students. Their clients were bright, often high-functioning people for whom pathology-oriented tests like the MMPI seemed inappropriate. As early as the 1960s, the Myers-Briggs was administered at Michigan State University, the University of Florida, and Auburn University in Alabama. In 1965, a graduate student at Auburn wrote the first PhD dissertation on the Indicator.

The test found fans in other odd corners: Japan, for example. Takeshi Ohsawa, an industrial psychologist in Tokyo, translated the Myers-Briggs into Japanese in 1968, and within a few years he was administering it to a quarter million people a year. (The test is still widely used in that country.) Psychologist Donald MacKinnon, a colleague of Henry Murray's at Station S—and a former neighbor of Myers's in Swarthmore—employed the Indicator to study creativity at his Institute of Personality Assessment and Research in Berkeley, California. But the test did not gain a firm foothold in mainstream psychology until it was discovered by a woman named Mary McCaulley.

McCaulley, a psychologist on the faculty of the University of Florida, stumbled upon the Indicator in 1968 while perusing the *Mental Measurements Yearbook*, a comprehensive catalogue of psychological tests. Intrigued by its description, she ordered a copy and was delighted by the response it generated from her students and clients. "That's just how I feel," they told her when she described to them their type, expressing relief that "it's okay to be my kind of person." One test taker told her, "I feel like it X-rayed my soul!" McCaulley contacted Myers to request more information, and a year later they met in person. The two women discovered that they were both INFPs (introverted-intuitive-feeling-perceivers)—the type, said Myers, shared by "everyone who has fallen in love with the Indicator without anyone else telling them about it."

Indeed, McCaulley conceived a passion for the test that rivaled Myers's own. "When I discovered your work," she wrote to Myers, "it seemed as if I had found something I was looking for all my life." Psychological type gave her a feeling of meaning and purpose, and a satisfying sense of belonging: "It was as if I had come home." McCaulley made a gratifyingly devoted disciple. "You have set a foundation" for future generations, she told Myers, and psychological type would continue to "inspire young people" for decades to come.

For Myers, the support of this reputable academic was an inestimable prize. She began visiting the University of Florida several times a year, and she and McCaulley started attending professional meetings together and collaborating on a revised manual for the Indicator. In 1972, the two women founded the Typology Laboratory, later renamed the Center for Applications of Psychological Type (CAPT). (Myers rejected the title Type Applications Center—TAC—vowing, "No one is going to call my work tacky!") Though early on the center was "a chewing-gum-and-string kind of operation," acknowledged McCaulley, its mission was unstintingly ambitious: it promised to use type "to promote personal development," "to manage conflict," and "to increase human understanding worldwide."

So enraptured was Myers by her new niche in the academy that Chief began complaining about her absorption. His wife's "Jungian disciples" in Florida now monopolized her attention, he grumbled to a friend, and it was difficult even to get her to go out to the movies. But by now the Indicator was gaining irreversible momentum. It received a powerful push in 1975 when a new firm, Consulting Psychologists Press, took over its distribution, making the test widely available for the first time. The change in publishers made an immediate difference: from 1976 to 1979, sales of the Indicator tripled, reaching one million by the end of the decade. In 1975, the first national type conference was held at the University of Florida. In 1977, a journal devoted exclusively to research on type was established. In 1979, a membership organization, the Association for Psychological Type, was founded.

That year also saw a bittersweet development: the publication of *Please Understand Me*, a popularization of Myers's ideas by psychologist David Keirsey. The book became a best seller, but Myers harbored no envy or ill will: her one aim was to share the benefits of psychological type with as many people as possible. Now in her eighties, she was slowed by age, but she never stopped working on her beloved test. Myers had battled recurrent cancer for many years, and was now waging what would be her last fight. In the months before her death in May 1980 she was still at work, correcting the proofs of *Gifts Differing*, a book about psychological type. (Said the book's publisher: "Isabel is the only author we've ever had who, when you send a manuscript you have carefully edited, reedits the whole thing back to her original form and sends it back to you.")

Six months before she died, she had been feted at a special meeting of the national type conference, held in Philadelphia in order to honor her eighty-second birthday. Almost a thousand people turned out for the event, just four years after the first such convention drew a handful of attendees. Myers was toasted as an intellectual "giant" and presented with a necklace, INFP spelled out in gold letters. Back at home that evening, she turned to Chief, now her husband of sixty-one years.

"I really should have burst the bubble by telling people that I have been extremely fortunate in being able to do just exactly what I wanted to all my life," Myers told him. "Doing what I did was my idea of fun."

———■———

Everyone in this room hates her job.

On a Sunday afternoon in November 2002, two dozen people have gathered at the 92nd Street Y on Manhattan's Upper East Side to learn how a personality test can help them change their lives. From the hallway float the bright notes of a music recital and the aroma of chocolate-chip cookies baked in the Y's kitchen, but in here the mood is tense.

"Every morning when I walk into my office, my stomach hurts," says Shana, an Internet salesperson with striking blue eyes and hair soft and short as velvet.

"I never thought that this is what I'd do when I grew up," echoes Stacy, a round-faced public-relations executive with pearl earrings and a faint Southern drawl.

"I'm in finance and I want to get out," declares Amy, a freckled twenty-two-year-old whose dark hair is pulled back in a knot. Going around the room, the story is the same. The workshop participants are marketing coordinators, human resource managers, information technology consultants—the kind of nebulous, new-economy jobs no kid dreams about and with which today's workplace is rife. Nodding sympathetically at the front of the room is Shoya Zichy, a large, comfortable woman with graying blond hair and an expressive face. She's heard all this before, and she knows how to help.

Zichy is a type expert, an executive coach who uses the principles of psychological type to help those struggling in their professional lives: people who want to change jobs, improve their skills, find their true calling. Her sympathy is genuine, since she's been there herself. Twenty years ago Zichy was a private banker for Citibank. Sent on a business trip to the Philippines, she was stranded late one night in the Manila airport when, she says, Imelda Marcos commandeered her plane to take an impromptu jaunt to Malaysia. Alone save for a janitor sweeping the floor around her, Zichy resigned herself to a long wait. Then, as she tells the story: "In the middle of a large pile of debris, I noticed a book. Dog-eared and well-used, it caught my attention. I picked it up, and from that moment on my view of the world was altered forever."

The book set out the fundamentals of psychological type, concepts which Zichy immediately applied to her banking work. Her new business increased by 50 percent over the next few months, she says, but ultimately type helped her recognize something else: she was in the wrong profession. "I spent fifteen years in an industry in which people like me were maybe one percent of the population," Zichy says. She is an ENFP, or an extroverted-intuitive-feeling-perceiver, which according to type theory usually describes a person who is warm and vivacious but also scattered and disorganized. Now she understood why hers was the only red suit in a sea of navy blue, why she enjoyed interactions with clients but dreaded management meetings: "It's all very clear when you look at my type." Zichy dropped out of finance and became a full-time painter for four years. This too proved unsatisfying, and "more and more I gravitated to the work I should have been doing to begin with, which is training and coaching and helping people develop." Now, says Zichy, "I'm endlessly interested in what I do."

Back at the Y, she gives each member of the workshop a personality test: the version of the Myers-Briggs popularized by David Keirsey. Heads bend, pencils scratch. There are whispered complaints about the forced-choice format of the questions, as two participants confer over an apparently impossible choice between (A) and (B). "Can I add (C)?" one asks, half-seriously. "Don't overthink this," Zichy announces, patrolling the room. "Your first instinct is usually the truest one." Once they're finished, Zichy arranges the class into four groups based on their results: sensing-judging, sensing-perceiving, intuiting-thinking, and intuiting-feeling. At first people sit stiffly in their seats, smiling awkwardly as Zichy begins to explain the four categories. One participant asks her if people's types ever change.

"No, they don't," she says firmly. "They are there from infancy, from cradle to grave. The difference is in how you learn to manage it." She offers herself as an example: "I'm an extrovert, but I've learned to shut up sometimes." Another person tries again: "Do you find that people oscillate between types depending on their comfort level?" "No, I don't," she repeats. "People don't change their basic orientation." Overmastered by her utter certitude, the group seems to yield, giving themselves over to Zichy and her neat system.

The conversion is complete once she turns discussion over to the small groups. People sprawl in their chairs; the talk grows loud and animated. Zichy has directed them to make lists: how they describe themselves, what they admire and what they find irritating about the other groups. There's a lot of laughing, even some trash-talking: "Look at those Girl Scouts over there!" snorts one intuiting-thinker about her sensing-judging neighbors. The intuiting-feelers are huddled together, conversing intimately. "I just met these people, and I feel like I've known them forever!" one exclaims. Zichy announces a ten-minute break, but no one gets up.

Regaining their attention at last, Zichy goes around the room once more, asking the workshop's members which type-appropriate profession they have selected from the list she passed out. Shana says she's contemplating a career as an Outward Bound instructor. Stacy says she's thinking of becoming a teacher. Amy turns to Zichy and beams. "I want to do what you do," she says.

This is type today: from a test created in one woman's living room, the Myers-Briggs Type Indicator has become a global phenomenon. Following Myers's death in 1980, the test's popularity continued to surge; it was given to 750,000 people in 1983 and to 3 million in 1993. It is used by thousands of companies, including eighty-nine of the Fortune 100. Almost unknown before the mid-1970s, it is now, according to its publisher, "the world's most popular personality assessment." It has been translated into sixteen languages, and chapters of the Association for Psychological Type have sprung up in places from Australia to Korea to South Africa (there are more than two dozen chapters here in the United States).

The Indicator—these days it's often referred to by the acronym MBTI—is now under the stewardship of Myers's son, Peter, and his former wife, Katherine Downing Myers. Growing up in Swarthmore, Kathy knew the Myers family well; she, like Peter, has memories of Isabel sitting in the living room, laboring over the Indicator. "She seemed to be in her chair working every morning by eight at the latest and she was frequently there when we went to sleep at night," Kathy recalls. "I mostly remember her in that chair." During Myers's lifetime, Kathy and Peter acted as her "apprentices," helping her develop and refine the instrument; after she died, they became "guardians" of what Myers called "my baby." Like Myers herself, they have great aspirations for the Indicator: in 1999 they established the Myers & Briggs Foundation, a nonprofit organization that takes as its mission "extending the benefits of psychological type throughout the world."

In 2001, Mary McCaulley stepped down as president of the Center for the Application of Type; more than three decades' acquaintance with Myers and her test had only deepened her devotion. At the twelfth biennial type conference in 1997, McCaulley gave a toast in honor of what would have been Myers's hundredth birthday, calling the Indicator's creator "one of the few authentic geniuses." (McCaulley died in August 2003.) The center's database now contains the records of more than a million test takers, and its Isabel Briggs Myers Memorial Library holds the world's largest collection of Indicator-related publications, dissertations, and theses. Consulting Psychologists Press (now known as CPP) is still the distributor of the instrument, which it calls a way to "build understanding and transform lives."

So popular is the Myers-Briggs that it has inspired myriad imitators. The earliest, of course, was David Keirsey's Temperament Sorter, the test that formed the basis of *Please Understand Me* (and that Shoya Zichy uses in her workshop). Still in print, Keirsey's book has sold more than two million copies, and three million people have taken an online version of the Temperament Sorter. It, and other Indicator knockoffs, further simplify what was already a popularization of Carl Jung's ideas. Many of them reduce Myers's sixteen types to four, and assign each a color, an animal, or another easy-to-remember handle. There's the Management By Strengths system, for example, which has found a niche at automobile dealerships around the country. While the cars in the lot may come in a rainbow of colors, the people who work there come in only four: red (the "direct" person); green (the "extroverted" person); blue (the "paced" person); and yellow (the "structured" person). Zichy herself has created a rival to the Myers-Briggs, using colors to represent *her* four types of people: guardians, pragmatists, rationals, and catalysts. She calls it the Color Q. "It's shorter" than the original, she says, "but just as accurate."

The Indicator and its imitators are now applied to an almost unimaginably broad variety of purposes. It's employed by counselors and coaches like Zichy to fit people to jobs. "I use the Myers-Briggs as a foundation for my counseling," reports Norma Zuber, a career adviser in Ventura, California. "It looks superficial, but it is a profound instrument." The tests are often administered by corporations themselves: AT&T, Exxon, General Electric, Honeywell, and Transamerica are among the many major corporations that have used the MBTI. Some businesses use the exams to identify job applicants whose skills match those of their top performers. The Similarity Index, for example, is a service offered by The Computer Psychologist, a company located in Atlanta, Georgia: test takers are assigned a number based on how closely their personalities resemble those of successful employees. "Cloning humans isn't an option," says president Frank Merritt, sounding almost regretful—but, he suggests, finding their personality doubles is. (In a sublime example of such coerced conformity, psychologist Rowan Bayne reports the case of a group of executives who were told by their boss that they had six months to "become ENFJs," their company's "designated management type.")

Other companies use the Myers-Briggs to develop communication skills and promote teamwork among current employees (one study finds that about 40 percent of the personality tests administered by large corporations are used for such purposes). The prominent consulting firm McKinsey & Company, for example, has made the test an integral part of its operations; McKinsey "associates" often know their colleagues' four-letter MBTI types by heart. Businesses also rely on personality tests to ease strains among coworkers with dissimilar backgrounds. As one North Carolina-based workshop leader, who administers the Indicator in the diversity seminars she conducts, put it: "People tend to react to each other based on race and gender without realizing that what they're responding to is personality characteristics." When the oil giant Texaco settled a race discrimination suit for $176 million in 1996, its intensified "diversity training" efforts included administering the Myers-Briggs to eight thousand of its employees.

The Indicator has also been embraced by academia (at least outside of psychology departments). Universities use the Myers-Briggs to match roommates, enhance career counseling, and enliven student orientation sessions. The MBTI has been incorporated into the curricula of military academies and colleges as well. For almost twenty years, for example, every freshman at the U.S. Naval Academy has taken the test; a 2003 report in the Proceedings of the United States Naval Institute blamed troop attrition on "type-preference conflict" between intuitive-feeling-perceiving sailors and sensing-thinking-judging officers. The Indicator has been given to medical students for decades, and is now spreading to business schools and law schools as well. Donald Baker is a University of Alabama law professor and MBTI proponent who received so many inquiries about the test from other schools that he set up an e-mail discussion network on the subject. Knowing their type "not only helps students with their reasoning, learning and writing abilities, but also trains them in those crucial 'people' skills that today's legal profession requires," he maintains.

Perhaps most surprisingly, the Indicator has found a welcome niche at churches and other religious organizations across the country. In workshops and on retreats, congregants take the Myers-Briggs to better understand their own spirituality and to improve communication with other worshipers. Lynne Baab of Seattle, Washington, conducts classes on the MBTI for churches in her area. An understanding of type, she says, can uplift everything from an individual's prayer style to a church's collective good works. "People of different types take on different kinds of volunteer opportunities," she offers as an example. "You don't want someone whose Myers-Briggs type ends in 'P' to be putting together the schedule for the food bank!" A shelf full of books now addresses the connection between type and theology; readers will learn from them that each of the world's major religions represents a different Myers-Briggs type, and that Jesus was a classic ENTP.

The list goes on: social service agencies, law firms, technology companies, professional sports teams, financial planners, marriage counselors, dating services—all use the Indicator or tests like it. Perhaps it's a good thing that the type-guided matchmakers now in business didn't exist in 1917. Isabel Myers once told a friend that if she'd known about type before she met Chief, she probably wouldn't have married him.

It's easy to see why the Myers-Briggs would appeal to businesses and other organizations; it does so for the same reasons that "people-sorters" appealed to the employers of the early twentieth century. The need to select strong applicants is as pressing as ever—and the need for these people, once hired, to get along is even greater. Today's employees are less likely to man an assembly line (and less likely, for that matter, to be only men, or only whites). Instead, they collaborate with coworkers, interact with clients and customers, accept and offer direction—all tasks that require them to relate, often closely, with a diverse group of other people. A benign way to describe differences is indispensable in a project-based, team-organized, service-oriented economy.

Original and independent-minded as she was, Isabel Myers managed to create a personality test that conforms perfectly to this twenty-first-century workplace. The Indicator's unfailingly positive tone blends seamlessly with the language of corporate political correctness and with our society's emphasis on promoting self-esteem. The euphemistic blandness of the Myers-Briggs, its mild vocabulary of "fit" and "gift," is the key to its success, and it has been widely copied by other, similar instruments.

Here's how one publisher promotes its personality test, the Omnia Profile: "That an employee's personality needs to 'fit' the duties of the job to be successful should come as no big surprise. The more 'natural' and comfortable the behavior required by the job for the employee, the better he or she will do the job." The nice folks at Omnia want to save workers from any unnatural, uncomfortable lack of fit: "For instance, having your reserved, accommodating assistant make coffee for a big meeting is easy for her because it allows her to be the helpful, team player she naturally is. Asking her to try and sell widgets to everyone who calls, though, requires her to be something she's not naturally—assertive, thick skinned and goal driven . . . Selling is 'unnatural' and potentially painful behavior for her. Making coffee isn't."

The sly brilliance of using the Omnia Profile, the Myers-Briggs, or any other personality test to label employees is that, by dint of answering the test's questions, employees appear to be labeling themselves. After all, the boss didn't arbitrarily assign them an Administrator personality or a Counselor-Advisor personality—workers chose it themselves with their responses to Omnia's fifteen-minute questionnaire. Once that tag has been affixed, certain capacities and limitations "naturally" follow, all of them defined and determined by the employer. The worker's freedom to shape her own identity at work ends with the choice between (A) and (B).

Employees are often encouraged to embrace this assigned identity, to wear it almost literally on their sleeve. The Management By Strengths system, for example, provides workers with color-coded name tags announcing their type to everyone they encounter. At the Brooks Group, a sales-management training firm in Greensboro, North Carolina, employees are given a framed copy of their personality profile to hang in their offices. (The boss, profiled as a "doer-talker," has his posted just outside his door—perhaps to offer his subordinates fair warning.) Such types and profiles were created for the convenience of the employer—but in time, it's hoped, employees will make them their own.

The administration of personality tests is frequently presented as a gesture of corporate goodwill, a generous acknowledgment of employees' uniqueness. Under this banner of respect for individuality, organizations are able to shift responsibility for employee satisfaction onto that obliging culprit, "fit." There's no bad worker and no bad workplace, only a bad fit between the two. It's a conveniently fatalistic philosophy: workers can't be trained in new skills or grow into new responsibilities, and workplaces can't be expected to accommodate their developing needs and abilities. Personality functions as an escape valve, letting off potentially explosive pressures for individual freedom and institutional change. Whether we are "thinkers" or "feelers," "sensers" or "perceivers" makes an effective distraction from other kinds of questions: whether the work we do is fairly managed and adequately paid, whether it's personally rewarding and socially useful. Looked at from this less entertaining perspective, our economy is full of jobs for which no one is really "fit."

But how to explain the most startling aspect of the Indicator's popularity—its ardent embrace by individuals? Almost alone among personality tests, the Myers-Briggs has developed a passionate following among laypeople who cherish the insights it provides into themselves and others. The epiphany Shoya Zichy and Mary McCaulley experienced upon first encountering type is so common, in fact, that in MBTI circles it has a name. Peter Myers explains that his mother "called it the 'aha' reaction, an expression of delight that so often came with a person's recognition of some aspect of their personality identified by the Indicator." He adds that "one of her greatest pleasures in giving feedback after scoring a person's Indicator was the occasional astonished response" she received from those who felt that its descriptions were uncannily accurate.

Of course, few test takers could find the Myers-Briggs actively objectionable; it's too determinedly innocuous for that. But for some significant number of people, the earth moves, the heavens open, the world suddenly makes sense. Although the observations offered by the MBTI often have an ingenuous, all-I-really-need-to-know-I-learned-in-kindergarten quality, they are greeted by this group as deeply profound. These are the people who immediately figure out the type of everyone they know, whose everyday speech becomes an alphabet soup of Indicator acronyms, who can explain just about every situation they encounter with reference to the types of the individuals involved.

Once their infatuation is in full bloom, type devotees may seek out others who share their passion. "The type community is like Machu Picchu," confides Shoya Zichy. "It's a hidden city. It's there, but it's not vis-

ible in the bookstores or the libraries." The faithful nevertheless find
their way to the hundreds of books about psychological type—many of
them published by CPP, the Indicator's distributor—which apply the
theory to everything from marriage to parenting to spirituality. They attend type conferences and workshops, the descriptions of which frequently place the instructor's four-letter type after his or her name like a
credential. They buy T-shirts, coffee mugs, tie tacks, license-plate
frames, and computer mouse pads emblazoned with their type or with
self-congratulatory slogans: "ENTJs Are Life's Natural Leaders," "INTPs
Incubate Ideas." They may even participate in chat rooms and e-mail
discussion lists specifically for their type.

Why do so many people fall in love with the Myers-Briggs? One of its
principal attractions is no doubt its reassuring confirmation of what we
already know about ourselves. Unlike projective techniques, which
claim to confront us with detritus dredged from our unconscious, the
MBTI repackages a shallow self-appraisal in a more appealing form. If a
test taker doesn't agree with the four-part type he or she is given, "we
must continue trying out type descriptors and questions until the person
feels comfortable, and the counselor feels comfortable," says Kathy
Myers. This process, known as "finding best-fit type," is intended to produce an identity as cozy and familiar as an old sweater.

Another aspect of the Indicator's allure is its comforting stability; as
Shoya Zichy insisted, a person's type does not change. The Myers-Briggs
instantly confers a clear, firm identity, often just at the moment when it
is most needed: when people are switching jobs, looking for a partner,
feeling lost and purposeless. And Myers's relentlessly positive orientation ensures that everyone's permanent personality is a good one. This is
a Lake Wobegon world, where all of the children (and all of the adults,
too) are above average. Faults and failings, when they are acknowledged, are put down to "a deficit of type development" or "falsification
of type." Type theory has no room for internal contradictions, inherent
flaws, base impulses. The only villains here are external pressures that
would pull us away from our "real selves," from our "own ideal path of
type development."

The Myers-Briggs also offers an attractive way to understand relationships with other people. No longer complicated and mysterious,
friends, family, and acquaintances are now easily understood with refer-

ence to their types: "She's a total ESFP," "He's such an INTJ." Conflicts are not due to genuine differences of opinion or interest, but simply to the divergent ways various types comprehend and communicate. Even as it elides real differences in philosophy, politics, and status, the Indicator offers test takers an imagined bond with others of their type. Although personality tests ostensibly isolate the ways in which we're unique, the Myers-Briggs often seems aimed at subsuming individuality in a convivial crowd. "It lets people know that they're not alone," explains career counselor Norma Zuber.

The Indicator, in short, is not so much diagnostic as therapeutic, not about exploring people's personalities but about making people feel better. In this sense, the "aha moment" experienced by many of its fans really does mark a transformation. The test taker is no longer an ambivalent, uncertain individual, struggling along in a confusing and sometimes unfriendly world. With the help of the Myers-Briggs, she's become a person with a firmly fixed identity, occupying a snug niche in an orderly universe full of people just like her.

The question, called out from the back of the packed meeting room, is really more like a compliment: "Is there anything that you *haven't* accomplished on behalf of the Myers-Briggs?"

But as Peter Myers slowly gets to his feet and takes a microphone unfamiliarly in hand, he seems full of sober urgency. "Yes, there is," he says meaningfully. Peter, seventy-seven, has his father's height and his mother's gentle features. "The supreme thing that has not yet happened is the acceptance of Jungian psychology and the MBTI by the academic community." He looks around at the crowd of more than a hundred people and speaks emphatically: "We need to prove to the scientists what everyone in this room already knows." He sits down amid a rush of applause.

Although the Myers-Briggs has certainly won over "everyone in this room"—a May 2003 gathering of New York City type professionals, hosted by Shoya Zichy—along with legions of organizations and ordinary people, scientists have remained stubbornly resistant to the Indicator's ingratiating charms. "An act of irresponsible armchair philosophy," writes one. "Too slick and simple, possessing an almost horoscope-like quality," demurs another. "A party game," "a Jungian horoscope"—when academic psychologists have evaluated the Indicator, their judgments have not been kind.

But the scientists' disdain is shown most clearly in their neglect. Myers-Briggs proponents like to point to the more than 7,800 studies that they say have been conducted on the MBTI. But a significant number of these articles were published in specialty publications like *The Journal of Psychological Type*, *MBTI News*, and *TypeWorks*. Many others appeared in books produced by CPP, the Indicator's distributor. And most research on the Myers-Briggs is concerned with exploring applications for the test—not with proving or refuting its basic legitimacy.

Scientific psychology takes issue, as it has from the beginning, with the very essence of the Myers-Briggs: type. The skepticism that greeted Isabel Myers when she introduced her type-based test has since grown only stronger. Most people's personalities, psychologists note, do not fall neatly into one category or another, but occupy some intermediate zone; this fact makes the assignment of type imprecise and even arbitrary. Scientists' doubts are supported by the frequency of changes in test takers' supposedly inborn and immutable types. One investigation (conducted by Indicator proponents, no less) found that the percentage of people who achieved the same four-part type across two administrations of the test was only 47 percent. In other words, more than half of those who took the Myers-Briggs were given a different type when they took the same questionnaire a short while later.

Another study discovered that individuals' types may change even according to the time of day. Its authors described one subject, for example, who "was a good intuitive thinker in the afternoon but not in the morning." One of the most thorough appraisals of the Myers-Briggs appears in *In the Mind's Eye*, an evaluation of "performance-enhancing techniques" commissioned by the National Research Council. Published in 1991, the report notes that a variety of studies have found that 24 to 61 percent of test takers receive the same Myers-Briggs type when reexamined at intervals ranging from five weeks to six years. That means, of course, that 39 to 76 percent are assigned a *different* type. Changes of this frequency, write authors Daniel Druckman and Robert Bjork, "suggest caution in classifying people in these ways and then making decisions that would influence their careers or personal lives." Although the test's champions claim that its feedback can make people

more sensitive to the ways they think and behave, "unfortunately, neither the gains in sensitivity nor the impact of those gains on performance have been documented by research," Druckman and Bjork point
out. "Nor has the instrument been validated in a long-term study of successful and unsuccessful careers." The authors conclude their examination of the MBTI with a recommendation that it not be used for career
counseling "until its validity is supported by research."

Even when an individual consistently attains the same type, that des-
ignation may not mean much. While there is limited scientific support
for some of Myers's basic dimensions (people do seem to differ in their
relative levels of introversion or extroversion, for example), there is no
evidence that her sixteen distinct types have any more validity than the
twelve signs of the zodiac. And research has found little connection between Indicator types and real-life outcomes. There is scant evidence
that MBTI results are useful in determining managerial effectiveness,
helping to build teams, providing career counseling, enhancing insight
into self or others, or any other of the myriad uses for which it is promoted.

But what about all those "aha moments"? Could thousands of Myers-
Briggs devotees have been deceived? Once again, science's conclusion is
blunt: yes, they could. Psychologists explain the test's overwhelming popularity with reference to what they call the "Barnum effect." The phenomenon is named after the famous showman P. T. Barnum, who liked to
say that a circus should have "a little something for everybody." MBTI
personality descriptions, it's suggested, also offer "a little something for
everybody": enough hedged statements and vague commonplaces to
allow any individual to read one and think, "Yep, that's me."

The first research on what would later be termed the Barnum effect
was conducted by psychologist Bertram Forer in 1949. After administering a personality test to a group of subjects, Forer handed back their
results—but the participants' ostensibly individualized personality descriptions were actually all the same, lifted from an astrology book
Forer had purchased at a newsstand. Some excerpts: "You have a great
need for people to like and admire you." "You have a great deal of un-
used capacity which you have not turned to your advantage." "You prefer a certain amount of change and variety and become dissatisfied
when hemmed in by restrictions and limitations." "You pride yourself

as an independent thinker and do not accept others' statements without satisfactory proof."

Participants were then asked how accurate they found their profiles. On a scale of 0 (poor) to 5 (perfect), the subjects gave their reports an average rating of 4.2, with more than 40 percent awarding a flawless 5. Subsequent research has demonstrated other intriguing aspects of the Barnum effect: that people are often unable to identify whether the results they're given are derived from a test they've taken or made out of whole cloth, for example, and that given a choice, we actually *prefer* the invented feedback. A finding with particular relevance for the Myers-Briggs is that individuals are more likely to endorse positive accounts of themselves, a phenomenon scientists call the "Pollyanna principle."

With this research in mind, read some descriptions drawn from the Myers-Briggs literature. Test takers may learn that they are: "Adaptable, flexible, and accepting unless a value is threatened." "Conscientious and committed to their firm values." "Loyal, considerate, notice and remember specifics about people who are important to them, concerned with how others feel." "When committed, organize a job and carry it through." "Loyal and committed to their values and to people who are important to them."

Contemplating these artful statements and the raptures of recognition they often inspire, one recalls another quip for which P. T. Barnum was famous: "There's a sucker born every minute."

The warnings of academic psychology seem to have dissuaded few admirers of the Myers-Briggs. Their passion for the test is a matter of emotion rather than rational analysis; they are engaged, it might be said, in a romance. Those who love type have been seduced by an image of their own ideal self, have fallen hard for a rosy vision of their own potential. In the blush of this infatuation, science's dour pronouncements are as little heeded as the admonitions of disapproving parents.

In any case, psychological type has built a private world around itself, an intimate universe that has no need for external validation (however much Peter Myers and others would like to have it). For those within its charmed circle, type provides an unwavering self-conception, a foundation for relating to others, a plan for success, and an excuse for failure. It even offers an explanation for why some people refuse to join in: it is, of course, because of their type. Perceivers don't want to be restricted, introverts don't want to reveal themselves, sensers find the theory too abstract, and so on. Type's professional orbit is similarly circumscribed: it has its own journal, its own library, its own network outside of psychological science's usual checks and balances. Not for nothing is the biennial gathering of Myers-Briggs devotees called "World of Type."

Still at the center of this world is the haloed figure of Myers herself, whom her many followers affectionately call "Isabel." It sometimes seems that her fierce ardor for the test she created has been passed on to these followers like a torch. They, like her, appear to value type more than the people type is supposed to describe. The Indicator was Isabel Myers's true love, more than Katharine, more than Chief, more than Carl Jung. Although Myers referred often to Jung, invoking him as a kind of wise godfather to the Indicator, her test does not really descend from his deeply humanistic approach to personality. Rather, its lineage is some unholy union of the human engineering that produced "people-sorters" like the Humm-Wadsworth with an older tradition of American self-improvement, an optimistic philosophy that stretches back to the phrenologists and beyond. If Myers truly was a "genius," her inspiration lay in marrying an industry-friendly management tool with a user-friendly form of therapy. The Myers-Briggs helps institutions find human cogs for their machines, and helps humans feel happy being cogs.

This odd-couple pairing carried the Indicator far away from the spirit of Carl Jung's thought. (That Jung can be understood in a very different way is apparent from what Henry Murray took from the same text, Jung's *Psychological Types*.) While Jung allowed that "type is nothing static. It changes in the course of life," Myers insisted that it was inborn and immutable. While Jung cautioned that "it is often very difficult to find out whether a person belongs to one type or the other, especially in regard to oneself," Myers asserted that personality is evident in "a few basic, observable differences in mental functioning." And while Jung was interested in complicating, even enchanting our world and the people in it, Myers seemed determined to tidy it up, make it neat. One critic of the MBTI has compared the type devotee to "the fisherman calmly fishing for minnows from atop the back of a whale"—ignoring the profound while seizing on the superficial.

Indeed, Jung's writings carried clear warnings to Myers, if she had cared to listen. "Every individual is an exception to the rule," he declared, and fitting such individuals into a rigid system is "futile." To "stick labels on people at first sight," he fulminated, was "nothing but a childish parlor game." But perhaps Jung foresaw that his words would go unheeded, that people would cherish their theories more than the flesh-and-blood individuals they purport to describe. "Everyone," he sighed, "is in love with his own ideas."

SIX

Child's Play

The cross-examination got off to a contentious start.

"You appear to be of rather light color," drawled the chief defense attorney, T. Justin Moore, eyeing the slender, dapper man on the witness stand before him. "What percentage, as near as you can tell us, are you white and what percentage some other?"

Dr. Kenneth Bancroft Clark returned Moore's gaze with a cool stare.

"I haven't the slightest idea," Clark responded, his diction formal and precise. "What do you mean by 'percentage'?"

"I mean, are you half white, or half colored, or half Panamanian, or what?"

"I still can't understand you."

"You don't understand that question?"

The more insolent the lawyer became, the more dignified was his witness. In due time, Moore elicited from Clark that he was born in the Panama Canal Zone, of Jamaican parents, and moved to the United States when he was four; that he grew up in Harlem, attended college at Howard University and graduate school at Columbia University; and that he was now an assistant professor at the City College of New York.

Earlier, under friendlier questioning by plaintiff's lawyer Robert Carter, Clark had been more forthcoming, talking freely about his work with black children in Harlem. Though he was a psychologist who studied personality, Clark did not focus on inborn preferences, or unconscious psychodramas, or modes of perception—any of the factors that his predecessors believed make people who they are.

Instead, he spoke of the unrelenting pressure of large social forces on the individual personality. "I have come to the conclusion that prejudice, discrimination, and segregation in general, each has a basic corroding and distorting effect upon the personality of the Negro child who is a victim of these," Clark testified. Racism, he continued, warps the personalities of its victims in different ways: "Some human beings may react by withdrawing, becoming submissive, seeking to avoid as many contacts with this punishing society as it is possible for them to avoid," Clark observed. "Others may react aggressively, become rebellious, and try to fight back against the society that is trying to tell them they are almost substandard human beings."

It was this novel approach to personality that had brought the thirty-seven-year-old Clark to the courtroom in Richmond, Virginia, in February 1952. Robert Carter was one of a small band of lawyers then working for the National Association for the Advancement of Colored People (NAACP), suing local governments to desegregate their schools. This particular case—*Dorothy E. Davis v. County School Board of Prince Edward County*—concerned a school for black children located in Farmville, Virginia, about seventy miles southwest of the courthouse. The facilities of Robert R. Moton High School were so miserably inadequate that they had prompted an angry walkout by students a year earlier. Their school had no gym, no cafeteria, no science labs; it was filled to bursting with pupils, some of whom were taught in a school bus or in tar-papered outbuildings known as the "chicken shacks."

The material deficiencies of Moton, and the many amenities of the all-white Farmville High School a few blocks away, made a mockery of Supreme Court rulings permitting public facilities to be "separate but equal." But the NAACP advocates didn't just want to secure equally good schools for black children. They wanted to overturn the whole regime of segregation, to force the public schools to educate white and black children together. To accomplish their bold aim, they would call on a surprising ally: a quietly passionate man and his revolutionary personality test.

To persuade hostile Southern judges to overturn segregation, NAACP staffers recognized, they would need to prove an elusive proposition: that segregation in itself was harmful. Such proof required a way to measure the nature and extent of the damage, a seeming impossibility until Carter heard about the work of Kenneth Clark. The psychologist claimed he had developed a technique capable of probing "the delicate, complex areas" of race and personality, a tool that made the wounds of racism visible to the eye.

In the Richmond courtroom, Carter now asked: "Dr. Clark, are there any methods which are scientifically accurate with which a psychiatrist can test a child and determine whether or not an isolated fact like racial segregation has any effect upon his personality growth or development?"

There were several ways such an assessment could be attempted, Clark replied: psychologists might conduct interviews or administer pencil-and-paper questionnaires. But "the most promising methods," he said, "which are being more and more used for this, are what are called projective methods. These are methods which have the advantage of eliciting certain responses from your subject which ordinarily you would not get in those cases in which you are dealing with the kinds of problems, or the kinds of ideas, or the kinds of attitudes which the individual might not want to deal with directly." The psychological scar of racism, in other words, was for many blacks the kind of shameful secret, half-hidden even from themselves, that projective tests were designed to reveal.

Clark cited the Rorschach and the Thematic Apperception Test as examples but noted that these instruments were less than ideal for work with school-age children. Rather than presenting youngsters with an inkblot or a drawing, Clark explained, he and his wife, Mamie (also a psychologist), gave them two dolls. Made from the same mold, the dolls differed only in the color of their skin: one was white, the other black. "Then we ask them questions such as, 'Which doll do you like best?' 'Which doll is a nice doll?' 'Which doll is a nice color?' " Clark said from the stand. "Well, on the face of it, this seems to be a kind of situation in which a child was just reacting to dolls. Actually, the results which we get are much more fundamental, more profound, in telling us not only how this child reacts to himself but how he reacts to himself in terms of the personal problem of the factor of race."

Under Carter's gentle prompting, the usually reserved Clark grew voluble. Throughout his testimony, an impatient Moore repeatedly interrupted, complaining that the witness was talking too much. (One of the three judges hearing the case agreed, asking irritably, "Can't you abbreviate, Dr. Clark?") At last it was Moore's turn to interrogate the psychologist from up North. Wasn't it a fact, Moore asked, that the NAACP was out to make trouble, to "stir up and foment critical situations?" Wasn't it true, he demanded, that "the Chinaman and the Indian have, in their own way, pride of race?" So why, he inquired, couldn't "the Negro" be happy in his place and not try, as Moore put it, to be "a suntanned white man"?

Working himself into a rhetorical lather, Moore mounted an attack on the NAACP's fragile new strategy, the claim that it was not only material deprivation but psychological harm that made segregation so invidious. He conjured up a vision of a sparkling new school, "just as good as any high school in Virginia," in which teachers, "every one of them," have twenty years' experience and a PhD in education, in which the students "have brand-new buses to ride to school every day in." If black children attended such a school, he asked, would Dr. Clark still insist that they were being damaged, just because there were no white children present?

Robert Carter and the other NAACP lawyers held their breath. Would their star witness, an able but mild-mannered psychologist, come through?

Kenneth Clark drew back to look his questioner in the eye. "I insist that, Mr. Moore. And I insist it most sincerely, because I do not believe material things are as important as your question would suggest that they are." In a tone of quiet authority, he continued: "No amount of that kind of material attempt at equality can ever substitute for the kind of essential dignity, acceptance, and humanity, which every human being, without regard to his color, his religion, or national background, must feel, if he is going to be a fully mature and fully adult human being. You cannot buy it with bricks and mortar."

The very presence of a psychologist in the courtroom was a sign of the times. In the years following World War II, the weight of cultural authority had shifted to men like Benjamin Spock and Alfred Kinsey, social scientists with expert knowledge of human nature. Increasingly, these doctors and professors took the place of ministers and priests, replacing religious dictates with commandments of a different kind. The NAACP became the latest cause to seek the blessing of social science when it entreated psychologist Kenneth Clark to testify on its behalf.

Clark had impressive academic credentials: a PhD from a prestigious university, a decade of research and clinical work, more than two dozen published papers. But his power as a witness followed from a less traditional qualification: those dolls.

Clark's doll tests were no dry laboratory experiments, but tiny dramas inflamed by the pain of racism. Responding to Clark's queries, black children did not just choose the white doll to play with; they actively disparaged the dark-skinned doll, calling it "dirty" and "bad." When he asked his young subjects which doll was "like you," they often became agitated. "A great many of the children react as if I were the devil in hell, myself, when I ask this final question," Clark recounted ruefully. "Some of them break down and leave the testing station; they cry . . . It is as if I had tricked them. We were all friendly before, they were expressing very freely their spontaneous reaction, and then I put them on the spot." Such reactions, he said, were proof that his technique was tapping "the flagrant damage to the self-esteem, the self-respect of the Negro child."

There were skeptics, of course, even within the NAACP. William Coleman Jr., an assistant attorney working on the desegregation cases, was one of the doubters. "Jesus Christ, those damned dolls!" he exclaimed later. "I thought it was a joke." He and others heaped ridicule on the test, but Robert Carter and lead lawyer Thurgood Marshall believed that the skillful use of psychology was their best hope for a legal victory.

As it turned out, Carter and Marshall were correct in predicting that psychological expertise would play a central role in the case of *Davis* v. *County School Board*—though in a way they had not anticipated. Two days after Clark offered his testimony, another psychologist ascended the witness stand. This was Henry Garrett, chairman of the psychology department at Columbia University and past president of the American Psychological Association. Garrett knew Clark and his work well; in fact, he had served as Mamie Clark's adviser and as a member of Kenneth Clark's doctoral committee. But if Carter and Marshall imagined that psychology would be a dependably loyal ally in their fight against segregation, they were mistaken: Garrett, an unapologetic racist, was testifying for the defense.

In the months before the *Davis* trial, the NAACP had called Kenneth Clark to the stand in two other desegregation trials, and the de-

fense in these cases had been unprepared to rebut his psychological testimony. Not this time. The powers who wanted to keep white and black
children separate had recruited their own social science experts. "If a
Negro child goes to a school as well equipped as that of his white neighbor," Garrett confidently professed, "if he had teachers of his own race
and friends of his own race, it seems to me he is much less likely to develop tensions, animosities, and hostilities, than if you put him into a
mixed school where, in Virginia, inevitably he will be a minority group."

Clark's tests did not persuade him otherwise, he said; in his testimony, Garrett spoke condescendingly of the "idealistic person" who is
"so strongly prejudiced on the side of abstract goodness that he does not
temper the application of the general principle with a certain amount of
what might be called common sense." (Clark in particular was "none
too bright," in Garrett's opinion: "He was about a C student, but he'd
rank pretty high for a Negro.")

In addition to Garrett, the defense called on another psychologist,
John Buck. Like Clark, Buck had created a personality test for children,
in his case while working at the Lynchburg State Colony, a Virginia
mental hospital. Buck believed that his own test, which required youngsters to draw a house, a tree, and a person, provided a revealing "self-
portrait" of the drawer. But he could see no connection between these
insights and larger social problems; he did not believe, he testified, that
personality tests had "any substantial validity as applied to the public
school situation in Prince Edward County."

In his closing statement, defense attorney Moore seized on Garrett's
and Buck's statements as proof that segregation was not psychologically
harmful, after all, and that Clark's tests were worthless. "In summary,"
he proclaimed, "the testimony of all our experts shows that these so-
called projective tests which are being used are really of very little value
in this field." One thing was certain, however: "We do know that a perfectly terrible situation would be created, which would be detrimental to
the colored children as well as the white, if by court decree the system
we now have were done away with."

The judges concurred. "It indisputably appears from the evidence
that the separation provision rests neither upon prejudice, nor caprice,
nor upon any other measureless foundation," wrote Judge Albert Vickers
Bryan, author of the opinion. "Rather the proof is that it declares one of

the ways of life in Virginia. Separation of white and colored 'children' in the public schools of Virginia has for generations been a part of the mores of her people. To have separate schools has been their use and wont." With finality he declared: "In this milieu we cannot say that Virginia's separation of white and colored children in the public schools is without substance in fact or reason. We have found no hurt or harm to either race. This ends our inquiry."

The decision did not, however, end a long-running tension in the use of psychology to mold the shape of society. Though the profession had only recently gained the general attention and approbation of the public (thanks in large part to the help it provided during World War II), it had a longer history of taking positions, and not always admirable ones, on matters of importance to public life.

Personality psychology and testing had an especially checkered past. As often as it had been used to question our ideas about who we are, it had offered a convenient prop for the status quo. Minorities and women, for example, were early on regarded as too undifferentiated even to possess unique personalities. Variations among ethnic groups began to attract more attention around the turn of the century, when changing patterns of immigration led researchers to compare Americans of Anglo-Saxon stock with newer arrivals from southern and eastern Europe (what one psychologist called "these oxlike men"). Not surprisingly, the results of their tests confirmed the assumed superiority of northern Europeans, leading some social scientists to urge restrictions on immigration from less-favored countries.

This was "race psychology," a doctrine that held that individuals' personality and other characteristics were determined by their ethnicity. The discipline, which made its first appearance in the *Psychological Index* (an annual listing of research studies) in 1912, expended its most vigorous efforts on documenting the differences between whites and blacks (and, sometimes, American Indians). An article in *Psychological Bulletin* described "the mental qualities of the Negro" this way: "lacking in filial affection; strong migratory instincts and tendencies; little sense of veneration, integrity, or honor; shiftless, indolent, untidy, improvident, extravagant, lazy, untruthful, lacking in persistence and initiative, and unwilling to work continuously at details." A book titled *Race Psychol-*

ogy: *A Study of Racial Mental Differences* reported that American Indians were "decidedly inferior" to whites in the areas of "judgement, breadth, intensity, reasonableness, independence, refinement, unselfishness, and integrity."

Within a few decades, however, beliefs about race and personality had begun to shift. First came the recognition that even if minority groups were, in fact, different from the white majority, it might be these groups' enforced role in society rather than some inherent defect that made them so. This insight animated an important book of the period, *An American Dilemma,* by the Swedish sociologist Gunnar Myrdal. Asked by the Carnegie Corporation to investigate America's "Negro problem," Myrdal in 1944 issued a report that noted personality differences between blacks and whites but posited a firm opinion on their source: such differences "have no basis in biological heredity" and "are of a purely cultural nature," he wrote. Though the personality traits he attributed to blacks were often unattractive (they are "more indolent, less punctual, less careful" than whites, Myrdal asserted), he offered a sympathetic explanation for such flaws: "They know that all the striving they may do cannot carry them very high anyway, and they feel the harshness of life—the caste pressures are piled on top of the ordinary woes of the average white man."

The next step was an acknowledgment that the environment shapes *all* of us, men and women, majority and minority. Social scientists now trained their attention on that "average white man," not in his customary role as benchmark of normality but as just another crooked creature of society. This was the perspective adopted by another classic of the era, *The Authoritarian Personality.* The product of a group of social scientists based at the University of California at Berkeley, the book, published in 1950, advanced the theory that "authoritarianism"—the propensity to blindly follow a reactionary leader—was actually a personality type rooted in childhood experiences. Led by the German philosopher and social critic Theodor Adorno, the group developed personality tests to identify the type, characterized by obsessive conformity, extreme rigidity, and deep insecurity expressed as a hatred of outsiders and minorities.

Their F Scale (for fascism) probed for signs of "underlying antidemocratic trends in the personality" with items like "America is getting so far from the true American way of life that force may be necessary to re-

store it," and "Too many people today are living in an unnatural, soft way; we should return to the fundamentals, to a more red-blooded, active way of life." The authors' psychoanalytic orientation led to a predictable emphasis on sexuality—for example, "The sexual orgies of the old Greeks and Romans are nursery school stuff compared to some of the goings-on in this country today, even in circles where people might least expect it"—but, interestingly, the item that yielded some of the most useful information concerned young people: "Obedience and respect for authority are the most important virtues children should learn."

Though the Berkeley group's work on authoritarianism was stimulated by some of its members' experiences as Jews in Europe (and by the increasingly appalling developments on that continent), research for the F Scale was conducted on Americans: ordinary citizens drawn from service clubs, public speaking classes, and adult education courses in West Coast cities like Oakland, California, and Eugene, Oregon. Studies employing the F Scale indicated that there was plenty of conformity, rigidity, and ethnic hatred right here at home—an unsettling observation that would be borne out by the often-violent reaction to the civil rights movement just then getting underway. Adorno and his colleagues used the conventional categories of normal and abnormal in an unconventional way: to suggest that it was the majority that was diseased, the whole society that was sick.

Social science's approach to personality had been spun around by a surge of strong historical and intellectual currents. The traumas of the twentieth century—two world wars, the Great Depression—made it abundantly clear that events could alter personality. Adolf Hitler's atrocities made horrifyingly real the dangers of classifying people by supposedly inherent characteristics. And the ascendance of psychoanalytic and anthropological perspectives on personality placed new emphasis on environmental influences, especially child rearing. "The majority of mankind quite readily take any shape that is presented to them," wrote anthropologist Ruth Benedict, whose work emphasized the role of culture in the formation of individual personality. "Human nature is almost unbelievably malleable," affirmed another anthropologist of this school, Margaret Mead. Such views seemed to have ready application to the dilemmas of minority children growing up in a racist country. Offered

only a cramped corner of society, the child contorts himself to fit it. "He is the little creature of his culture," Benedict observed, and "its habits are his habits, its beliefs his beliefs, its impossibilities his impossibilities."

By midcentury, social science's approach to personality was a swirl of exciting and provocative ideas. And in the middle of it all was Kenneth Clark.

Clark came late to an awareness of the relationship between culture and personality. Growing up in several different Harlem neighborhoods, attending an elementary school full of Irish and Jewish as well as black children, he rarely encountered racial segregation. That confrontation would occur when he enrolled in college at age seventeen, leaving New York City for the almost-South of Washington, D.C. "At Howard University was the first time in my life that I became aware of what it really meant to be a Negro in America," Clark said later. It was, he added, "an education in race relations which will stay with me for the rest of my life."

His dormant political consciousness was roused by the bigotry he met in Washington. When he was turned away from a public restaurant located in the Capitol Building because of his color, for example, he and a group of classmates returned with picket signs, "in order to see if we could not get them to treat us like the loyal Americans which we felt we were." Such experiences transformed him into "a quite different person," he reflected, someone with "a very intense feeling of race and with a very, I think decided tendency to be disturbed about racial problems."

Clark had arrived at Howard intending to become a doctor. In his sophomore year, however, he happened to take a psychology class. "To hell with medical school," he decided. "This is the discipline for me." For Clark, psychology held out the possibility of a "systematic understanding of the complexities of human behavior and human interaction"—including insight into "the seemingly intractable nature of racism." While at Howard he also met Mamie Phipps, the woman who would become his lifelong collaborator. Clark first persuaded Mamie to become a psychology major, and then persuaded her to marry him.

Following graduation, Clark moved back to New York to study for a PhD at Columbia University. His mentor there would be social psychologist Otto Klineberg, whose 1935 book, *Race Differences*, concluded that

"there is no adequate proof of fundamental race differences in mentality, and that those differences which are found are in all probability due to culture and the social environment." At the time, in fact, Columbia was buzzing with activity at the intersection of culture and human development, its anthropology department home to both Ruth Benedict and her (and Margaret Mead's) influential mentor, Franz Boas. Inspired by this heady atmosphere, Clark began exploring the ideas that would later emerge full-blown in his doll tests. He served on the staff of the Carnegie Corporation, doing research for Gunnar Myrdal. He consulted for the American Jewish Committee, the organization that underwrote the Adorno group's studies on the authoritarian personality. And he wrote articles of his own, notably a case study of an eighteen-year-old race riot participant, "R.," published in 1945.

Clark's sharp skills of observation were apparent in his description of the young man's distinctive clothing—"rusty brown shoes, striped blue socks, extremely pegged pants (narrow at ankles and wide at knee), a quite long jacket"—and his slangy speech: "John the Man" (for Mayor Fiorello La Guardia) and "Castle-a-Bunk-a" (for house). Looking for a vocabulary to describe the influence of racism on personalities of young people like R., Clark coined a phrase that made reference to his subject's audacious style. "The 'zoot effect' in American culture appears to manifest itself when the human personality has been socially isolated, rejected, discriminated against, and chronically humiliated," Clark wrote. "It is the consequence of the attempts of the individual to stabilize himself and maintain some ego-security in the face of these facts." As always, Clark's concern was for the way individuals fashion their personalities in response to powerful social forces.

Clark received his doctorate in 1940 and became an instructor at the City College of New York in 1942. Four years later, he and Mamie opened the Northside Testing and Consultation Center, a youth clinic in Harlem; eight years later, he prepared a landmark report on the effects of prejudice on children's personalities for the Midcentury White House Conference on Children. Without quite being aware of it, Clark had been preparing for years to play a major role in the nation's racial politics. He'd overcome many barriers along the way: he was the first black person to receive a PhD from Columbia's psychology department, the first black person to become a full professor at City College. When his side lost the *Davis* v. *County School Board* case in 1952, the defeat only strengthened his resolve. This was Kenneth Clark's reaction to racism: the harsher it was, the more determined he got.

The NAACP was determined, too. It appealed the *Davis* decision, which the U.S. Supreme Court bundled with four other suits to form the case known as *Brown* v. *Board of Education*.

On May 17, 1954, the U.S. Supreme Court handed down its verdict. Not only did it declare segregation unconstitutional, but it offered psychological reasons for doing so: "To separate [black schoolchildren] from others of similar age and qualifications solely because of their race generates a feeling of inferiority as to their status in the community that may affect their hearts and minds in a way unlikely ever to be undone." The opinion, written by Chief Justice Earl Warren, attributed this finding to "modern authority"—that is, psychology—and referred in a soon-to-be-famous footnote to a review of social science research (including the doll tests) that Clark had helped produce for the court.

Clark was teaching a class at City College when he was summoned to take a call from Thurgood Marshall. Learning of the unanimous ruling, Clark was swept by "tremendous exhilaration," he remembered. "I just felt so enthusiastic. I felt joy at being an American. I was full of hope and optimism." Across town, a celebration broke out at the Clarks' Northside Center when the news came over Mamie's radio. For the first few days after the decision, Clark recalled, "we were in the clouds." Many of Clark's professional colleagues shared his jubilation, viewing the decision as a victory not only for civil rights, but for psychology. The *Brown* judgment was the most important Supreme Court decision to rely so heavily on social science research, a gesture that constituted "the greatest compliment ever paid to psychology by the powers-that-be in our own or any other country," exulted Otto Klineberg, Clark's Columbia mentor.

Clark himself became an instant celebrity, known nationwide as "the doll man." For his contribution to the watershed case he received effusive plaudits, countless speaking requests, and a clutch of honorary degrees. Thurgood Marshall even insisted that those NAACP lawyers who had doubted the value of the psychologist's testimony bow down to Clark and admit their mistake. Energized by his stunning success, Clark allowed his expectations and ambitions to expand. He would become a "psychologist for society" engaged in "public therapy," a healer who would treat not only individuals but the country's entire population. "American children can be saved from the corrosive effects of racial prejudice," he declared a year after the *Brown* decision. "These prejudices are not inevitable; they reflect the types of experiences that children are forced to have. Such prejudices can be prevented—and those already existing can be changed—by altering the social conditions under which children learn about and live with others." Clark boldly concluded: "When human intelligence and creativity tackle the problem and bring about the changes in the society, then these prejudices and their detrimental effects will be eliminated."

For those who sought to heal society's ills, children made ideal patients. Still malleable, they readily accepted the impress of their environment, whether it was the pernicious racism of the segregated South or the enlightened egalitarianism promoted by Clark in books such as *Prejudice and Your Child*, published in 1955. Clark realized just how susceptible youngsters were to the biases of their elders while administering his doll tests. "The fascinating thing, the thing which we did not expect, was the getting of evidence that this damage began as early as it did," he reported. Earlier research had revealed the injuries that racism inflicted on adolescents, but "this was the first time we had evidence that it could begin as early as four or five years old, and the more sensitive and intelligent the child, the earlier it began."

If the personalities of blacks (and whites, for Clark believed that they too were deformed by bigotry) were not to be irreparably damaged, interventions must be made early. Facilitating his strategy was the fact that parents were by this time accustomed to accepting child-rearing advice from psychological experts; from now on that counsel would address not just sleep schedules and feeding times but issues of racial identity and self-esteem. Clark and other socially minded psychologists were going to change the world, and they were going to start with the children.

Before he could act as psychologist to America's youth, however, Clark had to prove that they needed his help. As he had noted during the *Davis* v. *County School Board* trial, using personality tests to examine children was fraught with difficulty. Their literacy was limited, so written questionnaires were of little use. They often lacked a grasp of abstract concepts that would allow them to compare themselves to a hypothetical norm: "more than most people," "as often as others." And they were frequently frightened or intimidated by the testing situation, leading to bashful reticence. Almost inevitably, the special demands of testing children led psychologists to employ projective techniques, which didn't require their young clients to read or perform abstract mental operations and which often resembled disarming forms of play.

Dolls were used to gather information about children's inner lives as early as the 1920s, when New York psychiatrist David Levy developed an approach he called "activity play therapy." Levy would actually "get under the desk and play with the child for perhaps an hour; that's where the patient put the interview, and that's where he went," recalls an observer. "He would say to the child, 'This is the mother doll, this is the father doll, this is the child doll. What do they say?' And the child would start talking." Psychoanalysts Anna Freud and Melanie Klein also introduced dolls into play sessions with young patients.

A more focused approach was taken by Ruth Horowitz of Columbia University's Teachers College. Horowitz was interested not in dispensing therapy but in exploring "children's emergent awareness of themselves, with reference to a specific social grouping"—that is, race. Her Show Me Test, published in 1939, was designed especially "to get below the level of active language, to utilize the vast reservoir of understanding which comes before the organization of verbal expression, the child's fund of passive language." Children aged two to five were shown pictures of a white boy and a black boy and told, "Show me which one is you." Minority children were more accurate in their selections, leading Horowitz to speculate that they early on developed a sense of being different.

The Show Me Test caught the attention of Clark, and with Mamie he embarked on a series of similar investigations (eventually employing dolls instead of pictures). Their early experiments were modeled closely on Horowitz's, but by the mid-1940s they had added a crucial component: asking their young subjects to "Give me the doll that you like best," "Give me the doll that is a nice color," and "Give me the doll that looks bad." Such requests were intended to establish the children's racial preferences, not just their capacity for racial self-identification. The results were sobering. In a 1947 study, two-thirds of the black children tested said they liked the white doll best; nearly as many said that the white doll was a "nice color" and that the black doll "looks bad."

The Clarks concluded: "It seems justifiable to assume from these results that the crucial period in the formation and patterning of racial attitudes begins at around four and five years." At this age, the psychologists wrote, minority children adopt attitudes about themselves that "conform with the accepted racial values and mores of the larger environment." By 1950, the Clarks were stating these views even more emphatically: "It is clear that the Negro child, by the age of five, is aware of the fact that to be colored in contemporary American society is a mark of inferior status." It was up to the educational system, they contended, to relieve "the tremendous burden of feelings of inadequacy and inferiority which seem to become integrated into the very structure of the personality as it is developing."

Dolls weren't the only playthings in the odd toy chest of children's projective techniques: balloons, blocks, dough, clay, and finger paints were all put to use as diagnostic devices. By far the most popular play technique, however, required just a piece of paper and a pencil or crayon. Clark himself often added a drawing component to his doll test, giving children a sheet with outlines of a girl and a boy and objects like a leaf and an apple, along with a box of crayons. He found that black children often colored the human figures yellow, pink, or white, even when they had chosen appropriate hues for the objects. Some applied to the girl and boy strange shades like red and green—indicating, Clark suggested, deep psychic conflicts on the subject of skin color.

The earliest drawing test, which asked children themselves to sketch a human figure, had been introduced in 1926 by psychologist Florence Goodenough. She intended her Draw-a-Man Test as a measure of intelligence, not personality, and awarded points based on the number of details—facial features, fingers, embellishments of hair and clothing—a child included in the drawing. Some psychologists who administered the test soon began to suspect, however, that the drawings children produced revealed far more than their IQ. One who saw a world of feeling and fantasy in a few penciled lines was Karen Machover.

Machover, a clinician at Bellevue and other New York City mental hospitals, was a brilliant but brittle woman who had herself survived a

singularly grim childhood. Her father died the same month she was
born; when she was eight years old, she emigrated from Minsk, Belarus,
to New York but was left to raise herself when her mother died a short
time later. Machover (then Sophie Karen Alper) supported herself
throughout her adolescence, managing to finish college and graduate
school. (Though she received a master's degree and not a PhD, she referred to herself as "Dr.," and most of her colleagues followed suit.)
While working as a clinician she also taught at New York University,
and in 1936 married one of her students, Solomon Machover. A year
later, their son Robert was born.

Only half-joking, Robert Machover today recalls his mother as "a
witch" (she died in 1996). "My mother had X-ray vision about drawings,
especially mine," he says. "What she could see in them were often truths
that were hidden from the person who did the drawing, including myself. I always assumed that there was something supernatural about how
she would interpret them." Karen Machover developed her own technique, similar to Goodenough's, which she named the Draw-a-Person
Test. The subject was given a blank piece of paper and a medium-soft
pencil; he or she was instructed simply to "draw a person," then to draw
a person of the other sex. She gave the test to her young son "hundreds"
of times, he says—until, as a self-conscious teenager, he refused to draw
for her, nervous about what his spookily perceptive mother could see.

In 1949, Machover published a book describing the interpretation of
the Draw-a-Person Test and laying out its theoretical rationale. There is,
she explained, "an intimate tie-up between the figure drawn and the
personality of the individual who is doing the drawing"; the sketches
children produce are less literal renderings of actual people than visual
metaphors for the fears and desires that populate their emotional lives.
Machover's interpretations of these metaphors were recklessly loose,
heavily Freudian, and occasionally (unintentionally) hilarious. She
looked first at the style of the drawing: shading was indicative of anxiety,
while erasures and dark, heavy lines suggested inner conflict. The size
and shape of body parts was significant. A small nose reflected a sense of
sexual inadequacy; a large head, "intellectual or perhaps moral vanity."

Clothes and accessories were also revealing: barrettes, bows, shoe-
laces, and other "restraining yet socially decorative devices," for example, hinted at a struggle for self-control. Ties, pipes, and cigarettes

signaled a preoccupation with sex, while buttons and pockets were tell-tale signs of an excessive dependence on mother. Machover gathered additional clues from the discussions she held with test takers after they had finished drawing. When a paranoid patient was asked why he had emphasized his figure's neck, for instance, he explained that without a neck, "you could not turn your head to see who was after you." In the course of her questioning, Machover often uncovered dark depths beneath an apparently innocent scribble. A girl's omission of one eye in the male figure she drew, Machover reports, "was admittedly associated with sadistic fantasies of annihilating a rival brother by gouging out one of his eyes with her knitting needle."

Machover's psychoanalytic bent led her to discover sexual perversities everywhere in the drawings: oddly shaped hands showed guilt about masturbation, while accentuated breasts were hallmarks of the "orally deprived." Boys who elaborated the waist and hips were suppressing "homosexual panic"; girls who drew wide shoulders were engaging in "masculine protest" (i.e., they wished they were male). Later in life Machover rejected Freud, however, renouncing psychoanalytic precepts with the same certitude with which she had once propounded them. She became a zealous feminist, and began accepting only women as therapy patients, a practice she described as "reparations." Though she remained proud of the Draw-a-Person Test and convinced of its accuracy, she came to regret her participation in "boxing people into categories," says her son—"this whole psychodiagnostic game of which she had been part."

Around the same time that Karen Machover sought to improve on the Draw-a-Man intelligence test, John Buck was becoming frustrated with the limits of another technique: the interview. Buck, a clinician at the Lynchburg State Colony in Virginia (and one of the psychologists who testified in defense of segregation), was trying "to persuade a nine-year-old girl to answer questions—any questions," he recalled. "She steadfastly refused." Finally, "in sheer desperation," Buck asked his young patient if she would be willing to draw instead. "She nodded assent. She was given paper and pencil, and she immediately produced a series of drawings in which sexual symbols predominated."

Buck took up his questions again, and to his astonishment, "the child responded with a fluency that contrasted strikingly with her previous stony silence." He resolved to create a test that would take advantage both of the insights offered by the drawings themselves and of what he called the "pencil-release factor," the fact that children spoke more freely while absorbed in the activity of sketching. Informal experiments revealed that asking clients to draw not just a human figure, but also a house and a tree, yielded the richest trove of information. Like Machover, Buck interpreted these designs with an imaginative abandon unburdened by evidence: the drawing of a person reflects how the test taker feels about herself, he decided; the house reflects how she feels about her family life; and the tree reflects how she feels about her general environment. Buck's first major publication on what he called the House-Tree-Person Technique appeared in 1948, and almost immediately became a favorite of clinicians working with children.

The success of Buck's and Machover's tests, not surprisingly, inspired many imitators: the Draw-a-Family Test and the Draw-a-School Test were two of the earliest, along with the Kinetic House-Tree-Person Test, which asked subjects to show the person in the drawing doing something active. These were followed by the Kinetic Family Drawing and the Kinetic School Drawing, and by now the floodgates were open wide to the Draw-an-Animal Test, the Draw-a-Car Test, the Draw-a-Person-in-the-Rain Test, even the Draw-a-Person-Picking-an-Apple-from-a-Tree Test.

As child psychology and psychiatry emerged as distinct disciplines, personality tests suited for use with young people proliferated. The Rosenzweig Picture-Frustration Study, introduced in 1948, was a set of cartoon panels depicting people in exasperating situations, such as missing a train or getting splashed with mud. The characters had empty bubbles above their heads, ready to express children's angry or destructive urges. The Blacky Pictures, appearing in 1949, were a set of cards presenting the exploits of a cartoon cocker spaniel. The stories children told about Blacky, his sibling Tippy, and their parents were analyzed for the presence of Freudian favorites like oral eroticism, anal sadism, Oedipal complexes, castration fear, and penis envy. Special adaptations of popular adult personality tests were eventually developed: child or adolescent versions of the Minnesota Multiphasic Personality Inventory, the Thematic Apperception Test, and the Myers-Briggs Type Indicator are available. (Teenagers may also be given the standard adult versions of the Rorschach and the TAT.)

Once relatively unusual, personality testing of children has now become routine, incorporated into the admissions process at private schools, the evaluation of learning and behavioral problems, and the investigation of child custody and child abuse cases. A 2002 survey of child psychologists found that they spent more than a quarter of their time testing their young clients; a recent poll of school psychologists revealed that they spend about 50 percent of their time conducting assessments (and only 19 percent offering treatment). Even more striking is the rapid rise of an industry based on healthy children's personalities: teaching to them, parenting to them, making them the basis of self-esteem and communication-skills programs. Kenneth Clark—who bought the dolls he used in his test at the Harlem Woolworth's for fifty cents each—might be surprised to see how widespread, and how elaborate, children's personality tests have since become.

———■———

Lancaster High School in Buffalo, New York, is the kind of place that the students at Virginia's Moton High School could only have dreamed of. Built in the years just after the *Brown* decision, it's a sleek, modern building with rows of lockers lining long hallways, floors buffed until they gleam. In the classrooms are banks of whirring computers; in the parking lot is a fleet of yellow school buses. But Lancaster's crowning glory is its field house: finished in 2000, the gymnasium spans 31,500 square feet and cost $1.7 million to build. On the last day of June 2003, it is quiet and dark—but in anticipation rather than disuse.

First the music starts up: a thumping beat so loud the air vibrates. Then the laser show begins, sending showers of light streaming over the walls and floor. Finally, at the back of the building two sets of double doors burst open, letting in a blast of midday sun. The kids come in stomping, cheering, chanting, dancing. They keep coming and coming until the space, chilled meat-locker cold, grows warm with the heat of almost two thousand pubescent bodies. These are "student leaders" from all over the country, here for the annual conference of the National Association of Student Councils. Lancaster High School is their host this year, and they've already been treated to awards ceremonies, motivational speakers, and a trip to Six Flags amusement park. Now it's time to learn about their personalities.

The crowd settles down and turns its attention to a stage, flanked by two huge video screens, set up at the front of the field house. The pounding rock music is replaced by a sprightly pop tune—"True Colors, green and blue/Gold and orange, which are you?"—as a young woman bounds onstage.

"Hi everybody, I'm Letitia Fox, host of the True Colors show!" she exclaims. Her amplified voice booms through the building and her gigantic visage grins from the two screens. "Stand up, everyone, and tell the people around you what color you are!" Earlier today, the teens participated in workshops in which they read descriptions of four personality types, each represented by a color, and chose the one that fit them best. "How many of you are fun-loving Orange?" Fox yells, pointing to her own orange shirt. The room fills with cheers and shrieks. "Let's give it up for the responsible Golds! What about the curious Greens? I feel the *love* in this room—who are the caring Blues?" More screams and whistles.

"Now, let's welcome the True Colors Players!"

The first actor to ascend the stage is a nerdish young man in a yellow button-down shirt. In a pinched voice, he tells the audience that he believes in being organized and planning ahead. "Otherwise, I won't get into Harvard," he explains. A moment later he's replaced by an actress in an orange tank top. "We spend too much time in class," she declares, bouncing on the balls of her feet. "I'm bored just sitting around talking!" She makes way for another woman, wearing green, who clutches a book to her chest and announces solemnly, "I prefer to work alone." Finally, a blue-shirted young man leaps onstage. "I'm sorry I was late," he says sweetly. "I was helping a friend."

The four actors proceed to put on a skit about planning a prom, a task that goes predictably awry. Green calls Gold a control freak; Orange agitates for a pizza break; Blue makes a mushy plea for a group hug. A few minutes later, they've worked it all out. "We're different, and that's okay," Blue concludes. Adds Orange: "We each have our own way of doing things—and together, we can have the perfect prom."

Letitia Fox reappears, wielding a microphone, and several audience members are called up onstage. "So, what did you learn?" Fox prompts a young woman.

"I learned more about myself and how I behave with other colors," the girl answers obligingly. A second girl chimes in: "I learned that I'm a Green, and so I have to be more patient with people." The microphone is passed to a smirking teenage boy.

"I learned . . ." he drawls, ". . . that Orange is number one!" Whoops and hollers fill the field house, right up to its expensive rafters.

True Colors is the brainchild of a California man named Don Lowry. Bluff and self-assured, with the craggy good looks of a soap-opera patriarch, Lowry admits that in his youth he was painfully insecure. He remembers, as a high school football player, taking a good look at his teammates. "I noticed that the most successful athletes were not necessarily the most gifted and talented," he says. "What they had was personal confidence. I felt I lacked that in a lot of areas." As an adult, Lowry became a teacher and a coach. Then, in 1978, his life was changed by a personality test: "All of a sudden I had an awareness of who I was and what I wanted and what I'm about. It was an awakening for me."

Looking for a way to share this epiphany with others, Lowry adapted his insights about personality to a format he calls "edutainment." He borrowed heavily from the work of psychologist David Keirsey (who had borrowed from Isabel Myers, who had borrowed from Carl Jung) in delineating four different personality types, then wrote a role for each in a short play. He put on the first True Colors show in the early 1980s, playing all four characters himself. "The reaction was phenomenal," he recalls. Twenty years later, there are half a dozen four-person casts of "True Colors Players," performing for children all over the country. The True Colors system, which now includes a line of products like books, games, and stickers (Orange kids get a sticker that says "Where's the action!"; Blue kids get one that reads, "Do you need a hug?"), has been used by more than fourteen thousand schools and by organizations like the Girl Scouts and the 4-H Club. Lowry has even worked with the writers of children's television shows to help them develop characters that represent all four personality types.

Lowry's ambitions for his creation, however, have barely been tapped. "We're now working with a whole town—Anaheim, California," he says proudly. "I intend to reduce all of the social problems in that city." He plans to introduce the True Colors approach to personality into every

Anaheim institution, from the Walt Disney Company (already a client) to the public schools and the city government. Even the Anaheim McDonald's, he says, will have placemats featuring True Colors games. "It will be a True Colors city," he says excitedly. "A True Colors city is a place where everyone is valued for who they are."

After Anaheim comes the whole country: Lowry dreams of designing a national personality test, to be aired on television on Sunday nights. (Perhaps this idea isn't so far-fetched: on October 25, 2003, more than 230,000 TV viewers in Austria participated in what was billed as the "world's largest personality test," and Britain's BBC is preparing a similar televised personality test to air sometime in 2004.) After America, the world: Lowry has already begun licensing the True Colors format for use overseas. "There are twenty million teachers in China," he says meaningfully. He seems to take seriously the injunction printed on a pamphlet distributed at Lancaster High School: "Make It a True Colors World."

In the fervor of his commitment and the scope of his ambition, he is not unlike Kenneth Clark. But Lowry has turned the psychologist's central insight on its head. Clark saw that human nature is formed in a complex interaction between the individual and his society, between who he might be and who his culture tells him he must be. In the case of black people living in America, this exchange was tainted by racism, producing personalities that were warped by anger or bitterness or passivity. The healthy development of every American demanded change on a society-wide scale, Clark asserted, and this was a duty all of us bore together. Lowry, by contrast, sees human nature as a set of simple, inborn preferences that vary only in superficial ways. Neither society nor its members require fundamental change; all that's necessary is that we recognize and celebrate our "differences." In a True Colors world, personality is an individual problem with an individual solution.

In fact, Lowry sees an ignorance of personality type at the root of every major social crisis, from poverty to school violence to terrorism. He has taken a special interest in bringing True Colors to the inner city, convinced that minority children in particular need to know if they are Orange or Blue, Green or Gold. A study conducted by his organization, says Lowry, concluded that personality type—and not, say, quality of educational opportunity—is the major determinant of academic success. A simple awareness of personality preferences can make a difference, the company promises, "from Harvard to the ghettos."

Don Lowry calls himself "a pretty far-out guy." But the idea of assigning children—even toddlers—a personality type is gaining mainstream popularity. In 1987, a youngsters' version of the Myers-Briggs, called the Murphy-Meisgeier Type Indicator, was introduced. Intended for use with children in grades two through eight, it labels kids on the same dimensions as the grown-up test: extroversion-introversion, sensing-intuition, thinking-feeling, and judging-perceiving. Parenting books emphasizing personality type have also begun to appear. "Type affects everything—the way you talk to your kid, the kind of activities you encourage them to do, how you discipline them," declares Paul Tieger, coauthor with his wife, Barbara Barron-Tieger, of the 1997 title *Nurture by Nature: Understand Your Child's Personality Type—And Become a Better Parent*. "It's helpful to start getting an awareness of type very early, when they're babies," he adds.

But it's in the nation's schools that personality testing has really taken off. Starting as early as the 1970s and gaining momentum through the 1980s and 1990s, the concept of "learning styles" has become enormously popular among teachers and administrators. The idea is that each child has a preferred way of taking in information, a preference that can be identified by one of the many learning-styles tests now on the market. Bold claims are made for the concept: it can boost students' academic achievement, raise their self-esteem, address attention-deficit disorder, even reduce delinquency and dropout rates.

Some of these questionnaires have a cognitive focus (claiming to determine, for example, whether kids are "visual," "auditory," or "tactile" learners). But others are personality tests by a different name. The Student Styles Questionnaire, for example, is also based on the four axes of the Myers-Briggs. Introduced in 1996 by Thomas Oakland, professor of education at the University of Florida and past president of the International School Psychology Association, it provides young test takers with a computer printout telling them "what their strengths are, and, toward the end of the report, areas that they want to work on," says Oakland. "Wouldn't it have been great to have had that at the age of ten?"

The Learning Preference Inventory is yet another children's test grounded in Jungian personality type. The Learning Styles Inventory, the Learning Style Identification Scale, and the Learning Style Inventory measure a mix of intellectual and personality characteristics. And the Style of Learning and Thinking test classifies children as "left-brain dominant" or "right-brain dominant" (the first group is said to be conforming, organized, and logical, the second explorative, intuitive, and creative). No matter which test they favor, however, learning-styles proponents must confront the fact that little evidence supports their claim that children learn better when "taught to" their preferred style, or that a test can identify what that style might be. And there's no proof at all that learning styles can ameliorate ADHD or rescue delinquents and dropouts.

Robert Brown, emeritus professor of educational psychology at the University of Nebraska-Lincoln, says he "is not aware of any instrument with sufficient theoretical or psychometric support to warrant use for making prescriptive statements for individual students." He adds, "Being attentive to and responding to the needs, interests, and abilities of individual students seems like a worthwhile goal for teachers. However, doing so is much more complex than administering a learning-style inventory and matching teaching strategies to student learning styles."

Other skeptics within psychology have weighed in with criticisms of specific instruments: the Murphy-Meisgeier's authors "propose many possible uses that are not warranted by the evidence." The Learning Preference Inventory "may be a futile and unwarranted exercise." The Learning Styles Inventory is so unreliable as to require "great caution in making educational prescriptions for individual students." The Learning Style Identification Scale "cannot be recommended for use." The Learning Style Inventory is "a psychometric disaster" with "no redeeming values." And the Style of Learning and Thinking test relies on a theory that is "too simplistic" and "not well supported."

Faulty science is only one hazard associated with giving personality tests to children. Such tests impose limiting labels on young people who are still developing a sense of themselves and their capacities. Asked if children are growing and changing all the time, Thomas Oakland retorts, "Nope. These are biologically based qualities. They are there from the beginning." Although such classifications are presented as a boon for kids—"Children typically say, 'My gosh, I wish every child in my classroom could know this about themselves!' " Oakland reports—in truth the labels seem to serve the convenience of adults. Fuzzy, feel-good rhetoric ("Just as each snowflake, tree, and star in the universe is different, so it is with children," coos the promotional materials for Oakland's Student Styles Questionnaire) disguises the fact that these tests are used to rank and track children in disturbing ways.

For example: according to Oakland, gifted students are 29 percent more likely than nongifted students to score as "imaginative" on his test. (The Student Styles Questionnaire substitutes the terms "imaginative" and "practical" for the Myers-Briggs's "intuitive" and "sensing.") It's troubling, then, to hear Oakland proclaim that "blacks and Hispanics generally prefer a practical approach to instruction, which generally focuses on facts and smaller details, while whites are more inclined to an imaginative style, dealing with theories and broad details." Oakland also contends that black students may drop out of school at a higher rate because they "are more likely than whites to base their decisions on 'thinking' rather than 'feeling' styles. 'Thinkers' value honesty even if it hurts the feelings of others, while people with a 'feeling' orientation are more inclined toward harmony."

Stereotypes of gender as well as race are reinforced by this personality test: starting as early as age eight, says Oakland, female students are more likely than their male counterparts to score as "feelers." In order "to be more effective in life," he opines, girls who are labeled "thinkers" "need to acquire a respect for harmony and for relying on and developing their feeling capacities and displaying other feminine qualities." In this way, the apparently benign personality testing of children provides convenient cover for the less appealing agendas of adults. Miriam Hanson is a counselor at Woodstock High School near Atlanta, Georgia, who uses Don Lowry's True Colors system with her students. "It doesn't pigeonhole or get offensive," she enthuses. "Instead of telling someone, 'You're not college prep material,' you can tell them what they might be interested in based on the color they are."

Alongside the relatively new learning-styles tests, projective and play techniques are still used to assess youngsters' personalities. Dolls continue to be employed by those who work with children, though the dolls are now likely to be anatomically detailed models designed to investigate the possibility of abuse. In one study, more than two-thirds of child protection workers used anatomically detailed dolls, along with about a third of law enforcement officers and mental health professionals. Storytelling tests such as the Blacky Pictures and the Children's Apperception Test still have their champions. And drawing tasks such as the Draw-a-Person Test and the House-Tree-Person Test continue to inspire a devoted following: on surveys of test use conducted over the past forty years, they're consistently ranked among the instruments psychologists use most often. (A 2001 survey of testing practices in custody evaluations suggests that projective drawing tests are being used *more* often than before; likewise, a recent study showed that 85 percent of graduate programs in clinical psychology require students to learn about projective techniques, an increase over past levels.) Their popularity persists despite the fact that, again and again, research has demonstrated these tests to be dangerously flawed.

For example: starting in the 1970s, anatomically detailed dolls have been used to identify abused children; sexualized play with the dolls is thought to indicate the experience of abuse. But as numerous studies have since shown, children who have *not* been abused (as well as those who have) often play with the dolls in a sexually suggestive manner. Two recent experiments—conducted by proponents of the dolls—found that a majority of children who had not been abused engaged in touching, rubbing, poking, and pinching body parts, and that a quarter of non-abused five-year-old boys responded to the request "Show me what the dolls can do together," by placing the dolls "in a position suggestive of sexual intercourse." Another study reported that, among a group of non-abused two- to six-year-olds given anatomically detailed dolls to play with, 75 percent spontaneously undressed the dolls and 71 percent touched the male doll's penis. Curiosity about sex and the human body, it seems, is more normal than not.

The Children's Apperception Test, an adaptation of the TAT introduced in 1949, was revised in 1991 and is still used by almost a quarter of clinicians. Researchers, however, have rendered an unequivocal verdict on the instrument: there is "no objective evidence to suggest that the responses to these pictures can be interpreted in a manner that is useful in any scientific sense," a reviewer concludes. "The use of the technique as a method of developing a personality description is entirely unjustified by any scientific standard." Declaring the test "an historical anachronism," another psychologist states that "despite its following, the CAT should not be available to clinicians in its present form." The Blacky Pictures Test, which has no norms and has not been updated since its creation in 1949, has even less to recommend it.

It is drawing tests, however, that have received the harshest rebukes from scientists. Calling the Draw-a-Person Test "embarrassing," one critic derides it as "phrenology for the twentieth century." Another asserts that the technique "more properly belongs in a museum chronicling the history of simpleminded assessment practices in school psychology."

Researchers point out that the "sign" approach to interpreting drawings—inferring personality characteristics from particular details—has no solid evidence behind it, while more global assessments of the sketches are likely to pass judgment on artistic ability and general intelligence rather than personality. The quality of the original research performed by test creators Karen Machover and John Buck has been judged extremely poor: a reviewer called Buck's manual "certainly one of the worst horrors ever perpetrated in the field of clinical psychology," displaying "incredible naïvete, fanaticism, and arrant disregard for any attempt at scientific validation of the material presented." More recent efforts to improve the accuracy of projective drawing techniques have also fallen short.

Yet clinicians who work with children continue to administer drawing tasks to their young patients: 27 percent of clinicians use the Draw-a-Person Test, according to a 1998 survey, and 34 percent use the House-Tree-Person Test. More important, they continue to believe that the conclusions they draw from the tests are correct. Psychologists have a name for this phenomenon: "illusory correlation," or the human tendency to associate two variables that are actually unrelated—to assume, for example, that test takers who draw figures with large heads must have an inflated sense of their own intellectual abilities. A 1995 study suggests that around nine out of ten psychologists who use the Draw-a-Person Test to make diagnoses generate such dubious conclusions.

The ease of arriving at these false assumptions was demonstrated in a classic 1967 experiment conducted by psychologists Loren and Jean Chapman. The Chapmans showed a series of Draw-a-Person sketches to undergraduates who had no knowledge of the test. The college students "discovered" the very same associations—large eyes indicate paranoia, and so on—claimed by the test's promoters and repeatedly debunked by research. "Again and again," the Chapmans write, "the DAP signs have failed to hold up." Still, they note, such connections seem so natural and obvious that we remain convinced of them even when we are shown evidence to the contrary. As a clinician assured the two researchers: "I know that paranoids don't seem to draw big eyes in the research labs, but they sure do in my office."

Kenneth Clark's most crucial point, the one he devoted his career to making, was that the personalities of children are invariably affected by the society in which they grow up. As he testified in the *Davis* v. *County School Board* trial, some people react with rage when confronted with the implacability of racism; others become helplessly passive. A few respond by fortifying their resolve, "by seeking to prove that they are not as inferior as people say." Clark himself was one of these few: in the face of prejudice, he became more ambitious, more industrious, more certain of his goals.

These characteristics served him well in the years following the historic *Brown* v. *Board of Education* victory. Clark was elected the first black president of the American Psychological Association. He taught at Harvard, Columbia, and the University of California at Berkeley. He wrote important, widely read books such as *Prejudice and Your Child*. But as time went by, and America did not become the just society he envisioned, Clark's determined optimism began to waver.

A major blow to his confidence was the country's vehement and often violent resistance to integration. In Farmville, Virginia, for example, whites closed down their own school rather than admit black students from Robert R. Moton, and then—with state funds—established a private academy for white children only. They shut Moton's doors as well, leaving blacks to fend for themselves; many never graduated and came to be called the "lost generation." The county kept its public schools closed for five years, until the federal courts forced it to open integrated institutions in 1964. In the elation that followed the *Brown* de-

cision, Clark had predicted that America would be rid of its racial problems "within ten years or so." A decade on, with peaceful civil rights
protesters being greeted by teargas and billy clubs, the situation seemed
more desperate than ever.

A blow struck closer to home was the stinging criticism directed at
his research after it was cited in the *Brown* ruling. Sociologist Ernest van
den Haag sneered that Clark's sample size was "too small to test the reaction to a new soap." Writing in the *Villanova Law Review* in 1960,
van den Haag patronizingly pronounced that "the best conclusion that
can be drawn is that he did not know what he was doing; and the worst,
that he did." Edmond Cahn, a law professor at New York University,
was less insulting but no less severe in his judgment: "I would not have
the constitutional rights of Negroes—or of other Americans—rest on
any such flimsy foundation as some of the scientific demonstrations in
these records," he wrote in the *N.Y.U. Law Review*.

Clark's critics were justified in their claim that the doll tests suffered
from serious weaknesses, a fact that even his supporters eventually came
to acknowledge. For example, Clark reported that black children from
the North often became upset when asked which doll was like them,
while those from the South "either laughed or tried to appear casual
about the whole question." Yet students in the second group were far
more likely to attend segregated schools. The psychologist explained his
results by reasoning that racism was still a raw subject for the Northern
children, while their Southern counterparts had more completely, and
more troublingly, absorbed racist assumptions into their identities. To
many observers, however, it seemed that Clark was intent on finding
psychological damage from segregation no matter what the responses of
his young subjects.

Specific criticisms of Clark's methods soon led to larger questions
about whether social science deserved a place at all in public affairs, especially the courts. Here Clark rose to offer a ringing defense of his profession and the importance of its insights. "Man's relations with his
fellow man," he declared, "involve matters far too grave and crucial to
be left to lawyers and judges alone." The nature of these relations could
be illuminated by a socially engaged psychology: "I believe that to be
taken seriously, to be viable, and to be relevant, social science must dare
to study the real problems of men and society, must use the real commu-

nity, the marketplace, the arena of politics and power as its laboratories, and must confront and seek to understand the dynamics of social action and social change," he affirmed.

But for all his resounding conviction, Clark was beginning to suspect a terrible truth. From its founding, psychology had been embraced by institutions eager to take advantage of its tools. "Should social scientists play a role in helping industry function more efficiently—make larger profits—develop better labor management relations—increase the sense of satisfaction among the workers?" he asked rhetorically. "Should social scientists play a role in helping governmental agencies and key policy makers make more effective and valid decisions? Should social scientists play a role in attempting to solve the many human and psychological problems faced by the military arm of our government?" Institutions had long answered yes. So why the shrill objections when social science ventured to participate in America's debate about race?

The answer was as dismaying as it was inescapable: because in this case, psychology supported the weak against the strong, the minority against the majority. Clark's research had abetted a legal ruling that demanded, in his words, "fundamental changes in the power alignments and group status patterns which prevail in our society." The many who resisted such fundamental changes now regarded psychology not as a useful ally, but a dangerous threat to the status quo. The contributions of social science were welcome, it seemed, only as long as they kept America's injustices intact.

As this sobering realization set in, Clark's sanguine determination slipped away, replaced by a weary sense of defeat. "To be quite candid about the success of my attempts at being a psychologist for society, I have to state that I have failed," he remarked in 1968. He had sought to heal what he called the country's "moral schizophrenia"—the way it promised equality for all, then denied true equality to many of its citizens. But, he discovered, the patient did not wish to be cured. "I fear the disease has metastasized," he lamented. Clark's despair seemed to deepen after his beloved Mamie died in 1983; a short while later he said in a speech: "Thirty years after *Brown*, I must accept the fact that my wife left this earth despondent at seeing that damage to children is being knowingly and silently accepted by a nation that claims to be democratic."

As he grew older, this once proud figure became almost bent with bitterness. He told an interviewer that when a friend asked him, "With your cynicism, your pessimism, as intense as it is, why haven't you committed suicide?" he replied, "I'm curious. I really want to see this process, this joke, up until I die." It was surely no comfort to him to know that the changes in his character were a tragic confirmation of his central thesis: social forces like racism have the power to distort individual personality.

On April 23, 2001, the town of Farmville, Virginia, held a celebration. It was the fiftieth anniversary of the student walkout at the Robert R. Moton High School, the pivotal event that led to *Davis v. County School Board* (and, some say, started off the civil rights movement). Spectators clapped as a ribbon was cut in front of the old school building, now a national historic landmark and a civil rights museum. They applauded again for a series of speakers whose inspiring words—given American race relations' freighted past and complicated present—sometimes seemed tinged with unintended irony. First at the podium was African-American journalist Juan Williams.

"It's always been about the children," he declared—though if history has taught us anything, it's that the clash of powerful social forces is almost always about the agendas of adults. After Williams came John Stokes, one of the students who walked out of his school in anger five decades ago. He read a poem taught to him by a favorite teacher at Moton, and again an awareness of past and present lent the verse's sweet words an unanticipated bitterness.

"Look not at the face nor the color of a person's skin, but look at that heart which is deep within," Stokes recited. "For the face and the skin will one day fade away, but the deeds of a good person will never decay."

SEVEN

The Stranger

In their search for truth, some researchers are so fanatical they inspire jokes about making science into a religion. Raymond Cattell was such an investigator, and in his case it was no jest. In 1972, the personality psychologist came out with a book titled *A New Morality From Science* in which he preached the strange doctrine of "Beyondism," a religion he invented.

An austerely logical man, with a long, narrow face and a high domed forehead, Cattell found traditional faiths "intellectually indigestible." The problem, he coolly explained, was that they had arrived at their principles "by processes with which no self-respecting scientist would want his work to be associated." Therefore, "since better truth-finding processes now exist"—namely, science and technology—"religious and ethical genius is better expressed through these new channels." He set out to develop a system of belief made "of the same metal as science itself" and had little doubt that it would replace the old creeds before long. Indeed, he predicted that one day it would be possible to render the tenets of his faith in mathematical formulas, "elegant equations" as compelling as any biblical psalm.

Along with reforming religion, Cattell was determined to impose order on another area he regarded as ripe with unscientific superstition: personality psychology. Trained as a chemist, he admired the rigor that men like Dmitri Mendeleev, creator of the periodic table, brought to the study of nature's elements. When Cattell switched to psychology, he brought with him a kindred desire to sort, classify, categorize. His goal was to create a periodic table of personality, to reduce each element of human nature to its purest essence. Cattell's unyielding commitment to rationality would produce groundbreaking research and an enormously influential personality test, but it would also lead him disturbingly, even dangerously, astray.

■ ■ ■

Cattell was a devoted acolyte of science, making prodigious offerings at
its altar. The publication of his book on Beyondism came near the end
of a long and astonishingly productive career: over the course of his professional life, he wrote more than fifty books and five hundred scholarly
articles and chapters. In a 2002 survey, he was ranked near the top of a
list of the most eminent psychologists. And he created one of the
world's most widely used personality tests, the Sixteen Personality Factor Questionnaire (16PF).

Such accomplishments were made possible by Cattell's fanatical work
habits. The researcher "is on the job night and day," he liked to say, and
he meant it: for many years he rarely left his laboratory until close to
midnight, and even then was so lost in thought that he could find his
car only because it was the last one in the lot. Once at home, he would
lie awake in bed, "utilizing the quiet of the night" to reason through
some mental experiment. In these off hours he would record his
thoughts on a tape and later give it to a secretary to transcribe; she often
didn't have time to finish one cassette before the psychologist arrived
bearing another. "Dr. Cattell writes faster than I can read," students and
even colleagues complained; another frequent lament was that "whenever you have an idea, Dr. Cattell has already written a paper on it."

He worked through holidays and vacations, the lights of his lab burning "on Christmas day and other unlikely times." He believed that "the
best recreation is a change of work," and when he did take time off, it was
almost comically compressed. He spent a single day painting one landscape every year. He played golf, but to avoid spending more than an hour
away from the lab he shot only nine holes, running from one to the next
and leaving his younger partner gasping for breath. Often his leisure time,
limited though it was, still managed to involve work. Cattell would walk
briskly around a local park, debating a research question with a colleague,
or he would swim the sidestroke while facing one of his graduate students,
also afloat, as they planned the next phase of their collaboration.

He worked so hard that his first wife divorced him. They were married in the difficult early years of his career, and the couple lived in a
dark, damp basement flat. "Busy as I was, she had to put up with neglect
as well as straitened circumstances," Cattell commented later. "I could

not blame her when she finally left me." He worked so hard that his health suffered (despite a change of apartments): "From overwork, snatched meals, and a cold attic, I fell ill with a stomach condition, which lasted some years." But this ordeal only toughened his resolve, making him "canny and distrustful," as Cattell reported. "It bred asceticism and impatience with irrelevance, to the point of ruthlessness."

Cattell's scorn for all things soft and sentimental extended from his professional to his personal life. Born in Britain, he had an imperious accent to accompany his aloof demeanor, and even his friends called him "aristocratic." His one weak spot, in fact, was for his beloved England. He adored bawdy limericks, London music hall ditties, and English folk songs like "Widdecombe Fair"; he would perform the Highland fling on request. Cattell had grown up by the sea and pined for it long after he moved away. During the many years he spent in the landlocked American Midwest, he built a swimming pool that was a one-inch-to-the-mile copy of the English Channel, complete with a two-foot-square Isle of Wight.

Always, he was something of a loner. "The researcher's life is a long wrestling with difficulties alone, oriented to remote and intangible rewards," he noted almost proudly. Coolly analytic, he once devised a test of one's sense of humor. He described even ordinary human behavior in highly technical language, often of his own invention—speaking, for example, of the various "ergs" (his word for instinct) behind our actions: the mating erg, the pugnacity erg, the food-seeking erg. Cattell thought, and worked, in a rarified realm he called "psychological hyperspace," and it was in this chilly sphere that he went looking for the basic elements of human nature.

He was, of course, joining a search long underway. For decades, psychologists had hunted far and wide for a key to personality. They had studied mental patients in hospitals in the Swiss mountains and on the Minnesota plains. They had tested students on Harvard's ivied campus and in the South's ramshackle segregated schools. They had displayed inkblots, distributed questionnaires, shown subjects drawings, asked subjects to make drawings of their own.

But what if, all along, the answer had been right there on their office shelf—in the dictionary?

The idea behind what is known as the "lexical hypothesis" is beauti-fully simple: if an important aspect of personality exists, people will have invented a word for it. The more significant a quality is, the more syn-onyms our language will offer to describe it. If a characteristic is less vital, words referring to it will be fewer, will be used less often, and may even drop out of the vernacular altogether. The lexical hypothesis pro-poses that people talking about other people—over back fences, on street corners, over a cup of coffee or a mug of beer—have created the most comprehensive catalogue of personality traits imaginable.

The notion that language holds the key to personality had been around for a long while. The English scientist Francis Galton was prob-ably the first to speculate on it, reporting in 1884 that *Roget's Thesaurus* contained at least a thousand words to describe character. His estimate was put to a far more rigorous test in 1936 by American psychologist Gordon Allport and a colleague. They painstakingly combed through a dictionary (*Webster's New International*, unabridged), counting every word with the capacity to "distinguish the behavior of one human being from that of another." The staggering result: 17,953 words. (By selecting those terms they considered most important, the researchers were able to pare the list down to 4,504.)

To be of any use to personality psychologists, the number would have to be reduced even further—and by this time, scientists had a tool to do so. Factor analysis, a statistical technique used to identify groups of re-lated items, is capable of sorting a welter of data into a few clean cate-gories. British psychologist Charles Spearman devised the method (which he first described in 1904) to assist in his search for *g*, or a gen-eral intelligence factor. Though many investigators followed Spearman in applying factor analysis to research on intelligence, few extended it to the much more complex and ambiguous domain of personality; for that it would take someone truly fanatical. Raymond Cattell fit the bill.

Raymond Bernard Cattell was born in 1905 in a village near Birming-ham; when he was six years old, his family moved to a seaside town in Devonshire, on England's southwest coast. Young Raymond developed a fierce love for Devon's severe landscape, spending his time tramping around its moors and building and sailing his own boats. He dabbled in science, too, making gunpowder in a chemistry shed constructed in his family's apple orchard. A bright boy, he was also headstrong and willful: "The headmaster divided his time between giving me special personal sessions in science and mathematics, and thrashing me for various original deviations from school regulations," Cattell remembered. He won a scholarship to a local boys' academy, then another to attend the University of London.

Cattell elected to study chemistry, graduating with first-class honors in 1924 at the age of nineteen. But he quickly became dissatisfied with the field and its limited scope. In these years following World War I, he explained, there was a "ferment of social and political ideas" in which he longed to take part. In addition, a sheltered, small-town upbringing had exposed him to "a certain shock at the poverty and poor morale I saw in big cities," and "soon my laboratory bench began to seem small and the world's problems vast."

Just about this time, Cattell encountered the ideas of an eminent psychologist. "Like the timely flash of a bell buoy, when one has tacked one's sloop to a new course in the dark, I had the illumination right then of hearing a lecture by Sir Cyril Burt," he later wrote. Inspired by Burt's vision of using psychological science to improve society, Cattell decided to switch disciplines, and chose as his mentor none other than Charles Spearman, the inventor of factor analysis. For his choice of a profession, Cattell suffered the disapproval of his parents and the teasing of his former classmates. "As I packed up my flasks and condensers, I had to endure some good-natured chaff from my fellow chemists, since psychology was then regarded, not without grounds, as a subject for cranks," he noted. At the time, he recalled, "it was said with some truth that two psychologists out of three were 'a bit strange.' "

Cattell himself had no regrets: "My choice seemed to me justified. It provided exactly what I had to have—a means of contributing more fundamental solutions to social problems, along with the intellectually esthetic fascination of pursuing a science." He wanted to help people, but in a characteristically remote fashion: he would use the precise tools of science to improve the lot of humanity in general. Cattell had active scorn, in fact, for those "do-gooders" and "social workers" who tried "to make up by the warmth of their hearts for the emptiness of their heads."

Unhappily for him, the only employment available once he became a psychologist was just such "soft-nosed" work with individuals. After receiving his PhD he took a series of jobs in teaching and counseling, becoming a college lecturer, director of a child guidance clinic, and advisory psychologist at a progressive school. He found these assignments enervating and dull, and took time when he could for his real passion: "Through all the experiences of the merely 'fringe' jobs in psychology that I was compelled to take I was able to keep some research and writing going."

For Cattell had conceived a great ambition: he would apply the statistical approaches he had learned under Spearman to create a science of personality. Watching his mentor investigate intelligence with the help of factor analysis, Cattell dreamed of "unraveling the structures of temperament and motivation by the same instrument." He wanted nothing less, a colleague later marveled, than to solve "the riddle of the universe."

Cattell's dream was grand, but his reality was far drearier. If he stayed in England, only more insufferable teaching and counseling awaited him. The resources he needed to achieve his bold aim simply weren't available—"there being then," he noted, perhaps "six men in Britain whose full-time profession it was to research in psychology."

Then salvation arrived: in 1937, Columbia University professor Edward L. Thorndike invited Cattell to come to the United States as a research associate. Departing his cherished country was the hardest thing Cattell ever had to do: "The broken marriage and the bleak future could be met. But could I disloyally uproot myself from that which had created the fiber of my being?" The opportunity was too good to forgo, and so with "the wrench of a tooth extraction," he traded his native land for the satisfactions of science, "a beauty of a more abstract and placeless kind."

As it turned out, Cattell flourished in America, procuring a succession of prestigious posts: from Columbia, he went on to Clark University, then Harvard. When World War II broke out, he even developed officer selection tests for the U.S. military. But work on his grand plan did not really get underway until he landed in what would be his permanent job: in 1945, he headed to the University of Illinois, where he was appointed Distinguished Research Professor of Psychology. The opportunity to engage at last in his long-imagined project made him almost ecstatic; the feeling, he said, was "close to that which great religions have called being 'reborn.' "

Cattell married again, and his new wife, Karen, helped him with his research, even becoming one of his guinea pigs. Some of his early studies of personality involved tests of thirty or forty different faculties, taken every day for a hundred days. Karen Cattell became "the literally long-suffering subject" of these investigations, her grateful husband noted: "Every day for nine weeks she endured the electric shocks and other indignities of the experiment."

Together they had four children (Cattell had one son by his previous marriage), but his kin didn't see much of him in these years. As he once remarked, not entirely apologetically, "there is a kind of absentminded-ness about the scientist, arising from an exaggerated singleness of pur-pose, which makes him terribly prone to throw away the family with the bathwater." Though Cattell loved his wife and children, his deepest af-fections lay elsewhere. "There is no place like home," he wrote warmly, but by "home" he meant "the small community of three or four research associates at a time, as in my laboratory spontaneously going into a hud-dle whenever an intriguing possibility requires discussion. The family life of discoveries and failures shared, of emergencies calling for mid-night work, and of problems solved, leave few dull moments."

Blinkered though they may have been, Cattell's hardworking habits were necessary to even attempt the monumental task he had set for himself. He planned to start with the list of 4,504 words assembled by Gordon Allport a decade earlier, agreeing with proponents of the lexical hypothesis that "all aspects of human personality which are or have been of importance, interest, or utility have already been recorded in the substance of language." He would then reduce this total by several methods, including factor analysis. Cattell likened the technique, which identifies related terms by tracking their values as they are subjected to a series of mathematical operations, to discerning dim shapes in "the chaotic jungle of human behavior." In an actual jungle, he asked, how does an explorer decide "whether the dark blobs which he sees are two or three rotting logs or a single alligator? He watches for movement. If they move together—come and disappear together—he infers a single structure."

While working at Harvard, Cattell had managed to start on some of this factor analytic work, but he was assisted there only by a crude, manually operated card-sorting machine. At Illinois, he had the

tremendous advantage of access to one of the world's first computers—
the Illiac I (or as he reverently referred to it, the "Sacred Illiac"). This
hulking piece of equipment, then cutting-edge technology, made the
analysis of large amounts of data possible. Even so, the quantity and
complexity of Cattell's investigations made for work that was intellectually grueling and almost physically taxing, like felling trees or quarrying
rock. Slowly, his labors began to reveal patterns beneath the layers of
human language. Between 1940 and 1950, Cattell published more than
three dozen papers in which he began to lay out his master plan for measuring and explaining human nature.

His research identified sixteen factors, building blocks of personality that he claimed constituted "natural elements," "logically equivalent to an element in the physical world." Cattell called these sixteen
basic attributes the "Universal Index," numbering them UI 1 to UI 16,
just as chemists using the periodic table would label oxygen or hydro-
gen. He believed that he was not reinterpreting but actually discovering these bedrock traits of personality—and so, like an astronomer
naming a new star or a biologist naming a new species, he invented
an original vocabulary to describe human nature. "New concepts need
new terms," he explained; these concepts could be "precisely referred
to only by abandoning the battered, changing coinage of popular language." The words he concocted were indeed novel, and entertainingly
odd, like the dialect spoken by an alien in a mediocre science-fiction
movie: *Autia* meant imaginative, *Harria* meant no-nonsense, *Parmia*
meant uninhibited, *Zeppia* meant energetic.

To measure these characteristics he created the Sixteen Personality
Factor Questionnaire, a 187-item test that aimed, said Cattell, "to leave
out no aspect of the total personality." It posed questions such as "Do
you tend to get angry with people rather easily?" and "Would you prefer
the life of (a) an artist (b) a Y.M.C.A. secretary?" Test takers were
graded on qualities ranging from "worrying suspiciousness" to "calm
trustfulness," from "independent self-sufficiency" to "lack of resolution,"
from "bohemianism" to "practical concernedness." The questionaire's
broad inclusiveness, focus on normal personality, and apparently solid
scientific foundation made the 16PF an immediate commercial success,
especially popular with the large corporations then poised on the edge
of postwar expansion. In 1949, Cattell founded his own company to de-

velop and promote the test, the Institute for Personality and Ability Testing, Inc.

Unknown to his customers and colleagues, however, alongside this work on personality Cattell was pursuing another endeavor: one just as ambitious, but far more controversial.

In the England of Cattell's youth, eugenic ideas were widely held and perfectly respectable, even progressive. Once again, Francis Galton had been first on the scene, coining the term *eugenics* in 1883 from the Greek word for "good in birth." The evolutionary theories of his cousin, Charles Darwin, persuaded Galton that human beings ought to approach the business of procreation more deliberately, taking pains "to increase the contribution of the more valuable classes of the population and to diminish the converse." We mate animals with the intention of enhancing their genetic stock, he pointed out, so just imagine "the galaxy of genius" that might be created if only "a twentieth part of the cost and pain were spent in measures for the improvement of the human race that is spent on the improvement of the breed of horses and cattle." Galton even fantasized about a government-sponsored eugenic competition in which the ten fittest men would be married off to the ten fittest women, in a state wedding at which the Queen herself would give away the brides.

Interest in eugenics grew in the early decades of the twentieth century as Britain's leading thinkers became concerned that the country's aristocracy was producing fewer children, while its impoverished "underclass" was multiplying out of control. Cyril Burt, the scientist who drew Cattell into psychology, was an enthusiastic eugenicist, as was Charles Spearman, Cattell's academic mentor. Spearman foresaw a felicitous union of eugenics with his own work on intelligence testing: "An accurate measurement of everyone's intelligence would seem to herald the feasibility of selecting better endowed persons for admission into citizenship—and even for the right of having offspring," he enthused. Through such a coordinated campaign, a utopia would soon be achieved: "Perfect justice," Spearman predicted, "is about to combine with maximum efficiency."

With his reverence for science and his lofty ideals of helping humanity, Cattell, too, found eugenics appealing. Early in his career, he authored several books promoting eugenic solutions to social problems. One of these, *The Fight for Our National Intelligence*, was funded by a grant from the Eugenics Society and published in 1937. It warned that people of inferior ability were having larger families, resulting in a steady decline in England's average intelligence. He recommended that government provide incentives for those of greater aptitude to produce more offspring and for those of lesser aptitude to produce fewer. The book succeeded in generating sensational newspaper headlines like "English Children Getting More and More Stupid!" and "Ban Balmy Babies!," but it did not, as Cattell had hoped, "start a chain reaction leading to a formal government investigation" of falling intelligence test scores.

In this book Cattell, like Burt and Spearman, focused on the inheritance of intellectual ability. But he also advocated the application of eugenics to personality. "One may ask why so much trouble has been taken to find out what specifically is happening in regard to intelligence, when it is possible to argue that other traits are equally socially important," Cattell later wrote. "The reason is that one must begin with something, and something indeed validly measurable and of obvious importance to the group. However, there are hundreds of other psychological and physiological attributes that need improving, and which doubtless will soon be better understood eugenically."

When he arrived in the United States in 1937, Cattell was surprised to discover that eugenic views, though hardly unknown here, were less generally acceptable. "I was astonished when I came to America to find that eugenics was almost a bad word," he recalled. He did not renounce his beliefs, however, even after Adolf Hitler's attempted genocide of the Jews during World War II made eugenics all but universally reviled. Cattell regretted that Hitler's activities had given eugenics "the tang of inhumanity," since "actually, in the history of human movements, it takes second place in humanitarian movements in the last two thousand years only to Christianity and Islam." And he was impatient with the slow pace of social change. As a young man, he had expected the eugenic revolution to be swift: "I never dreamed that it would take so long to get the rear guard to catch up."

In time, he did modify his opinions somewhat, becoming an advocate of voluntary—rather than state-enforced—eugenics. (Cattell encouraged his graduate students to have more children, for example, believing that it was the moral responsibility of intelligent citizens to generously propagate their genes.) He continued to maintain that the wide adoption of eugenic practices "would surely eliminate very rapidly the totally unnecessary poverty, petty ignorance, and unfulfillment one sees in so many sections of society." For years Cattell published little on the subject, though all the while he was developing and refining his ideas. They emerged full-blown in his 1972 book, *A New Morality From Science*.

Here eugenics, and the evolutionary theories behind it, became the basis of Cattell's invented religion. "Beyondism is based on the principle that evolution is good," he stated bluntly. "From this principle I derive many other beliefs, because anything that advances the evolution of our species is good, and anything that hinders evolution is not good." Francis Galton had also mused on the possibility of basing a religion on evolutionary principles, but Cattell was prepared to lay out the canons of his church in careful detail. The god he worshiped was "the Evolutionary Purpose," and in order to faithfully serve this higher calling, he proposed setting up a "grand experiment."

"Grand" is something of an understatement. Cattell imagined that the entire globe would serve as a huge laboratory in which "the variation and natural selection which now take place in our world haphazardly" would be consciously monitored and managed. Human beings would be divided into discrete ethnic and cultural groups; these groups, kept separate from one another, would be encouraged to engage in unfettered competition. Each group's success or failure—its ability to prosper economically, remain physically healthy, reproduce abundantly, generate great works of culture—would provide the ultimate judgment on its fitness.

This deliberate harnessing of the forces of evolution would bring about a race of super-people, Cattell promised. By "co-operating with Nature in its vigilant and ruthless elimination of the less fit," the experiment would produce the "genetic and cultural patterns with the highest survival potential in a changing and indifferent universe." It was *Lord of the Flies* on a monstrous scale, with a band of "qualified elites" supervising the vicious play.

The scheme, he acknowledged, would turn traditional morality on its head, since the ethics preached by Beyondism "are apparently the exact opposite of those which religion and humanity have bred into our bones." For example, human groups must be let alone to flourish or founder; helping people in groups other than one's own would be a sin, because it impedes the free functioning of evolution. The "outright transfer of gains from one group to another frustrates and confuses the feedback of proper reward to good cultural habits and genetic inventions," Cattell admonished. "It thus constitutes not an equivalent of 'charity' between individuals but a pernicious and evil interruption of group evolution."

Another example: there may come a time when a group should be forced to eliminate itself, for its own good and for the good of humanity. "The wider intergroup morality requires that a society which shows itself obstinately unable or unwilling to change vicious habits that are killing it should be phased out," he calmly explained. Always fond of new words, Cattell coined the term *genthanasia* to describe the merciful act by which "a moribund culture is ended, by educational and birth control measures, without a single member dying before his time."

Perhaps anticipating readers' reactions to such drastic measures, Cattell urged them not to waste pity on the suffering of evolution's castoffs. This, he reminded them, is simply the way of nature, "red in tooth and claw"; the people who truly deserve our sympathy are the brave adherents of Beyondism. Although all humans are involved in the "triumphs and the tragedies of the evolutionary process," he noted, only Beyondists are "aware of the process in which they are participating," giving them "a common tragic sense of life." He concluded: "Here is the need for all the compassion we can summon—the compassion for the courage of those who strive, together, for more light in this darkness."

A year after he published *A New Morality From Science*, Cattell retired from the University of Illinois and moved to Colorado, where he built a house shaped like a sailboat that jutted from a mountainside overlooking Denver. The altitude and the cold weather aggravated his already poor health, however, and five years later he moved to Hawaii. (Oddly enough, the islands' rocky coasts and sea breezes reminded him of his native Devonshire.) Cattell continued to proselytize for his new-fangled faith, publishing a second book on Beyondism in 1987. He noted with satisfaction that science seemed to be moving in his direction, with the emergence of sociobiology signaling a shift in emphasis from environmental influences to genetics as the basis of behavior. He could now glimpse the day when everyone would be a convert to Beyondism:

"With good fortune we shall before long see the revealed religions fading out of the more advanced countries," he prophesied. "Out of the superstition-ridden night of the past two thousand years will gradually dawn the light of science-based evolutionary religion."

Gravely important though it was to Cattell, most of his colleagues in psychology remained ignorant of his work on eugenics, intent instead on his factor analysis of personality and his still-popular personality test. Though many were initially impressed by his dogged efforts—"By far the most systematic and rigorous attack on the problems of personality measurement is led by Cattell," wrote an admiring Starke Hathaway in 1965—several aspects of his approach soon fell out of favor. Cattell's idiosyncratic language, called "neologic gobbledegook" by one psychologist, was first to go. His yield of sixteen factors also came under scrutiny, as numerous researchers determined that sixteen was still too many. The reception of Cattell's ideas was not eased by his dense writing style, which produced articles "so abstruse," remarked one observer, as to be "little understood by the majority of psychologists."

Many in the field eventually came to regard him with a mixture of respect and pity, as a hardworking mule of a scientist distinguished mostly by the indefatigability of his labors. One psychologist drew this stinging conclusion: "If the worthiness of a theory is to be assessed by its impact on the field of psychology, rather than by critical reviews that politely praise the theorist's tireless research efforts and impressively complicated network of ideas, it would seem that Cattell's success has been at best minimal." Still, some features of his work survived. The 16PF has been translated into or adapted for use in more than fifty languages and is still frequently administered, especially for career counseling and employee selection; by some estimates it is second in use only to the MMPI. More important—though the man himself did not want the honor—Cattell has been acclaimed as the father of the biggest development in personality testing in decades.

In the years following Cattell's major publications on personality, a number of other researchers pursued the possibility that personality could be described by fewer than sixteen factors. As scientists in various laboratories began conducting independent investigations, a funny thing started happening: over and over again, the same number kept showing up. In 1949 a University of Chicago psychologist, Donald Fiske, applied factor analysis to a pool of personality descriptors and identified five factors. In 1958, Ernest Tupes and Raymond Christal, working at Lackland Air Force Base in Texas, also located five factors. In 1963, University of Michigan researcher Warren Norman reported he'd found five factors. In 1981, John Digman at the University of Hawaii came up with . . . five factors.

These researchers gave the factors different names, but the essence of each was the same across experiments. There was Extroversion, the inclination to actively reach out to others. Neuroticism, the disposition to feel negative emotions. Agreeableness, the tendency to be good-natured and cooperative. Conscientiousness, the propensity to be organized and goal oriented. And Openness, the proclivity to be imaginative and curious. The striking persistence of these five factors led some psychologists to make a bold suggestion: perhaps the key to personality, the solution to the "riddle of the universe," had at last been found. Could this handful of traits grasp the heart of human nature?

In a 1981 paper, Lewis Goldberg of the University of Oregon named the factors "the Big Five." He intended the phrase to indicate that the five dimensions covered big, broad domains of personality, but it soon took on another meaning: the Big Five was a big development, a major new theory. It appeared just in time, at a moment when the entire enterprise of personality testing looked doomed.

In 1968, an earthquake had hit personality psychology. This was the year *Personality and Assessment* was published: a small, unassuming book with an utterly devastating impact. Its author, a Stanford University psychology professor named Walter Mischel, simply pointed out that personality tests don't do a very good job of predicting how humans will act. Mischel's review of the literature showed that the correlation, or statistical relationship, between personality tests and people's actual behavior was only about .30. This meant that less than 10 percent of the variance in a person's behavior was explained by personality as measured by personality tests. "Most traditional clinical assessments have ignored the individual's actual behavior in real life situations," Mischel noted. "It is as if we live in two independent worlds: the abstractions and artificial situations of the laboratory and the realities of life."

In life, he observed, our actions are driven not only by our personalities, but by the situations in which we find ourselves. We adjust our behavior according to our role (worker, parent, friend), to the occasion (a meeting, a family outing, a party), and to a thousand other details of our ever-changing environment. Such mutability, though "acknowledged in the abstract" by personality researchers, was ignored by them in practice, largely because it seemed to defeat the possibility of accurate measurement. From the time the very first personality tests were developed, psychologists attributed stable, consistent personalities to their subjects—not because they had proof such personalities existed, but because the task of assessment would be much easier if they did.

Mischel's point was, in a way, stunningly obvious: people are complicated, and their behavior is influenced by a number of forces. "Unlike rats and other lower organisms who have been psychology's favorite subjects," he noted dryly, "humans do exceedingly complex and varied things." Researchers' willful neglect of that fact had led them "to a grossly oversimplified view that misses both the richness and the uniqueness of individual lives." Yet the effect of his commonsense argument was seismic. Personality psychology was shaken, its practitioners consumed with self-doubt and self-recrimination. With almost masochistic fervor, some carried the critique much further than Mischel himself: there was no such thing as a personality, they declared, only a shifting array of responses to environmental stimuli.

The years following the appearance of *Personality and Assessment* are universally described as "dark" ones for the field: it was "experiencing a major crisis," "paralyzed in agonizing reflection," "mired in Mischellian mud." To make matters even more dire, personality psychology had already been in a state of contraction at the time of the book's publication. After the sweeping theories of human nature proposed in the 1930s and 1940s—and the scientific skepticism that often greeted them—the discipline made a bid for intellectual respectability by addressing itself to more limited, more provable hypotheses about personality. In the 1950s and 1960s, psychologists generated a host of "mini-theories" or "theories of the middle range," and the tests they designed followed this modest course. Instead of trying to map the entire personality, as had Hermann Rorschach, Starke Hathaway, and Henry Murray, researchers now tried to isolate and investigate small areas: for example, "Machiavellianism," or the propensity to act in the shrewdly self-serving ways recommended by the sixteenth-century political operator Niccolò Machiavelli.

Mischel's piercing criticisms made this self-effacing practice even more pronounced. For more than a decade, personality psychologists shrank from making the bold claims about human nature that had always enlivened their enterprise. But their irrepressible penchant for grandiosity could not be restrained forever. The field eventually brokered a truce with Mischel's position: behavior is the product of an *interaction* between personality and situation. Heading into the 1980s, this compromise seemed to satisfy all sides; as one observer noted wryly, "Nowadays almost everyone is an interactionist." But once that grudging concession was made, personality psychology hastened back to its longtime quest, the search for a single key to human nature. The Big Five looked like it might be it.

If psychologists Paul Costa Jr. and Robert McCrae were to be measured on the Big Five, they would no doubt emerge with very different results. Costa is forceful and energetic, "big and bluff, like a bear," as one colleague describes him. He held positions at Harvard and the University of Massachusetts before joining the government's National Institute of Aging, working in its Laboratory of Personality and Cognition (he has been chief of the lab since 1985). McCrae, by contrast, is modest and reserved. "Jeff," as he's known, "is sweet and quiet," says this same acquaintance. "When he writes, though, he's a fiery tiger." He arrived at the NIA in 1978, two years after receiving his PhD from Boston University.

Yet these two men, so dissimilar in temperament, have formed one of the most intense and lasting partnerships in personality psychology— "an astonishingly fruitful research collaboration," in the words of one observer. When they began working together in the 1970s, they published papers on a wide variety of subjects: psychological maturity, coping mechanisms, high-risk behaviors. Very soon, however, they set their sights on a much larger project: identifying the basic ways in which people differ from one another. They started with Raymond Cattell's Sixteen Personality Factor Questionnaire, subjecting its items to another round of factor analysis. They reduced Cattell's sixteen dimensions to just three—neuroticism, extroversion, and what they called "openness to experience"—and in 1978 Costa and McCrae introduced a test to measure this trio. Taking the first letter of each trait, they called it the NEO Personality Inventory.

It wasn't long before they realized their mistake: powerful evidence was emerging that suggested that agreeableness and conscientiousness were also important elements of personality. The pair wasted no time in adding these factors to their original three, and by 1989 their joint articles carried titles like "More Reasons to Adopt the Five-Factor Model." McCrae and Costa changed their test as well, publishing a new version of the questionnaire under the stuttering name of NEO PI-R (NEO Personality Inventory-Revised).

The NEO PI-R contains 240 questions that are answered on a five-point scale, from "strongly agree" to "strongly disagree." Although it has been promoted as the latest word in personality assessment, to the test taker it may appear little different from the 16PF or even the MMPI. Its items share the older tests' odd, floating-in-space kind of contextlessness—"I believe that the 'new morality' of permissiveness is no morality at all," "I would rather be known as 'merciful' than as 'just' "—and their oddly phrased negatives, as in "I'm not crafty or sly," "I have never literally jumped for joy." Test takers are asked to compare themselves to a vaguely defined group of others: "Some people think of me as cold and calculating," "I have fewer fears than most people." The NEO also contains a number of fairly straightforward self-descriptions: "I am dominant, forceful, and assertive," "I often feel helpless and want someone else to solve my problems."

Starting in the early 1980s, Costa and McCrae mounted a relentless campaign to promote the Big Five and the NEO. The five-factor model, they claim, is the key for which personality psychologists have been searching for almost a century. "After decades of debate on the number and nature of major dimensions of personality, a consensus is emerging," they declare. Five factors are "both necessary and reasonably sufficient for describing at a global level the major features of personality."

Though each factor may subsume many other related qualities (Agree-ableness, for example, might also cover Kindness, Trust, and Warmth), every important personality trait in existence is substantially related to one of these five. Raymond Cattell's sixteen factors were too many, and their original three too few; five, they conclude, are "just right."

Costa and McCrae believe (as Cattell did) that their five factors are objects found in nature, as solid as iron or zinc. Their reality "is an em-pirical fact, like the fact that there are seven continents on earth or eight American presidents from Virginia," they write. So persuaded are they of the value of their model that they have begun reanalyzing other major personality tests, such as the MMPI, the TAT, and the Myers-Briggs, to show how they are "really" measuring the Big Five—though not as well, of course, as their own NEO PI-R. "Those who use the Myers-Briggs Type Indicator will miss Neuroticism," they warn, "while those who use the Minnesota Multiphasic Personality Inventory will not measure Conscientiousness." Like some kind of fevered numerolo-gists, McCrae and Costa see the same digit everywhere they look: five, five, and again five.

Their confident advocacy has successfully created an aura of in-evitability around the Big Five. As two of their supporters proclaim, "The research leading to the Big Five structure simply constitutes a body of findings too powerful and crucial to be ignored by anyone who seeks to understand human personality." And indeed, the five-factor model has produced "an explosion of interest," in the words of one psychologist. Since it was introduced in the early 1980s, the Big Five has inspired hun-dreds of research studies, applying the model to everything from Aus-tralian soldiers to Italian politicians, from how citizens vote to how college roommates get along, from how attractive young people will find each other to how well laid-off executives will fare.

So broad is the Big Five's appeal that it has even begun spreading be-yond personality psychology. Recent studies have looked for evidence of the five factors in at least a dozen "nonhuman species," including don-keys, hyenas, pigs, rats, guppies, and octopuses. A similar analysis per-formed on fifty-six breeds of dogs came up with only three factors: reactivity, aggression, and trainability. "It is unclear why there were only three canine factors instead of five," muses the author of the article. Per-haps, he concludes, "the inner life of a dog is simply not equivalent to the inner life of a human." The Big Five has even been applied to the effort to endow products with particular "personalities." The five personality factors found among brands, one marketing professor reports, are Sincerity, Excitement, Competence, Sophistication, and Ruggedness; Hallmark cards ooze Sincerity, while Guess jeans perfectly embody Sophistication.

Though surveys have not yet documented the frequency of its use, the NEO PI-R already appears to be the test of choice for psychologists conducting personality-related research, and there are signs that the questionnaire is being embraced by industry as well. (With the usual dumbing-down, of course: an article about the Big Five, appearing in 2002 in a magazine for human resources professionals, reported that "you can account for 99 percent of the differences in human behavior with five words: stress, stimulation, novelty, dominance, achievement.")

Costa and McCrae have themselves come out with a test called the NEO-4, which lops off the Neuroticism scale in an apparent effort to make the test more attractive to career counselors and workshop leaders. Perhaps emulating the hugely popular Myers-Briggs, Costa and McCrae have identified six "personality styles," complete with snappy nicknames, based on the interaction of the four remaining dimensions. For example, low Openness to Experience plus high Conscientiousness equals the kind of person the authors term a "By-the-Booker"; low Openness to Experience combined with low Conscientiousness produces what they call a "Reluctant Scholar."

Among personality psychologists, so recently resigned to the collapse of their field, enthusiasm for what some have called "the magic five" can reach a quavering pitch: we are now, breathes one expert, "poised on the brink of a solution to a scientific problem whose roots extend back at least to Aristotle." But while the Big Five's grateful fans are applauding all that their model can do, they may be overlooking all that it leaves out.

Clambering aboard the Big Five bandwagon, as many personality psychologists are now eager to do, means accepting a whole host of assumptions about human nature—many of which ignore or contradict the insights of earlier personality theorists.

Five-factor proponents, for example, firmly reject Henry Murray's contention that we are driven by forces that are deeply rooted and incompletely understood. "Human beings are fundamentally rational," counters McCrae, adding that "people generally understand themselves and those around them and act in ways that are consistent with their conscious beliefs and desires." Hence the straightforward self-report format of the NEO PI-R: the surreptitious strategies of projective techniques, its authors maintain, are simply unnecessary.

Also dismissed is Starke Hathaway's notion that some test takers will deliberately misrepresent themselves. Costa and McCrae assert that with few exceptions people tell the truth, and they assume a relationship of "candor and cooperation between administrator and respondent." The NEO PI-R has no "lie scales" like those in the MMPI, only a single item at the end, asking respondents outright if they have answered all questions truthfully and accurately.

Repudiated as well is Kenneth Clark's conviction that we are all molded by powerful social forces. For the most part, Costa and McCrae are remarkably incurious about the origins of personality: "It is probably not meaningful or profitable to ask why there happens to be just five such dimensions," McCrae and a coauthor note nonchalantly. But it's clear where they think the research on personality traits is headed: "Genetic factors are expected to play a major role in their origin and development," predicts Costa, "whereas environmental factors like culture should play a minor role."

Along with spurning these features of previous personality theories, advocates of the Big Five make proudly explicit some assumptions that in earlier tests were quietly implied. For example, they deny that behavior varies much across situations; as the title of one of Costa and McCrae's articles trumpets, "Personality Is Transcontextual." (So much for the amiable compromise of interactionism; it's as if Walter Mischel never made his critique.) Neither do they believe that personality changes much over time. "Barring such events as dementia and major depressive episodes," McCrae declares, personality is fixed once our twenties are past. He and Costa like to quote William James on the subject: "In most of us, by the age of thirty, the character has set like plaster." (It's sobering to note that the usually open-minded James approved of this inflexibility, since "it keeps different social strata from mixing.")

McCrae reports that in a study he conducted in which individuals were given personality tests six years apart, 15 percent of participants thought their personalities had shifted significantly in the intervening years. The tests showed otherwise: "They thought they had changed, but they hadn't," says McCrae. (What about his earlier avowal that "individuals are knowledgeable and intelligent observers of their own thoughts, feelings, and behaviors"? Apparently that's only when their observations agree with those of his test.)

Emboldened by their swift success, champions of the Big Five have dared to make the ultimate claim: "The Five-Factor Model," intones Costa, "may be a human universal." McCrae reports that "very similar five-factor solutions" have been identified in German, Spanish, Portuguese, French, Dutch, Croatian, Russian, Japanese, Chinese, and Korean. "The fact that the five factors are found in many different cultures," he and Costa write, "suggests that they are basic features of human nature itself."

They add that support for the supposed universality of the five factors is emerging from still another direction: our prehistoric past. The Big Five, propose some evolutionary psychologists, represent the five qualities most important to human survival. Our ancestors' reproductive success might have turned on their degree of extroversion, agreeableness, conscientiousness, neuroticism, and openness—and on their ability to perceive such traits in others. Through natural selection, these theorists say, our brains are wired to ask five key questions of every individual we encounter: Is this person dominant or submissive? Is this person agreeable or unpleasant? Is this person responsible or unreliable? Is this person stable or unpredictable? And is this person smart or dumb?

In the Big Five, psychologists have advanced the most comprehensive personality theory imaginable: one that holds true across time, across situations, across culture, even across evolutionary epoch. A century-long search for a key to personality has been resoundingly, triumphantly concluded.

Or maybe not.

Though many personality psychologists see the Big Five as the salvation of the discipline, others aren't so sure. It may be time to halt this merry bandwagon, one skeptic suggests, "while the contents of the wagon are examined and its direction considered."

Some critics of the five-factor model are irritated, in fact, by the presumptuousness of its promoters. This "imperialistic" army, one psychologist complains, heralds "the trait kingdom to come, when even the 'yet to be convinced' will see the errors of their ways and come home to the Big Five." Cautions another dissenter: "We must all be a little more humble in this regard." Some of the Big Five's more outspoken detractors, like UC Berkeley professor emeritus Jack Block, offer a nudge at Costa and McCrae's motives: "They have a commercial, proprietary inventory they want to sell," he says, referring to the NEO PI-R. Block and others assert that—Costa's and McCrae's claims notwithstanding—the field is very far from a consensus on what constitutes the basic elements of personality. "There are lots of fads in psychology, and this is a fad," he states bluntly. "It's popular. But I don't think it has legs."

The enthusiasm with which the Big Five and the NEO PI-R have been received "is a social phenomenon, fueled by a prolific research team," agrees New York University psychologist Samuel Juni. "It is not indicative of superlative theorizing or psychometric workmanship." He and others fault the test for its sloppy construction, as well as its omission of scales that would identify test takers who misrepresent themselves. A study published in 2003 reported that subjects instructed to "fake good" on the NEO PI-R successfully lowered their Neuroticism score and boosted their Extroversion score; another investigation found that as many as 88 percent of job applicants actually hired after taking the NEO PI-R had intentionally raised their Conscientiousness score. As the test is used more frequently in the world outside the lab—to choose among job applicants, for example—the ease with which the NEO PI-R can be manipulated will become more problematic. Juni also chides the test's authors for "getting carried away" with the notion (not supported by solid evidence) that the NEO PI-R is useful for everything from vocational counseling to facilitating a physician's care to diagnosing mental illness.

Other critics' reservations go deeper, reaching down to the lexical hypothesis that provides the foundation for much of the work on the Big Five, as well as on Raymond Cattell's sixteen factors. Language, they point out, may not provide an accurate representation of personality:

the words that make it into a dictionary are likely to be those that afflu-ent, educated groups find useful, or that describe social and commercial intercourse rather than more intimate or even interior transactions. Similarly, we have many terms to describe human qualities (more than seventeen thousand, according to Gordon Allport), but very few to de-scribe situations, infinitely varied as they are.

The use of factor analysis to identify underlying patterns in that mass of terms has also been questioned. We must be aware, Block con-tends, of "the rigid logic of the method and its consequent quirkiness when it is unwarily set down in the real world. The method can issue marvelous, previously obscure connections; it can also issue mindless results." Quoting psychologist Paul Meehl, he warns that "no statistical procedure should be treated as a mechanical truth generator." Block takes issue even with the use of individual words as a starting point: "It is my belief that, for scientific purposes, single-word descriptors, al-though useful for many purposes, cannot convey crucial features of per-sonality," he states. "We need to use sentences, paragraphs, pages, chapters, and books to begin to do justice to the understandings we have or must develop."

Other researchers suggest that claims for the universality of the Big Five are premature. Lewis Goldberg was one of the model's early cham-pions, but his more recent studies have made him doubt whether it will hold up in languages other than English and its lexicographical cousins. While "the Big Five is a model that characterizes northern Indo-European languages very well," he says, "as you get farther south, the replication gets rattier." In a 2001 article authored with University of Oregon colleague Gerard Saucier, Goldberg concluded that the Big Five "is reproduced better in some languages than in others," and noted that other investigators had identified an alternative set of five factors in Ital-ian and Hungarian, and had found seven factors in both Hebrew and Tagalog, a language spoken in the Philippines. (Interestingly, the five-factor model—founded as it is on the expression of personal styles and preferences—appears better able to predict behavior in autonomous, in-dividualist cultures than in collectivist, community-based ones.)

In any case, five factors strike many observers as too few to ade-quately describe the infinite variety of human nature. Where does the kind and intensity of one's religious beliefs fit in? The nature of one's sexuality? The specific culture in which one was born, or which one has come to embrace? Such important features of personality find no place among the shallow categories of Agreeableness and Conscientiousness, Neuroticism, Openness, and Extroversion. Costa and McCrae boast that perhaps "the most impressive achievement of the [five-factor model] is its reduction of conceptual jangle." But what if that hubbub is itself a vital element of personality?

The most compelling critique of the Big Five, offered by Northwestern University psychologist Dan McAdams, begins by acknowledging the usefulness of the model. An awareness of where a person stands on the five factors, he says, "is indeed crucial information in the evaluation of strangers and others about whom we know very little. It is the kind of information that strangers quickly glean from one another as they size one another up and anticipate future interactions." But this aspect of the model's utility, McAdams continues, is precisely its limitation. Once it has yielded its effective speed-read of personality, it cannot offer any deeper or more profound knowledge of an individual's character. The Big Five thus traffics, in McAdams's resonant phrase, in "a psychology of the stranger."

To get beyond a psychology of the stranger, he says, several additional types of information are required—the kinds of insights that all of us habitually seek out when getting to know a new person. One of these is *contingent* information: the way an individual responds in different moods or situations. How would the Big Five classify a man who is usually passive, McAdams asks, but becomes pugnacious when directly challenged? How would it label a woman who is customarily reserved, but turns talkative when she's nervous? What would it do with a person who is generally unemotional, but who falls apart when offered sincere sympathy? Just as we don't really know a new acquaintance until we're versed in such subtleties, McAdams suggests, psychologists can't know a subject until they look past the static Big Five.

Other sorts of information cited by McAdams include knowledge about how people's personalities have changed and developed over their lifetimes; the cultures—ethnic, religious, social, professional—in which they are immersed; the current concerns and anxieties they harbor; the political beliefs and value systems to which they subscribe;

the desires and goals they hold for the future. A theory of personality assessment that takes heed of such variables has some claim to true intimacy and familiarity; a theory that neglects them will find itself among strangers.

In the summer of 1997, many psychologists encountered a stranger, though he was a man they thought they knew: Raymond Cattell. In June of that year, the ninety-two-year-old Cattell was chosen to receive a Gold Medal Award for Life Achievement in Psychological Science from the foundation operated by the American Psychological Association. This laurel had been bestowed only a dozen times, and never before on a personality psychologist. Glowing praise of his work was published in the APA's flagship journal, *American Psychologist*: "In a remarkable seventy-year career, Raymond B. Cattell has made prodigious, landmark contributions to psychology," the citation read. "He must be considered among a very small handful of people in this century who have most influenced the shape of psychology as a science." In August, Cattell traveled from his home in Hawaii to Chicago, where the annual APA convention was being held, in order to accept this glorious capstone to his career.

But then, just two days before the presentation of the award, it was abruptly suspended by the foundation's board of trustees. Scrambling to explain this unforeseen development, an APA spokeswoman noted that the board had voted to honor Cattell "before it knew of the information that has since come to light," she said carefully. "This new information has raised a lot of concerns, and we want to be thorough in making a judgment."

What had "come to light," of course, were Cattell's writings on eugenics. They were brought to the board's attention by Barry Mehler, founder and executive director of the Institute for the Study of Academic Racism, an organization that "monitors campus racism and serves as a resource center for legislators, civil rights groups, and journalists." Mehler, also a professor of humanities at Ferris State University in Michigan, warned in a letter to the APA that "the potential awardee has a lifetime commitment to fascist and eugenics causes." He was soon joined in his protest by Abraham Foxman, national director of the Anti-Defamation League. The prize, Foxman charged, would give the

APA's "seal of approval to a man who has, whatever his other achievements, exhibited a lifelong commitment to racial supremacy theories."
In response, the APA appointed a "blue-ribbon panel" to evaluate the
accusations and review the psychologist's work.

The public frenzy that ensued was deeply distressing to the fastidious
Cattell. "As a result of an award I never requested," he fulminated, "I
was appalled to find myself accused of racist beliefs in newspapers worldwide." At first he vigorously defended himself, sending a strongly
worded statement to news organizations. "I am not and have never been
a racist," he declared. Cattell went on to explain that "my views of eugenics have evolved over the years," and that he now believed in it only
on a voluntary basis. Far from being motivated by racism, he added, his
work on the subject stemmed from his belief that "important policy decisions should be based on scientific information and knowledge rather
than prejudice, superstition, or political pressure." As the controversy
continued, however, and as his health worsened (he was suffering from
colon cancer, prostate cancer, and congestive heart disease), he decided
to be done with it. Five months after he was to have received the award,
he sent a letter to the APA withdrawing his name from consideration.
A few weeks later, on February 2, 1998, he died.

Cattell's defenders, still angry about the way the psychologist was
treated, insist that he was not a racist. They may well be right. Although Cattell's beliefs grew out of a eugenicist tradition that indisputably regarded whites as superior to people of color, in later years his
philosophy was informed not by hot-tempered prejudice but by something more chilling: an unwavering devotion to the cool logic of science, no matter what the human cost. Science was literally Cattell's
religion, and he believed in practicing it without regard to the pleasure
or suffering of the individuals involved—a striking sort of indifference
in a personality psychologist, whose very subject is individuality. But
Cattell had always cared more about the grand abstraction of humanity
than about the specific human beings it encompassed. He beheld people
as if from a great distance, faces blurred and voices mute.

Something similar can be said of the proponents of the Big Five,
though they of course have no ties to Cattell's more extreme views. In
their impatience to find a system that will explain all of human nature,

they have overlooked the human herself; she remains a stranger, dim and indistinct. Says one thoughtful critic of the model: "The Big Five makes me think of being up in a spaceship, looking down at the planet below and seeing five continents. That's useful to know, but once you're back on Earth, it won't help you find your way home."

EIGHT

Uncharted Waters

In their century-long hunt for the key to personality, researchers have never glimpsed the elusive object of their pursuit. "No one has ever *seen* personality," as an early tester once stated the obvious.

But don't tell that to Turhan Canli. Sitting in his office at the State University of New York in Stony Brook, Long Island, the neuroscientist clicks open a richly detailed image on his computer screen.

"Here, look," he says.

The picture, captured with a technique known as functional magnetic resonance imaging (fMRI), is of a brain: a ghostly apparition, its folds and furrows rendered in sepulchral shades of gray. "This is the brain of an introverted person," Canli announces. He clicks again. "And this is the brain of an extroverted person." Another picture appears, and this time the pallid form is dappled with red and yellow spots that look like a flock of butterflies. Here, in vivid color, is visual evidence of a difference about which human beings have speculated for more than two thousand years.

Canli, boyish and slight with curly black hair and wire-rimmed glasses, performed this particular experiment in 1999 while a postdoctoral fellow at Stanford University. Subjects were given an abbreviated version of the NEO PI-R to determine their relative levels of introversion and extroversion. Then their brains were scanned using an MRI machine, which exposes the brain's tissues to a magnetic field. Molecules in the brain respond differently to the magnet depending on factors such as how much oxygen they're carrying, and these differences are used to generate images like the ones on Canli's screen. Cells that are full of oxygen (and are therefore not being used at the moment) show up as gray; cells that are depleted of oxygen (and are therefore being given a workout by some kind of brain activity) show up in color.

While their brains were being scanned, subjects were presented with positive and negative stimuli—that is, shown photographs of happy and unhappy things. Canli brings up these pictures with another click of his mouse: the cheerful photos depict babies, puppies, ice cream; the grim ones, snakes, spiders, and piles of human skulls. When Canli and his colleagues looked at the resulting brain scans, the effect was striking. When shown the sunny pictures, the brains of people who tested as introverts remained quiescent, while the brains of people who tested as extroverts fairly bloomed with activity.

Canli, now an assistant professor of psychology at SUNY Stony Brook, believes that discrepancies like this one reveal an intrinsic difference in the way people with varied personalities process information about the world. Extroverts, it seems, are wired to respond automatically and affirmatively to positive stimuli, while introverts are not. Such individual differences in brain reactivity, he says, amount to a person's "neural signature." Though Canli warns, "I'm cautious about the overinterpretation of this data," he confesses that he and his lab assistant at Stanford used to play a game: the assistant would show him a brain scan, and Canli would guess whether the person to whom it belonged was an introvert or an extrovert.

"If a life-or-death decision was based on that kind of assessment, I wouldn't be comfortable making it," he says firmly. Then he relents. "But just for fun? Yeah, I can make that distinction, and I'm usually right."

Turhan Canli is only one of many scientists now exploring the biological underpinnings of personality. "Personality research in general is moving away from woolly psychology into real biology," says Sam Gosling, a personality psychologist at the University of Texas. Since fMRI and other advanced brain-scanning technologies became widely available in the mid-1990s, investigators have used them to make intriguing connections between the way people behave and the way their brains operate. High levels of activity in the right hemisphere of the brain, for example, have been linked to optimism and extroversion, while greater activity in the ventromedial prefrontal cortex (an area of the brain a few inches behind the bridge of the nose) has been associated with negativity and neuroticism.

While no one has used brain scans as the basis for a personality test—yet—researchers are already pointing to their potential value in spotting mental illness. Carl Schwartz, a psychiatrist at Harvard Medical School, has found increased activity in a part of the brain called the amygdala in introverted adults, and suggests that MRI scans of children might identify those at risk of anxiety disorders later in life. Joseph Matarazzo, a leading behavioral neuroscientist, predicts that people suffering from panic attacks and other psychological conditions will one day be diagnosed by their brain scans.

In the meantime, other biological approaches are yielding additional insights into personality. For example, research indicates that the nervous systems of introverts are more sensitive than those of extroverts, making them more likely to startle at a loud sound, jitter after a cup of coffee, or pucker at a drop of lemon juice. Measures of heart rate show that depressed people have a relatively slower heartbeat, while fearful people have a faster one. Analyses of the electroconductivity of the skin demonstrate that anxious and neurotic individuals settle down less quickly after they've been stressed. Even eye movements can provide clues to personality. Scientists have found that when we pause to think something over, our eyes habitually glance to one side or the other. People who look to the left tend to be affected more deeply by negative stimuli, while people who look to the right tend to respond more intensely to the positive.

Assays of the various chemicals swimming in our bloodstreams offer another source of information about personality. Studies of immune-system reactions, for example, reveal that in response to hepatitis B vaccinations, neurotics produce fewer antibodies than well-adjusted people. High levels of the hormone testosterone have been tied to aggressiveness, sensation seeking, social dominance, and sexual activity. (In one recent study, members of college fraternities with elevated average testosterone were more "rambunctious," more "wild and unruly," and "outstanding in the crudeness of their behavior," while brothers in low-testosterone frats were more academically successful, more socially responsible, and came across as "friendly and pleasant.") Measures of cortisol, another hormone, show that high-cortisol individuals tend to be solitary, depressed, and "appreciative of fantasy, aesthetics, ideas, and values," while low-cortisol people are usually brash, exuberant thrill seekers.

Chemicals at work in the brain seem to be especially closely associated with temperament and behavior. Scientists suspect that the neurotransmitter norepinephrine helps regulate the upbeat feelings we get in response to positive activities or achievements, leading those with lower levels to seek additional stimulation from the outside world. Monoamine oxidase (MAO), an enzyme that breaks down norepinephrine and other neurotransmitters, is another substance that has attracted the attention of researchers. Low levels of MAO (suggesting accelerated breakdown of feel-good chemicals like norepinephrine) have been correlated with criminality, drug use, sexual promiscuity, and other "norm-breaking behavior."

In tandem with such findings have come striking discoveries in the genetics of personality. Studies of identical twins raised apart suggest that about 50 percent of individual differences in personality can be traced to our genetic inheritance. Now DNA analysis has begun to connect specific genes to particular personality traits. One of the strongest of these links concerns a gene that controls the development of sites in the brain known as dopamine receptors. Individuals who inherit one form of the gene tend to be excitable and impulsive; they may be diagnosed with higher rates of attention deficit disorder, and they may be more likely to abuse drugs. Scientists have also identified a gene that affects the way serotonin is transported in the brain (serotonin is the brain chemical influenced by the class of antidepressant drugs that includes Prozac, Paxil, and Zoloft). Research indicates that people with a particular version of this gene are more anxious and neurotic, and more focused on avoiding potential harm.

Surveying such developments, scientists like Roger Brent of the Molecular Sciences Institute in Berkeley, California, anticipate the day when it will be possible to "look at all the genes in an organism and predict its behavior"—to locate the key to personality in the body's flesh and blood.

Even ordinary personality questionnaires are now primed for dramatic change, thanks in this case to advances in computing technology. The move from pencil and paper to keyboard and screen promises to change the very nature of the tests, from inert lists of items to dynamic programs that monitor and even interact with their subjects.

For example: psychologists have long suspected that the length of time a person takes to reply to a question—what they call "response latency"—is a revealing fact. (Carl Jung acted on this possibility when he timed his word-association test.) Now they are at work on software that will measure, to a fraction of a second, how quickly we punch in (A) or (B). Keyboards may also be equipped to gauge the degree of pressure applied (imagine a forceful "True!" or "False!" in response to the MMPI item "I loved my mother"). The flexibility of computerized administration could even allow the test to modify itself as a person takes it—exploring in more depth, for example, an area that appears from early answers to be problematic. More unsettlingly, a computer can be programmed to cut short a testing session when it becomes clear that the subject won't meet a preset standard. Called the "countdown method," this tactic is reminiscent of vaudeville's hook: fail to perform, and you're yanked off the stage.

Pushing the potential of technology even further, psychologists are beginning to use computers to test "automatic" or unconscious reactions—split-second responses that are beyond our control and so may be more revealing than our premeditated choices. Participants are asked to make judgments about a series of words or images: the stimulus flashes on the screen, and the test taker must immediately classify it as "good" or "bad," "me" or "not me." The speed with which a subject makes the selection—regardless of his ultimate answer—is thought to impart information about his unconscious beliefs.

This approach, known as the Implicit Association Test (IAT), was early on used to investigate people's underlying feelings about race. Results demonstrated that people who consider themselves to be unprejudiced—even, in fact, minority-group members themselves—actually show signs of unconscious bias. Though subjects may eventually enter "good" in response to a black face, for example, it often takes them longer to do so than to make the same judgment about a white face. Used this way, the IAT is like a high-tech version of Kenneth Clark's doll studies.

The technique has also been employed to study personality-related characteristics like anxiety, shyness, self-esteem, depression, and phobia, to surprising effect. The test picks up tendencies toward shyness, for example, in people who do not register as shy on conventional personality questionnaires and who speak without shyness in observed interactions with others (both behaviors that are more or less under conscious control)—but who *do* betray shyness in their nonverbal behavior, gestures that remain outside control and even awareness.

Another innovative use of computers applies linguistic analysis to samples of speech. The way people talk reveals much about their personalities, says psychologist James Pennebaker of the University of Texas. He and his colleagues have developed a program that calculates the frequency with which individuals use certain types of words: pronouns, prepositions, conjunctions, articles, auxiliary verbs. "People who talk in the present tense and use a lot of first-person pronouns are different from people who employ the past tense and who don't often use pronouns," reports Pennebaker. "The first group tends to be very direct and immediate, while the second is made up of more psychologically distanced people."

If biological markers, genetic analysis, and computer technology continue their rapid development, the familiar pencil-and-paper personality test may soon be completely obsolete—supplanted by a syringe, a swab, or a click of the mouse.

Impressive as they may seem, however, none of these advances in assessment have yet approached a key to human nature. Many of them are notably inexact—James Pennebaker himself calls his word-counting program "shamelessly crude"—and many rely on approximate or indirect measures. Levels of neurotransmitters in living humans, for example, can only be estimated from the quantity of by-products (produced when they are broken down) found in blood, urine, or cerebrospinal fluid. The illuminated patterns produced by fMRI are not literal pictures of the brain at work, but visual models based on statistical analyses of quantitative data.

Even more precise measures can provide only a piece of the puzzle of why people are the way they are. Testosterone, for example, rises and falls in response to specific situations, and it works in concert with a host of other hormones. Likewise, the action of the dopamine receptor gene or the serotonin transporter gene can account for only a tiny part of an individual's total personality. Hundreds of genes are involved in every complex human behavior, and a single gene may explain just

1 percent or 2 percent of the variance in the way people act. "The most replicated associations have been between the dopamine D4 receptor gene and 'novelty seeking' and between the serotonin reuptake transporter gene and anxiety," notes researcher Jonathan Benjamin of Israel's Ben-Gurion University of the Negev. "But even these reports are controversial, and their effects are too small to add to existing scientific theories or allow for clinical use in psychological counseling."

The tools of science are so elegant, its authority so unimpeachable, that we may be tempted to accept its pronouncements without question. As Turhan Canli says of his fMRI scans: "People see pictures of the brain and they get seduced into thinking that this is the absolute, unbiased truth." Especially when the object of study is human nature itself, however, there's less absolute truth than assumptions, guesses, and wishful thinking at work. Nikos Logothetis, a neurobiologist at Germany's Max Planck Institute for Biological Cybernetics, has gone so far as to call much of the recent research using magnetic resonance imaging a "new phrenology." MRI technology is less reliable than scientists have claimed, he says, and the interpretations scientists draw from its data are oversimplified. The technique may fail to pick up a significant amount of activity going on in the brain, and in any case, scientists aren't even completely sure what it means when a region of the brain "lights up" on their screen.

The potential applications of personality genetics may likewise be oversold, says Dean Hamer, a geneticist at the National Institutes of Health who helped discover the serotonin transporter gene. He is asked if he can imagine a day when a personality test will be performed on a DNA sample. "I can imagine a day when people will be selling that, sure, in much the same way that people today sell personality profiles derived from paper-and-pencil questionnaires," he replies. "The genetic personality tests will contain about just as much voodoo as the current ones do—a sort of semi-science."

The next time we gape at the moony glow of an MRI scan or marvel at news of another genetic discovery, we may do well to remember the certain faith people once placed in bumps on the head.

A look back at the history of personality testing can feel like one long wave of déjà vu. The cycle, repeated endlessly, goes like this: psychologists devise a novel way of assessing personality and boldly declare it a key to human nature. The method is widely acclaimed; then, inevitably, it's debunked; at last, it's superseded by the next new thing. "We never seem to solve our problems or exhaust our concepts; we only grow tired of them," observed Gordon Allport of his colleagues' ever-changing "fashions." But why? Why do psychologists participate in this perpetual merry-go-round, taking the rest of us along for the ride?

The answer can be found in the pivot on which the whole enterprise turns. This axis is not a genuine desire to understand the individual in all her depth and nuance; it is the imperative to meet the needs of powerful institutions, and it has had profound consequences for the way all of us understand ourselves. One of the earliest exigencies to spur the creation of personality tests was doctors' need to diagnose the mentally ill. Hermann Rorschach and Starke Hathaway developed their assessments within the walls of mental hospitals, and though the tests have since been extended to the rest of us, they still bear the odor of disease and dysfunction. The Rorschach and the Minnesota Multiphasic Personality Inventory imagine us as an assemblage of ailments, the sum of our sicknesses; they are like "mental thermometers," in the words of one critic, equipped to detect illness but incapable of describing health.

Coming just after the doctors were corporate and government bureaucrats, with their need to sort and manage large groups of people. Isabel Myers and her many imitators obliged with tests that treated the individual like an interchangeable part, a cog that could be fit neatly into the general assembly. Though he had not intended it, Henry Murray, too, became a partner in the commodification of personality, his test turned into a marketing tool. As they're used today, the Myers-Briggs Type Indicator and the Thematic Apperception Test imagine us as the useful minions of institutions, our activities limited to laboring and purchasing, getting and spending.

And all along there were psychologists themselves, driven by their own powerful need: to be regarded at last as real scientists. Raymond Cattell pursued this aim with passionate intensity, determined to distill human nature down to its purest essence. His successors in this quest, Robert McCrae and Paul Costa Jr., have reduced the complexity of human nature even further. The Sixteen Personality Factor Questionnaire and the NEO Personality Inventory imagine us as inert objects of study, laboratory specimens with no more agency or individuality than a particle under a microscope.

The three strands of medicine, industry, and science wove themselves tightly together over the course of the last century, forming the web of ideas and assumptions that we know today as personality. These institutional interests made personality what *they* needed it to be—inborn, unchanging, easily quantified, precisely measurable—rather than what it actually was. Yet again and again, human nature proved itself too wily, too complex and changeable to be ensnared in their net. Hence the endless procession of new theories, new techniques, new tests, each as superficial and short-lived as the last. The inadequacy of these efforts becomes apparent when we consider that not one of the complicated, contradictory people whose stories are told in this book could be captured by their own test.

We might well give thanks that personality has proved so ingeniously elusive—except for two sobering facts. First, these tests have serious real-life consequences, in our classrooms, courtrooms, and workplaces. And second, the narrow, self-interested way we've been imagined by institutions has left us without a satisfying way to imagine ourselves. Personality tests provide a quick, simple take, stamped with the impressive imprimatur of science. Some possess a glib attractiveness, promising instant insight, illumination on the cheap. But they cannot offer a prospect from which to view ourselves whole. The vistas they afford are too restricted, obscured by the objectives and agendas of others. In this sense, all personality tests engage in "a psychology of the stranger."

Is there another way? The answer begins to come clear when we consider how any one of us gets to know a stranger: he tells us his story.

———■———

Dodge Morgan was born in Malden, Massachusetts, in 1932. His father died when he was a small child, and his widowed mother did whatever was necessary to support the family, including shoveling coal in a shipyard. Growing up fatherless during the Depression, Morgan faced daunting hardships, but he maintained a cheerful disposition. "He is such an optimist," says his wife, Manny, "that he will honestly tell you that the fact that his father died when he was three years old was the best thing that ever happened to him. He is absolutely determined to make something good out of everything."

As a young man, he worked at his uncle's boatyard, a frustrating existence for someone who longed to set sail himself. "From an early age, I was surrounded by boats I could not use," Morgan notes wryly, recalling "watching others sail off and wishing I could." Whenever he got the chance, he took it: "What I loved most about sailing was to go alone beyond the tether."

Morgan's older brother, Russ, and his grandfather, "Cap," were dominant figures. "Russ really filled the role of my father," he reflects. "He and Cap were my male role models, and no one ever had anyone more male than they." Russ was "handsome, strong, athletic, decisive, competent in so many ways," while Cap "simply was hell-bent and eccentric. He drank hard, did all the male things hard." His grandfather spoke in salty adages, among them: "The four most beautiful things in the world are a ship under sail, a full bottle of rum, a woman's body, and a field of wheat."

Following high school Morgan went on to the University of New Hampshire, where he was later expelled for a prank involving firing a cannon in the Dean of Women's bedroom. Morgan joined the Air Force, graduating second in his cadet class and flying fighter planes for five years. Following his stint in the service he returned to college, graduating in 1959 with a degree in journalism. Morgan's first job as a reporter was in Alaska, writing for the *Anchorage Daily News*. For three years he lived as frugally as possible, in a cabin without running water, and managed to save $23,000. The money went for a wooden schooner named Coaster, which Morgan proceeded to sail alone for two and a half years, from Maine to the Caribbean to Hawaii to Alaska.

By now, Morgan had married his first wife, but she left him during one of his maritime adventures. As would be the case throughout his life, he had a complicated relationship to intimacy and solitude. "I have a natural tendency to put the blinders on to the needs of other people," he acknowledges, though he was also "afraid of ending up old and alone in some harbor." Reluctantly, Morgan sold the boat and came ashore, but he promised himself then that he would one day return to the sea.

Morgan now got a job at a manufacturing firm in his home state. Three years later, when the company sold off its electronics division,

Morgan bought it himself. He and three employees set up shop in a garage, assembling devices like police radar detectors. The company, Controlonics, grew prosperous, generating annual sales of more than $25 million a little over a decade after Morgan took it over. By now he was married again, to Manny, with whom he had a son, Hoyt, and a daughter, Kimberly.

Successful as he was, Morgan started to feel restless and began fantasizing about a return to the sea. He became so preoccupied that Manny worried about another woman. "When he finally told me he wanted to sail around the world, it was almost a relief," she says. Morgan's brother was less generous: "You're out of your goddamn mind," Russ told him.

Morgan—fifty-one years old, an accomplished businessman, the father of two small children—knew his plan seemed preposterous, but he felt compelled to follow it anyway. "My place in the customary order of things is secure," he mused at the time. "But the customary order of things is not enough. How much more is there? It is time to try again to find out. There is so little time left."

This need to see himself as an active and vigorous hero formed an important part of Morgan's personality; his greatest fear was growing effete and coddled. "Sailing a boat alone is such an uncomplicated way to stay on the edge. I think it allows you to sort out what is important in life," he explains. "I think there are a lot of overcivilized people out there drinking coffee out of a Wedgwood cup." In 1983, he sold his business for $32 million. The next two years were a focused period of anticipation as he supervised the building of his boat and prepared himself physically and psychologically for the journey. At last, after a two-decade wait, he was ready to make good on his promise.

Morgan set off on his trip around the world on a clear, sunny morning in November 1985. His departure from St. George, Bermuda, was actually his second, after mechanical problems forced him to make a false start—but on this day the crisp sails of *American Promise* filled with wind and its sleek white hull sliced neatly through the water. As people and land and then even other boats disappeared into the horizon, Morgan contemplated the challenge he'd set for himself: to sail alone around the world without stopping, in 220 days or less. He had another goal, too: "I want to come back knowing myself in a deeper way than I do now," he said, adding in his sober fashion, "I'm afraid of some of the things I'm going to learn."

Morgan, a rugged man whose impassive countenance occasionally breaks into a boyish smile, had in mind the kind of self-reflection that only prolonged periods of solitude can induce. But he also had available a more conventional forum for introspection. On board his 60-foot sloop were 1,600 pounds of food and drink, 650 pounds of tools and spare parts, 300 pounds of clothing—and more than two hundred personality tests, sealed in waterproof packets.

The tests were Manny's doing. Looking for a way to make her husband's venture more than a vain self-indulgence, she had contacted two professors at Boston College to ask if they could use him as a case study. The psychologists, William Nasby and Randolph Easton, jumped at the chance. Morgan would become their captive subject, expected to take a personality test every day of his potentially life-changing journey.

By the time they were done, Dodge Morgan would have perhaps psychology's most-studied personality, documented not only in hundreds of test results but in interviews and correspondence with the two investigators, a daily journal and ship's log kept during the trip, and reels and reels of film taken by the six cameras mounted on Morgan's boat. This one man would become the subject of two dissertations and half a dozen scholarly articles, including an entire issue of the *Journal of Personality*. Though Easton would eventually drop out of the project, it became a kind of obsession for Nasby, a puzzle that demanded to be solved. His approach to studying Morgan eventually shaped itself into a comparison. On one side were the insights into his subject Nasby gleaned from pencil-and-paper tests. On the other side was a very different technique, a "life story" approach that examined Morgan through the stories he told about himself and his life.

From the tests (which included the TAT, the 16PF, and a close cousin of the MMPI) Nasby learned some useful, though limited, information: Morgan scored high on Exhibition, Endurance, and Dominance, low on Affiliation, Play, and Harm Avoidance. "Morgan is understood to be a man of great emotional stability and high conscientiousness who is highly focused on autonomy, endurance, dominance, and achievement," Nasby noted. "Morgan is not particularly extroverted; neither is he particularly agreeable. Although his score indicates a relatively high level

of openness to experience, his openness is limited by his strong preference for consistency and certainty." He added that Morgan's behavior
was occasionally antisocial and narcissistic.

When Nasby shared a preliminary sketch with Morgan, his subject
was unimpressed: "I don't think I want to spend much time with the guy
you are describing, and I sure as hell don't want him living with my family." The nuances of Morgan's personality would emerge only from his
story.

Morgan made good time in his first few days: heading south across the
Atlantic Ocean, pointed toward the tip of Africa, he averaged 175 nau-
tical miles a day. His emotional state, however, was not nearly so buoy-
ant. With nothing to see but water and sky, nothing to hear but the
snap of sails and the growl of his autopilot, Morgan suffered the "painful
postpartum of leaving." He felt seasick, anxious, lonely. "The cold reality of six months alone at sea hits me again with puzzling suddenness,"
he wrote in his journal. "I am amazed I can prepare so intensely and be
so acutely aware of this challenge and then be so abruptly shocked when
I actually get under way."

Each day, his routine was the same: rise, inspect the boat, fix things
that were broken, scan weather and instrument gauges, read a bit, eat
some of the freeze-dried food prepared by Manny. Even at night he got
up every two hours to check on the boat and its progress. It was during
his downtime that his feelings got the best of him: he read a sentimental
story and cried uncontrollably. He turned off his tape player because
music reminded him of people he loved. He was able to call home occasionally, but only felt worse after talking to his family. "It seems I cope
better with the loneliness when I do not remind myself of the delicious
alternative," he noted forlornly.

Morgan devised ways to break up the solitude. He sang show tunes;
he made shadow animals by the light of the moon; he walked the deck,
looking for shooting stars. He was thrilled by the sight of any living
creature: porpoises, albatrosses, flying fish. When he spotted a family of
dolphins, he whistled, yelled, jumped up and down. "They like it when I
make a fool of myself," he smiled. But even as he was adjusting to the
unrelenting aloneness, another dilemma arrived when the wind died,
the sails grew slack and the boat bobbed uselessly. This predicament

brought out the flip side of Morgan's need for action: his restlessness, his rage and despair when there was nothing to be done.

"A storm, frightening as it often is, can somehow be dealt with by actions. The calm sets my nerves right on the edge," Morgan wrote. "When *Promise* wallows, I feel each violent jerk of the lines as if they are my own sinews. I am under high tension. I hunt for any whiff of breeze, not only with my eyes but with my very soul . . . At least once per hour I let go, vent the pressure to scream curses into the west. And then I tense up again and plead, plaintively beg, for some wind . . . At midnight I give up the struggle to brood. Alone we sit in the middle of the ocean, eleven thousand miles from our destination, powerless." Morgan was led to a deeper realization: "I need a sense of progress. It is the only dimension I have for life."

In the midst of this emotional turmoil, he took his daily personality test, usually when his chores were done and the sun was setting. His account of a typical evening: "2030: Eat dinner straight from cooking pot. Sit on deck if good weather, in pilothouse if not. Contemplate state of world. Maybe more reading or writing. 2345: Time for science and a few laughs; take psychological tests." He found the tests amusing in their total disconnection from the life he was leading. "They are so irrelevant to my world now," he observed. " 'Do I like my parents? Would I rather be an engineer or an actor? Do I enjoy playing practical jokes? Am I the life of the party?' Who really gives a shit? I am the only party here."

But "surely the psychological pros will be able to learn something useful from these hundreds of strange and irrelevant pieces of paper I scribble out for them," he added slyly. "Oh yes, surely they will."

The life story approach has been around as long as any personality test, but it has never quite managed to join the mainstream. It shows up on no surveys of test use. No company owns the right to distribute it. There are no workshops, textbooks, or videos to teach its interpretation. And its most prominent practitioner did his important work in the area almost six decades ago.

But then, Gordon Allport was never quite mainstream, either. Born in Indiana in 1897, he grew up near Cleveland, Ohio, as the youngest of four sons. From the beginning he was a bit different, not like his rowdy, boisterous older brothers. "I never fitted the general boy assembly," he reflected. "I was quick with words, poor at games. When I was ten a schoolmate said of me, 'Aw, that guy swallowed a dictionary.' " (It was a fitting gibe at someone who would later go on to comb the dictionary in the service of the lexical hypothesis.)

Allport went to Harvard and studied psychology, mostly because his brother Floyd had done so first. As Floyd became an enormously successful scholar—he founded the discipline of experimental social psychology—Gordon continued to play the role of dutiful understudy. Even as he himself enrolled in graduate school, Gordon was typing Floyd's papers and assisting him in his research. Together the two brothers devised an early personality test measuring social dominance and submission—a ticklish subject for siblings engaged in intense, though submerged, competition.

After obtaining his PhD in 1922, Gordon broke away from Floyd's powerful influence to study on his own in Germany. Gradually he became disenchanted with his brother's highly quantified and mechanized conception of human nature, and enamored of European psychologists' more flexible and holistic approach. "Floyd's astoundingly neat system will not suffice," Gordon decided, and set about writing what he candidly conceded was an "attack" on his brother's theories. In an even bolder act of intellectual aggression, he submitted the finished article to the *Journal of Abnormal and Social Psychology*—edited by Floyd Allport.

His brother got the message. "You seem to be developing a type of Psychology somewhat different from mine," Floyd observed, adding with malice disguised as magnanimity: "It is the next best thing to mine." Gordon was enraged by his condescension—"He writes to me as he would to an unknown prof, in some distant dinky college," he fumed—and resolved to cut his ties with Floyd and with conventional psychology. "I truly do not care if I never see my brothers and sisters-in-law again," he declared, as he embarked on a career he would proudly describe as "maverick."

Though Gordon Allport helped establish personality psychology as an academic discipline, teaching the first course and authoring the first textbook devoted to the subject, he always retained the role of bumptious younger brother, pointing out its flaws and pressing his own case. He believed that the field focused too much on dysfunction and disease, and not enough on the normal, healthy human. He was after something quite different: "I wanted an 'image of man' that would allow us to test in full whatever democratic and humane potentialities that he might possess. I did not think of man as innately 'good,' but I was convinced that by and large American psychology gave man less than his due."

He thought, too, that personality psychology was excessively concerned with measurement and with the search for universal laws. Measurement is a useful tool, he noted, "but if it makes one think that one has embraced the totality of a personality by having a series of scores, then it has gone too far." Allport deplored psychologists' slavish imitation of biology, chemistry, and physics. "Following the lead of the older sciences they assume that the individual must be brushed aside," he lamented. "Science, they insist, deals only with general laws. The individual is a nuisance. What is wanted are uniformities. This tradition has resulted in the creation of a vast, shadowy abstraction in psychology called the generalized-adult-human-mind. The human mind, of course, exists in no such form; it exists only in concrete, intensely personal forms." He added, in what might have been his professional motto: "Personality is never general; it is always particular."

But Allport rejected, as well, the byzantine complexity of Freudian psychoanalysis and its insistence on finding hidden motives behind ordinary actions. He chided the analysts' determination to take "the long way around," asking, "Has the subject no right to be believed?" In fact, Allport found little in American personality psychology that met his approval, becoming a critic of Starke Hathaway's empirical test construction *and* Henry Murray's theories of projection *and* Raymond Cattell's methods of factor analysis. As one reviewer of an Allport book noted, "There is something in it to irritate almost everyone."

What Allport did endorse was an approach to personality assessment that paid close and respectful attention to the individual. The best vehicle for such attention, he believed, was the story, and he demonstrated how it might be used with a long, intense investigation of a woman named Jenny. Allport had in his possession (he declined to say just how) more than three hundred letters from a middle-aged woman, written to a friend of her son's. These documents formed the basis of Allport's exploration of her personality. "The letters deal with a mother-son tangle and are written in a fiercely dramatic, personal style," he noted. "Here surely is a unique life, calling for psychological analysis and interpretation." Whenever Allport found himself "wishing that I could take refuge in vague generalizations," his memory of Jenny's complicated character "pins me down with the unspoken challenge, 'And what do you make of *me?*' "

In the correspondence, which he used to teach generations of Harvard psychology students and which he published in 1965 as a book, *Letters From Jenny*, Allport employed pseudonyms: "Jenny" was not the woman's real name, he acknowledged, and neither was "Glenn" the true identity of her younger confidant. Allport claimed that he made the changes to protect the correspondents' privacy, but recent scholarship hints at another motivation: evidence dug up by psychologist David Winter strongly suggests that "Glenn" was Allport himself, and "Jenny" the mother of his own college roommate. Perhaps one reason Allport's analysis of the letters is so compelling, writes Winters, is that they bear "the imprimatur of his own personal experience."

Compelling or not, few psychologists were persuaded to go in the direction urged by Allport. Compiling life stories took a long time and didn't yield the kind of neat categories and confident predictions preferred by science (and by industry). While an array of other assessments—self-report inventories, projective tests, factor-analyzed questionnaires—went on to join psychology's mainstream, the life story approach still had a long way to go.

Now Dodge Morgan was sailing east around the bottom of the world, heading into the feared Southern Ocean. The "roaring forties," as these latitudes are known, are difficult and dangerous ones for even the most experienced sailor. Storm after storm beat down on *American Promise*. Enormous waves rocked the boat more than forty-five degrees to each side, so that "the gray-green water rolls by the pilothouse windows as if we were a submarine," Morgan observed. Cyclones whipped up the wind; icebergs loomed in the distance.

"Breaking waves are washing over the deck and often I stand in solid water to midcalf," Morgan reported in his journal. "The day wears on painfully. The seas are up and very steep again and *Promise* slams into them like a tank into a trench." He was tired, cold, and seasick. "I can't help but think that anyone who willingly submits to this kind of awful punishment is either crazy or masochistic," he added. "Which, I wonder, am I?"

Christmas Day arrived. Morgan sat on his bunk, humming Christmas carols to himself and opening the gifts his family placed on board months ago. He received a rum cake, a toaster, and some Super Glue, but "I do not have any Christmas spirit," he noted glumly. Six days later, it was a party of one on New Year's Eve. Looking into the camera in his pilothouse, he made some resolutions: not to covet his neighbor's wife, not to argue with his boss, not to stray too far from home—and joked that they wouldn't be hard to keep, at least for the next three months. "Happy New Year," he said, waving wanly at the camera. "Sorry I don't have a funny hat."

On February 22, Day 103 of the trip, the cameras recorded Morgan again as he opened one of the psychologists' waterproof packets. "Let's see what they have for us, the world of science," he muttered. The miserable weather had kept him inside for days, and he was plainly going a little stir-crazy. "It looks like . . . ho-ho! A personality profile." He considered its first question—"How have you been feeling the past week, including today?"—and belligerently retorted, "Cold as the southern end of a well digger!"

Next he mock-helpfully explained the test to the whirring camera. "I have to say 'not at all' up to 'extremely,' and grade these things: 'friendly, tense, angry, worn out, clearheaded, lively, sorry for things done, on edge, uncertain, full of pep.'" He paused and gave a slightly deranged grin. "Well, I could figure these out *easy*! Am I 'light-hearted, unsure, jittery, bewildered, horny . . .'" He stopped again and looked impishly toward his imagined audience. "No, it doesn't say 'horny' here," he admitted. "I wish it did, because I would be able to answer that one."

More fruitful was Morgan's informal self-examination, periods of reflection that led him to a rewarding realization: for all its hardships, there was something solid and true about the strange life he was leading. "My world is naturally obvious and simple and direct, lived as it should be lived," he asserted in his journal. "Existence belongs to creatures and elements with quick honesty, snap action, and interminable patience. Nothing else counts in this realm. Not intrigue or duplicity, rationalizations or negative wisdom, or life that needs change or senses that need constant stimulation. An individual human being belongs in this world. Humans' institutions do not. Institutions have lives of their own, burdened by symbols and rites and castes that obscure any view of the truth." He worked himself into a fevered denunciation: "Fuck them all, these institutions, from religions to college fraternities, organizations dedicated to dividing people and blurring the image of truth. We all must stand in our own space and see with our own mind the farthest horizon, and perhaps there we will see the source of our nature."

Morgan's spirits rose further as the weather cleared and he approached Cape Horn, the last great milestone on his long journey. As *American Promise* drew closer, he confessed, "I'm like water drops skittering on a hot skillet." At last the imposing land mass heaved into view, and Morgan seemed stunned, his customary detachment dropping away. "What a sight, what a sight," he whispered. Shaking off his awe, he pulled out a tuxedo jacket and three splits of champagne. He popped a cork, took a swig. "That one's for me, but there's three of us here." He opened another bottle and poured it on the deck: "This one's for *Promise*, a truly great boat." One more pop. "This one's for you, Cape," he said, and he hurled the bottle toward the far-off bluffs.

"Now we are going *home!*"

When Gordon Allport died in 1967, the life story approach lost its most vigorous champion, and personality psychology—which would be thrown into crisis by Walter Mischel's astute critique a year later—showed little interest in reviving it. Then a surprising thing happened: just around the time that the Big Five began its spectacular ascent, the life story approach, too, showed signs of life.

This resurgence is due in large part to one man: Dan McAdams, the same psychologist who has warned of the limits of the Big Five. McAdams, now fifty years old, began his research career using cards from the Thematic Apperception Test to study subjects' "intimacy motivations." Starting in the mid-1980s, however, he realized that what he really wanted to hear were stories from people's actual lives. And so just as many of his fellow psychologists were turning to the Big Five—or even to brain scans and gene assays—as the newest way to understand personality, McAdams was returning to the oldest: telling stories.

From the outset, he was concerned with applying rigorous scientific standards to the often-fuzzy life story approach. He and his Northwestern colleagues developed a structured protocol for documenting life stories, a guided interview process that lasts about two hours. Interviewees are asked to divide their lives into "chapters": childhood, adolescence, starting a family, building a career. They recount the leading events of each chapter, identifying main characters and describing specific scenes; they pick out turning points, high and low moments, most significant memories. They talk about recurrent struggles and conflicts, about their politics, values, and religious beliefs. Finally, they are asked to discern a dominant theme or message in their story, and to predict what future chapters might bring.

What matters in these investigations, McAdams stresses, is not the absolute veracity of the accounts, but the way they are presented. "Although these stories are grounded in reality, they are really fictions that we make up," he explains. "What I want to know is not exactly what happened in your childhood, but what *you* think happened." A fact such as "I was born prematurely on February 7, 1954," says McAdams, is not as significant as its accompanying lesson: "My father always said I was lucky to survive that premature birth; I beat the odds once, and now I am going to make my life count in a big way."

McAdams has worked out an objective system for coding these narratives, employing criteria such as complexity and coherence. Since 1997, he and his collaborators have used the system to evaluate hundreds of stories under the auspices of Northwestern's Foley Center for the Study of Lives. Some intriguing findings have begun to emerge from their work: for example, a positive relationship between the coherence of individuals' stories and their psychological well-being. This is a remarkable standard by which to gauge a person's mental health: not according to an expert's opinion or a norm group's average, but according to that person's degree of internal consistency. (It's not an entirely novel standard, however: as McAdams himself points out, Sigmund Freud and other pioneers of talk therapy had as a conscious goal making their patients' life stories at once more coherent and more complex.)

Even more telling than the stories' unity, says McAdams, are the basic themes at their core. His research has focused especially on two divergent motifs: "redemption" stories and "contamination" stories. In a redemptive story, negative life èvents—even awful tragedies—are perceived as sowing the seeds of positive developments to come. By contrast, contamination stories describe good times that are subsequently spoiled, euphoria followed by a crash. McAdams has found that people who tell redemptive stories tend to be happier and more "generative"—more likely to contribute to their communities and to succeeding generations. It's important to note, he says, that either of these templates can be applied to the very same series of events. He is interested not in actual incidents but in how they are interpreted; not in fixed states but in movement and its direction.

McAdams's life story approach is, in many ways, the un-test. It has no norms; subjects are not assigned numbers or types. The model explicitly acknowledges that people change and that their stories develop along with them. It views individuals as active shapers of their own personalities, "coauthors" of their life story along with the time and place in which they live. Culture, along with factors such as race, class, and gender, are seen as integral elements of life stories. For this reason, there can be no universal key to personality, only unique, particular personalities, and shifting, evolving ones at that. McAdams relinquishes the grand goal that has propelled personality psychologists for almost a century: "There is no simple, single key to understanding the individual person," he states bluntly, "no fundamental level of rock-bottom truth."

For all these reasons, the life story approach is almost defiantly resistant to the requirements of institutions, just about useless for the purposes of sorting and screening and labeling. McAdams allows as much: "Life narratives are about knowledge for knowledge's sake," he says. "They don't fit the agendas of industry or government." Even within psychology, the approach is often viewed as hopelessly impractical. Vociferous champion of the Big Five Robert McCrae seems uncharacteristically confounded by life stories: "I do not yet know quite what to make of them," he admits.

And yet they may be the only way to adequately describe or understand human beings as they genuinely are. Traditional personality tests present us with the world in microcosm, life with all its ambiguous stimuli, forced choices, and leaderless groups. But just as these tests' questions and simulations cannot begin to capture the real world's complexity, neither do the personalities they hand back to us begin to resemble the richness of our actual selves. The danger is that we may mistake their wan, washed-out copies for the lush, tangled beauty of the real thing. In contemplating an entity as intricate and enigmatic as personality, it seems wise to follow Gordon Allport's counsel to be "tentative, eclectic, and humble." On the subject of human nature, he liked to quote William James: "Our knowledge is a drop, our ignorance a sea."

Dodge Morgan sailed into the blue waters of Bermuda on April 11, 1986. By now his skin was deeply tanned, his hair shaggy and bleached by the sun. A brisk fifteen-knot wind blew, whipping the waves into six-foot swells and puffing *Promise*'s sails as it coursed its last few miles. Closer to shore, a chase boat scanned the horizon for the first sight of Morgan's vessel; at last it appeared, a tiny white dot. Grant Robinson, a shipbuilder who supervised the construction of Morgan's boat, was sitting at the controls. "*American Promise, American Promise*," he radioed, his voice trembling just a little. "We have a visual."

A brief silence, then a crackle. "Well, at least I haven't become invisible," Morgan radioed back, his laconic voice unmistakable.

He crossed the official finish line, about three miles from shore, at 12:17 p.m. He had sailed around the world, alone, in 150 days, one hour, and six minutes—cutting the previous record nearly in half. Proud as he was of his achievement, Morgan mostly wanted to see his family and friends. Once on shore, he will announce to the cheering crowd, "I have made up my mind that the race I really want to belong to is the human race."

Now, as *American Promise* glided fully into view, the chase boat pulled up alongside. On board were Manny and Hoyt and Kimberly, waving furiously. Morgan leaned over the side as they drew near.

"You're the first human beings I've seen in a hundred and fifty days!" he shouted. "You can't believe how beautiful you look."

Epilogue

An X-ray of personality." Since the early days of personality tests, this has been the testers' favorite metaphor, and no wonder: it calls to mind a precise and powerful instrument, capable of penetrating mere surfaces to produce an image of what's within. And yet this metaphor has never been more than an alluring fantasy, or perhaps a willful delusion. The reality is that personality tests cannot begin to capture the complex human beings we are. They cannot specify how we will act in particular roles or situations. They cannot predict how we will change over time. Many tests look for (and find) disease and dysfunction rather than health and strength. Many others fail to meet basic scientific standards of validity and reliability.

The consequences of these failures are real. Our society is making crucial decisions—whether a parent should receive custody of a child, whether a worker should be offered a job, whether a student should be admitted to a school or special program—on the basis of deeply flawed information. If these tests serve anyone well, it is not individuals but institutions, which purchase efficiency and convenience at the price of our privacy and dignity. Personality tests do their dirty work, asking intrusive questions and assigning limiting labels, providing an ostensibly objective rationale to which testers can point with an apologetic shrug.

But perhaps the most insidious effect of personality testing is its influence on the way we understand others—children, coworkers, fellow citizens—and even ourselves. The tests substitute a tidy abstraction for a real, rumpled human being, a sterile idea for a flesh-and-blood individual. No doubt these generic forms are easier to understand (and, not incidentally, to manipulate) than actual people, in all their sticky specificity. But ultimately they can only diminish our recognition and appreciation of others' full humanity, only impede our own advance toward self-discovery and self-awareness.

The current prevalence of personality testing, of course, is evidence that many feel otherwise—that such testing is filling a need, or at least a perceived need. And so a reconsideration of our reliance on personality tests must begin with an acknowledgment of their potency. Tests are powerful; the categories in which they place us are powerful. That's exactly why they must be employed with caution and care. These days a personality test may serve as a corporate icebreaker, a classroom game, a counseling exercise. Though such uses may seem harmless, we ought to be wary of the tendency of tests and their apparently definitive judgments to take on a life of their own. When our objectives—to get a discussion started, to stimulate self-reflection, to offer guidance—can be met without a test, they should be.

There's no question that this approach asks more of us as a society: the work that a test makes so smoothly automatic must be replaced by an effort of sympathetic curiosity and attention. But the rewards will be proportional to our exertions, an equation that also holds for the time and energy we invest in trying to understand ourselves. A guide to applying the life story approach pioneered by psychologist Dan McAdams can be found in his 1993 book, *The Stories We Live By: Personal Myths and the Making of the Self* (William Morrow). Recalling and analyzing in depth the principal events of our lives is far more intellectually challenging and emotionally involving than penciling in a series of bubbles—but at the end of it, we'll have a self-portrait that is more than a diagnosis, a job description, or a glorified horoscope.

When some kind of formal assessment is necessary (as evidence in a court case, for example), personality tests are not the only option. Alternatives include the structured interview (a dialogue guided by an established protocol); the collection of relevant biographical information; ratings provided by people who are familiar with the person being assessed; and behavioral observations made by multiple trained observers. Also available are targeted instruments developed for the situation at hand (as opposed to global measures that make sweeping statements about personality in general). A psychologist evaluating a mother or father seeking custody, for example, might administer the Parent-Child Relationship Inventory or the Parenting Stress Index—tests designed especially for this purpose—rather than the Rorschach or the Thematic Apperception Test.

Likewise, assessments of workers and students should be concerned with their specific abilities, not with overarching judgments of their personalities. The most effective evaluations are made by observing the individual in a situation as close as possible to the one in which he or she will be expected to perform. If personality tests must be used, they should be chosen carefully—free of invasive questions, fair to all groups, proven scientifically valid and reliable—and interpreted cautiously, with an acute awareness of their limitations. Their results should be kept strictly confidential.

Some of these caveats can be found in the guidelines produced by a coalition of testing organizations in 1998 (available online at www.apa.org/science/ttrr.html). According to the "Rights and Responsibilities of Test Takers," all of us have the right to be tested "with measures that meet professional standards and that are appropriate, given the manner in which the test results will be used"; to have tests administered and interpreted "by appropriately trained individuals who follow professional codes of ethics"; and to have test results "kept confidential to the extent allowed by law." But the ringing sound of "rights" in the statement's title fades to a whimper in its fine print: the so-called rights proclaimed by the guidelines "are neither legally based nor inalienable," its authors admit.

More stringent rules are set out in the American Psychological Association's Ethical Principles of Psychologists and Code of Conduct (available online at www.apa.org/ethics/code2002.html). This document sternly declares that "Psychologists use assessment instruments whose validity and reliability have been established for use with members of the population tested . . . Psychologists do not base [their] decisions or recommendations on tests and measures that are obsolete and not useful for the current purpose." Yet recent surveys show that many psychologists are doing just that—making the invalid, unreliable, obsolete and all but useless Draw-a-Person Test and House-Tree-Person Test, to cite two examples, among the field's most frequently used instruments. The statement alludes ominously to "potential sanctions" for those who violate the principles, including termination of APA membership, but the latest report of the APA Ethics Committee reveals that only ten of its more than one hundred and fifty thousand members were sanctioned in the year 2002; in none of these cases was "test misuse" the primary factor.

In any case, all these admonitions may be safely ignored by the majority of test publishers, distributors, and administrators who are not psychologists and so operate outside even the APA's toothless authority. Their interests are aggressively promoted by the Association of Test Publishers, an advocacy organization concerned largely with fighting off legislative and judicial challenges to the unlimited use of tests. Such efforts have been stunningly successful, resulting in a sprawling testing industry that is almost entirely unregulated. The list of legal protections for personality test takers is short indeed: Massachusetts and Rhode Island have passed laws limiting or banning the use of integrity tests; privacy provisions in some state constitutions offer very limited barriers against invasive questions; the Civil Rights Act outlaws tests that have an adverse impact on protected groups such as blacks and women (not usually an issue with personality tests); the Americans with Disabilities Act prohibits medical examinations (the Minnesota Multiphasic Personality Inventory qualifies) before a job offer is extended. And that's about it.

Significant new legal safeguards seem unlikely to be instituted (though optimists might envision a federal ban on personality tests in the workplace, similar to the 1988 law that prohibited polygraph examinations by most private employers). The responsibility for breaking away from our society's cult of personality testing lies first with the people who produce the tests. It would be unrealistic to expect them to relinquish a profit center that generates an estimated $400 million a year in this country alone, but perhaps not unreasonable to think that many might consent to the collective application of basic quality controls—if only to prevent another crash of the personality-testing industry under the weight of unmet promises, as has happened more than once in its history.

Psychologists are the second piece in this puzzle. As many observers have noted, there is a serious disconnect between what academic researchers demonstrate in the lab (the poor showing of most projective techniques, for example) and what clinicians keep doing in their offices. Professional organizations like the American Psychological Association need to scrupulously enforce among their members the rules their codes of ethics already profess. More persuasive still would be a move by the holders of psychologists' purse strings—managed care companies—to re-frain from reimbursing practitioners for the use of invalid or unreliable tests (a development already underway). The training of new psychologists could point out the pitfalls of traditional personality testing, and offer expanded instruction in alternative forms of assessment.

Users of personality tests who are not psychologists—employers, teachers, guidance counselors, workshop leaders—also have an obligation to educate themselves about the potential for personality tests to limit and stereotype. A careful examination of a test's psychometric properties and a healthy skepticism toward its claims might lead them to choose better instruments—or to forgo testing altogether in favor of some old-fashioned conversation.

And finally, there's us: the people who take the tests, voluntarily or otherwise. When confronted with a personality test we are obliged to complete, a few questions of our own are in order. Begin by finding out which test you will be given; if it's not one covered in this book, make your way to the nearest large public or university library, which should have a set of *Mental Measurements Yearbooks* on its shelves. In these doorstop-heavy volumes you'll find basic information about most personality tests, along with careful critiques by psychologists. Test reviews are also available online at a cost of fifteen dollars each: http://buros.unl.edu/buros/jsp/search.jsp.

Thus armed with information, you'll be better prepared to take the test, or, perhaps, to refuse it. (This more extreme stance is advocated by Carnegie Mellon University psychologist Robyn Dawes: "If a professional psychologist is 'evaluating' you in a situation in which you are at risk and asks you for responses to ink blots or to incomplete sentences, or for a drawing of anything, walk out of that psychologist's office," he urges. "Going through with such an examination creates the danger of having a serious decision made about you on totally invalid grounds. If your contact with the psychologist involves a legal matter, your civil liberties themselves may be at stake.") If you go ahead with the test, inquire about how its results will be used, ask for feedback once it is scored, and request an assurance that your answers will be kept confidential. You won't have subverted the cult of personality entirely, but you will at least be an informed participant.

And for those of us who have sought the help of personality tests in understanding ourselves: remember that promoters of the tests—from the Rorschach to today's inventories of the Big Five—have claimed for nearly a century that they possess an X-ray of personality. But in truth (as psychologist Joseph Masling once put it) the X-ray is more like a mirror, reflecting mostly the testers' own needs and wants. The tests say more about them than they do about us.

Acknowledgments

My sincere thanks are due to a number of people who helped, in different ways, with the making of this book. Dominick Anfuso, Rachel Klayman, and Philip Rappaport expressed spirited enthusiasm for the book early on in its development. Jack Block, Daniel Druckman, Thomas Fagan, Lewis Goldberg, John Hunsley, Howard Knoff, Scott Lilienfeld, Scott Meier, Wesley Morgan, Reuben Robbins, Brad Seligman, and James Wood shared their extraordinary expertise, answering questions and offering comments. Nancy Gottesman extended endless patience and unfailing good humor. Myriam Bucatinsky and Anna Christensen supplied crucial insight. Joan Konner provided an inspiring example, and Andie Tucher proved both an admirable teacher and a capable adviser. Ali Price made having my picture taken almost fun.

For their generous interest and encouragment, I thank fellow writers and editors Michael Agger, Solange Belcher, Hilary Black, Lexy Bloom, Susan Burton, Katie Darnton, Amelia Hansen, Nadya Labi, Hara Marano, Kat McGowan, Lois Morris, Jodie Morse, Joey O'Loughlin, Matthew Price, Paul Raeburn, Amanda Schaffer, Chuck Staresinic, and Anastasia Toufexis.

For their supportive and sustaining friendship, I thank Jenny Brown, Alison Burns, Camille Chatterjee, Rachel Doft, Ariela Dubler, David Engstrom, Robert Frumkin, Jesse Furman, Drew Hansen, Jessica Kaufman, Anne Martin, Meg Martin, Andy Moffit, Gina Raimondo, Luis Roth, Alyson Schenck, Michael Seeber, and Jon ten Oever.

My warmest and most grateful thanks go to Julie Cooper, Marguerite Lamb, Pamela Paul, Alissa Quart, Steve Schreiber, Rebecca Segall, and Debbie Siegel.

My agent, Andrew Blauner, has been a kind and thoughtful friend as well as a loyal and skillful ally. My editor, Martin Beiser, joined this project when it was well underway, but soon made himself indispensable with his sharp eye and steady guidance. His assistant, Stephen Karam, has been a model of cheerful efficiency.

My family has been a source of unstinting love and support during the writing of this book. For their lively welcome, I thank Loretta and Tom Witt, Chris and Satya Witt, Susee Witt, Margaret Cooper, and Dinka Majanovic. For her humor and high spirits (and some great music), I thank Sally Paul. And for—well, just about everything, I thank my wonderful parents, Nancy Murphy Paul and John Timothy Paul.

My deepest appreciation is reserved for the emotional and intellectual sustenance given me by my husband, John Fabian Witt. He has all of my heart, and a part of every word in this book.

Notes

INTRODUCTION

xii   *"a key to the knowledge of mankind"*: Quoted in Diane E. Jonte-Pace, "From Prophets to Perception: The Origins of Rorschach's Psychology," *The Annual of Psychoanalysis*, 1986.

xii   *"overpathologizes"*: Author's interview with James Wood, coauthor of *What's Wrong with the Rorschach? Science Confronts the Controversial Inkblot Test* (John Wiley, 2003), January 6, 2003.

xii   *used by eight out of ten clinical psychologists*: Cited in James M. Wood, Howard N. Garb, and Scott O. Lilienfeld, "The Rorschach Is Scientifically Questionable," *Harvard Mental Health Letter*, December 1, 2001.

xii   *nearly a third of emotional injury assessments*: Marcus T. Boccaccini and Stanley L. Brodsky, "Diagnostic Test Usage by Forensic Psychologists in Emotional Injury Cases," *Professional Psychology: Research and Practice*, June 1999.

xii   *almost half of child custody evaluations*: Francella A. Quinnell and James N. Bow, "Psychological Tests Used in Child Custody Evaluations," *Behavioral Sciences and the Law*, September 2001.

xii   *"we permitted the patients to design their own test"*: Starke R. Hathaway, videotaped interview conducted by W. Grant Dahlstrom, "Measuring the Mind: Psychological Testing: A Conversation With Starke Hathaway," Center for Creative Leadership, 1976.

xii   *an estimated 15 million Americans each year*: Eugene E. Levitt and Edward E. Gotts, *The Clinical Application of MMPI Special Scales*, 2nd ed. (Lawrence Erlbaum, 1995), 1.

xii   *administered by 30 percent of American companies*: Management Recruiters International, "Drug Testing a Prominent Part of the Hiring Process," Business Wire, April 30, 2003.

xii   *"woefully short of professional and scientific test standards"*: John Hunsley, Catherine M. Lee, and James M. Wood, "Controversial and Questionable Assessment Techniques," in *Science and Pseudoscience in Clinical Psychology*, ed. Scott O. Lilienfeld, Steven Jay Lynn, and Jeffrey M. Lohr (Guilford, 2003), 53.

xiii   *used by 60 percent of clinicians:* Wayne Camara, Julie Nathan, and Anthony Puente, "Psychological Test Usage in Professional Psychology: Report to the APA Practice and Science Directorates," American Psychological Association, May 1998, 19. All figures drawn from this survey are based on clinicians who spend at least five hours a week on testing.

xiii   *two-thirds of police and fire departments and state and county governments:* Phillip E. Lowry, "A Survey of the Assessment Center Process in the Public Sector," *Public Personnel Management,* fall 1996.

xiii   *the test she called "my baby":* Quoted in "Eminent Interview: Katherine Downing Myers," *Journal of Psychological Type,* vol. 61, 2002.

xiii   *given to 2.5 million people each year:* Personal communication from Siobhan Collopy, marketing communications manager, CPP.

xiii   *used by 89 of the companies in the Fortune 100:* CPP, "CPP Celebrates 60th Anniversary of Myers-Briggs Assessment," PR Newswire, October 28, 2003.

xiii   *what devotees call the "aha reaction":* Peter B. Myers, preface in Isabel Briggs Myers with Peter B. Myers, *Gifts Differing: Understanding Personality Type* (Davies-Black, 1995), xiii.

xiii   *as many as three-quarters of test takers achieve a different personality type:* Cited in "In the Mind's Eye: Enhancing Human Performance," ed. Daniel Druckman and Robert A. Bjork, Committee on Techniques for the Enhancement of Human Performance, National Research Council (National Academy Press, 1991), 96.

xiii   *the sixteen distinctive types described by the Myers-Briggs have no scientific basis:* See, e.g., M. H. Sam Jacobson, "Using the Myers-Briggs Type Indicator to Assess Learning Style: Type or Stereotype?," *Willamette Law Review,* spring 1997.

xiii   *"again and again," the results of drawing tests "have failed to hold up":* Loren J. Chapman and Jean P. Chapman, "Test Results Are What You Think They Are," *Psychology Today,* November 1971.

xiii   *the Draw-a-Person Test is still used by more than a quarter of clinicians:* Camara, Nathan, and Puente, "Psychological Test Usage in Professional Psychology," 19.

xiii   *the House-Tree-Person Test by more than a third:* Ibid.

xiv   *there are some 2,500 others on the market:* Cited in Margaret Talbot, "The Rorschach Chronicles," *New York Times Magazine,* June 24, 2001.

xiv   *a $400-million industry, one that's expanding annually by 8 percent to 10 percent:* Cited in ibid.

CHAPTER ONE: A MOST TYPICAL AMERICAN

1   *"Combativeness, six":* Quoted in Walt Whitman, *Walt Whitman: Selected Poems 1855–1892* (Stonewall Inn Editions, 2000), 114.

1   *"You are one of the most friendly men in the world":* Quoted in Madeleine B.

Stern, *Heads & Headlines: The Phrenological Fowlers* (University of Oklahoma Press, 1971), 103.

2   *"Breasting the waves of detraction"*: Quoted in Edward Hungerford, "Walt Whitman and His Chart of Bumps," *American Literature*, January 1931.

3   *"An American bard at last!"*: Quoted in ibid.

3   *"In America an immense number"*: Walt Whitman, *The Neglected Walt Whitman: Vital Texts*, ed. Sam Abrams (Four Walls Eight Windows, 1993), 161.

3   *"Never offering others"*: Walt Whitman, *Walt Whitman: Poetry and Prose*, ed. Justin Kaplan (Library of America, 1996), 677.

3   *"They shall arise in the States"*: Ibid., 590.

3   *"who would talk or sing to America"*: Ibid., 477.

4   *"very learned and erudite, fond of philosophical dissertations"*: Anonymous, "Bright, Passionate, Harmful, and Helpful Stars," trans. by Daria Dudziak, www.cieloeterra.it/eng/eng.testi.379/eng.379.html.

4   "The chief reason why Asiatics are less warlike": Quoted in Jacques Jouanna, *Hippocrates*, trans. M. B. Debevoise (Johns Hopkins University Press, 2001), 221.

5   *"Those maddened through bile"*: Quoted in Morton Hunt, *The Story of Psychology* (Anchor, 1994), 18.

5   *"Persons who have a large forehead"*: Quoted in ibid., 312.

6   "I collected in my house": Quoted in Stern, *Heads & Headlines*, x.

6   *"Gall's Passionate Widow"*: Quoted in Raymond Fancher, *Pioneers of Psychology*, 2nd ed. (W. W. Norton, 1990), 77.

6   *"mechanical aptitude"*: Quoted in D. B. Klein, *A History of Scientific Psychology: Its Origins and Philosophical Backgrounds* (Basic Books, 1970), 672.

7   *"practical system of mental philosophy"*: Quoted in Stern, *Heads & Headlines*, xii.

7   *"the professors were in love with him"*: Quoted in David Bakan, "The Influence of Phrenology on American Psychology," *Journal of the History of the Behavioral Sciences*, July 1966.

7   *"When Spurzheim was in America"*: Quoted in Stern, *Heads & Headlines*, xiii.

7   *"one of the world's greatest minds"*: Quoted in Minna Morse, "The Much-Maligned Theory of Phrenology Gets a Tip of the Hat from Modern Neuroscience," *Smithsonian*, October 1997.

7   *"a calamity to mankind"*: Quoted in Thomas Cooley, *The Ivory Leg in the Ebony Cabinet: Madness, Race, and Gender in Victorian America* (University of Massachusetts Press, 2001), 17.

7   *"Ode to Spurzheim"*: Cited in Paul Lafarge, "Head of the Class: The Bumpy Road From Phrenology to Public Schools," *The Village Voice*, January 17–23, 2001.

7   *"Nature's priest"*: Quoted in Karla Klein Albertson, "Phrenology in the
        Nineteenth Century," *Early American Life*, June 1995.

8   *"a strong social brain"*: Quoted in Stern, *Heads & Headlines*, 11.

8   *"a practical knowledge"*: Quoted in John D. Davies, *Phrenology: A 19th-
        Century American Crusade* (Yale University Press, 1955), 162.

8   *"Phrenologize Our Nation"*: Quoted in Stern, *Heads & Headlines*, 35.

8   *"the prosperity and material good"*: Quoted in ibid., 39.

8   *"Surely, [a reading] will point out"*: Quoted in Bakan, "The Influence of
        Phrenology."

8   *"two wizards of manipulation"*: Quoted in Stern, *Heads & Headlines*, 16.

8   *"No Conscientiousness!"*: Quoted in ibid., 17.

9   *"would veto bills"*: Quoted in ibid., 23.

9   *"what the great dome"*: Quoted in Justin Kaplan, *Walt Whitman: A Life*
        (Simon & Schuster, 1980), 149.

9   *"How can the value"*: Quoted in Stern, *Heads & Headlines*, 22.

9   *"It is not at all likely"*: Quoted in José Lopez Delano, "Snaring the Fowler:
        Mark Twain Debunks Phrenology," *Skeptical Inquirer*, January–February
        2002.

9   *"By and by the people"*: Quoted in Stern, *Heads & Headlines*, 17.

10   *"A correct Phrenological examination"*: Quoted in Bakan, "The Influence of
        Phrenology."

10   *"A most typical American"*: Quoted in Hungerford, "Walt Whitman and His
        Chart of Bumps."

10   *"painful confusion's derangement"*: Quoted in Robert H. Azbug, *Cosmos
        Crumbling: American Reform and the Religious Imagination* (Oxford University
        Press, 1994), 177.

10   *"a complete mental daguerreotype"*: Quoted in Bakan, "The Influence of
        Phrenology."

10   "AN APPRENTICE WANTED": Quoted in Davies, *Phrenology*, 50.

11   In October 2003, Emode renamed itself Tickle, Inc. and added a focus on
        social networking.

11   *"Man of the Internet"*: Quoted in Deborah Giattina, "Geek Love," *The
        Industry Standard*, February 12, 2001.

11   *"I saw that it was a tremendously meaningful experience"*: Author's interview
        with James Currier, March 18, 2003.

12   *"just for fun"*: Ibid.

12   *"Everyone is interested in themselves"*: Quoted in Anita Hamilton, "What
        Breed of Dog Are You?," *Time*, September 30, 2002.

12   *"Since the beginning of man"*: Quoted in Kathryn Balint, "Online Tests Try to
        Give You the Inside Information on Yourself," *San Diego Union-Tribune*,
        January 4, 2001.

12   *"Emode will use Internet technology"*: Emode.com, "Our Story," www.emode.com/emode/about/story.jsp.

12   *"It takes a really distracted and imprecise, scary process"*: Quoted in Alex Salkever, "In the Emode for Love," *Business Week*, March 10, 2003.

12   *"We take information"*: Author's interview with Currier.

14   *"Depress the adhesive nature"*: Quoted in Christopher Lehmann-Haupt, "Portrait of Whitman as a Product of His Times," *New York Times*, May 29, 1995.

14   *"I know what [Oliver Wendell] Holmes"*: Quoted in Kaplan, *Walt Whitman: A Life*, 153.

14   *"Not even his manuscripts"*: David Cavitch, *My Soul and I: The Inner Life of Walt Whitman* (Beacon Press, 1985), 26.

15   *"I went there often"*: Quoted in Philip Callow, *Walt Whitman: From Noon to Starry Night* (Allison & Busby, 1992), 186.

CHAPTER TWO: RORSCHACH'S DREAM

17   *"respectful eagerness of a young student"*: Quoted in Henri Ellenberger, "The Life and Work of Hermann Rorschach (1884–1922)," *Bulletin of the Menninger Clinic*, September 1954.

17   *"key to the knowledge of mankind"*: Quoted in Diane E. Jonte-Pace, "From Prophets to Perception: The Origins of Rorschach's Psychology," *The Annual of Psychoanalysis*, 1986.

19   *"the other world"*: Quoted in James M. Wood, M. Teresa Nezworski, Scott O. Lilienfeld, and Howard N. Garb, *What's Wrong with the Rorschach? Science Confronts the Controversial Inkblot Test* (John Wiley, 2003), 23.

19   *"Klex"*: Cited in Ellenberger, "The Life and Work of Hermann Rorschach."

19   *"What might this be?"*: Hermann Rorschach, *Psychodiagnostics: A Diagnostic Test Based on Perception*, 10th ed. (Verlag Hans Huber, 1998), 16.

19   *"angels with fluttering wings"*: Ibid., 25.

20   *"The funny part was that everything I saw"*: Julia Lytle, quoted in Earl J. Ginter and Joseph J. Scalise, "A Perspective on Hermann Rorschach: An Interview With a Personal Acquaintance," *Psychology—A Quarterly Journal of Human Behavior*, August 1978.

20   *"passing through hundreds of hands"*: Rorschach, *Psychodiagnostics*, 20.

20   *"The gloomy person is one to whom everything looks 'black' "*: Ibid., 99.

20   *"nothing other than the ability to create new"*: Quoted in Marvin W. Acklin and Jill Oliveira-Berry, "Return to the Source: Rorschach's Psychodiagnostics," *Journal of Personality Assessment*, October 1996.

20   *"penetrate by way of the test"*: Gertrud Behn-Eschenburg, "Working With Dr. Hermann Rorschach," *Journal of Projective Techniques*, March 1955.

21   *"provides a diagnosis so accurate"*: Quoted in John E. Exner Jr., *The Rorschach Systems* (Grune & Stratton, 1969), 6.

21   *"In all the languages of the world"*: Quoted in Ellenberger, "The Life and Work of Hermann Rorschach."

21   *"The test itself is technically so simple"*: Rorschach, *Psychodiagnostics*, 97.

21   *"a key to the knowledge of mankind"* Quoted in Jonte-Pace, "From Prophets to Perception."

22   *"a method of discovering the possibility"*: Quoted in ibid.

22   *"In Vienna they are soon"*: Quoted in Pierre Pichot, "Centenary of the Birth of Hermann Rorschach," *Journal of Personality Assessment*, December 1984.

22   *"Although Rorschach tended to stick"*: Behn-Eschenburg, "Working With Dr. Hermann Rorschach."

22   *"a tiny king from a fairy tale"*: Rorschach, *Psychodiagnostics*, 137–140.

23   *"Unfortunately we are still having difficulties"*: Quoted in Jonte-Pace, "From Prophets to Perception."

24   *"Few destinies are more pathetic"*: Ellenberger, "The Life and Work of Hermann Rorschach."

24   *"he was in the midst of his promising elaboration"*: Emil Oberholzer, introduction in "The Application of the Form Interpretation Test," in Rorschach, *Psychodiagnostics*, 184.

24   *"Being permitted to watch Rorschach"*: Behn-Eschenburg, "Working With Dr. Hermann Rorschach."

25   *"Well, he's a Jew"*: Author's interview with Fred Klopfer, February 18, 2003.

25   *"did a little wishful thinking"*: Pauline G. Vorhaus, "Bruno Klopfer: A Biographical Sketch," *Journal of Projective Techniques*, September 1960.

25   *"Whenever he walked into a room"*: Quoted in Leonard Handler, "Bruno Klopfer, a Measure of the Man and His Work," *Journal of Personality Assessment*, June 1994.

26   *"Persons who were intelligent"*: Samuel J. Beck, quoted in Roderick D. Buchanan, "Ink Blots or Profile Plots: The Rorschach Versus the MMPI as the Right Tool for a Science-Based Profession," *Science, Technology & Human Values*, spring 1997.

26   the richly detailed portraits: See, e.g., James M. Wood, M. Teresa Nezworksi, Scott O. Lilienfeld, and Howard N. Garb, "The Rorschach Inkblot Test, Fortune Tellers, and Cold Reading," *Skeptical Inquirer*, July 1, 2003.

27   *"I saw some of the best murderers"*: Samuel J. Beck, oral history interview, conducted by J. A. Popplestone, April 28, 1969, transcript located at the Archives of the History of American Psychology at the Unversity of Akron, Ohio.

27   *"find out what it's all about"*: Ibid.

27   *"what there is to know by scientific method"*: Ibid.

27   *"I had to have evidence"*: Ibid.

28   *"there was feverish activity"*: Marguerite Hertz, oral history interview, conducted by Robert N. Sollod, August 4, 1985, transcript located at the Archives of the History of American Psychology at the University of Akron, Ohio.

28   *"a psychological microscope"*: Zygmunt A. Piotrowski, "On the Rorschach Method of Personality Analysis," *The Psychiatric Quarterly*, July 1942.

28   *"a fluoroscope into the psyche"*: Samuel J. Beck, "The Rorschach Test: A Multi-Dimensional Test of Personality," *An Introduction to Projective Techniques*, ed. Harold H. Anderson and Gladys L. Anderson (Prentice-Hall, 1951), 103.

28   *"blueprint of the personality's structure"*: Samuel J. Beck, *The Rorschach Test Exemplified in Classics of Drama and Fiction* (Stratton Intercontinental, 1976), 4.

28   *"a foolproof X-ray of a personality"*: Cited in Walter G. Klopfer, "The Short History of Projective Techniques," *Journal of the History of the Behavioral Sciences*, January 1973.

28   *"Rorschach workers"*: Edwin I. Megargee and Charles D. Spielberger, "Reflections on Fifty Years of Personality Assessment and Future Directions for the Field," in *Personality Assessment in America: A Retrospective on the Occasion of the Fiftieth Anniversary of the Society for Personality Assessment*, ed. Edwin I. Megargee and Charles D. Spielberger (Lawrence Erlbaum, 1992), 170.

28   *"By 1950, more dissertations and journal articles would be written about the Rorschach"*: Cited in Wood et al., *What's Wrong with the Rorschach?*, 84.

28   *between 1955 and 1965, research on the Rorschach was streaming forth*: Cited in Arthur R. Jensen, "Rorschach," *The Sixth Mental Measurement Yearbook*, ed. Oscar Krisen Buros (Gryphon Press, 1965), 236.

29   *"two men talking about a crime"*: Douglas M. Kelley, *22 Cells in Nuremberg: A Psychiatrist Examines the Nazi Criminals* (Greenberg, 1947), 29.

29   *"a funny bear, fur spread out"*: Douglas M. Kelley, "Preliminary Studies of the Rorschach Records of the Nazi War Criminals," *Rorschach Research Exchange*, March 1946.

29   *"Oh, those crazy cards again"*: Quoted in José Brunner, " 'Oh Those Crazy Cards Again': A History of the Debate on the Nazi Rorschachs, 1946–2001," *Political Psychology*, June 2001.

29   *"had not had available such excellent testing techniques"*: Kelley, "Preliminary Studies of the Rorschach Records of the Nazi War Criminals."

29   *"wept unashamedly when I left Nuremberg"*: Kelley, *22 Cells in Nuremberg*, 12.

29   *"Nazi Rorschachs"*: Brunner, " 'Oh Those Crazy Cards Again.' "

29   *"Strong, dominant, aggressive, egocentric personalities"*: Kelley, *22 Cells in Nuremberg*, 238.

29   *"There are undoubtedly certain individuals"*: Kelley, "Preliminary Studies of the Rorschach Records of the Nazi War Criminals."

30   *"on the altar of a fetishistic goddess"*: Quoted in Wood et al., *What's Wrong With the Rorschach?*, 70.

30   *"It would go far towards clearing up the present state of confusion"*: Samuel J. Beck, "Rorschach," *The Fifth Mental Measurements Yearbook*, ed. Oscar Krisen Buros (Gryphon Press, 1959), 274.

31   *This is an ordinary classroom:* Author's reporting.

31   *"an experimentally induced dream"*: F. L. Wells, quoted in Beck, *The Rorschach Test Exemplified in Classics of Drama and Fiction*, 79.

33   *"I was awestruck at the prospect"*: John E. Exner Jr., *The Rorschach: A Comprehensive System*, vol. 2, 2nd ed. (John Wiley, 1991), ix.

33   *"What's that?"*: Quoted in Leonard Handler, "John Exner and the Book That Started It All: A Review of The Rorschach Systems," *Journal of Personality Assessment*, June 1996.

33   *"I fell in love with both those guys"*: Quoted in ibid.

33   *"I had hoped that because they were so very nice to me"*: Quoted in ibid.

33   *some warned, it was becoming too ungainly for routine use:* See Exner, *The Rorschach Systems*, 26.

34   *"a very, very good politician"*: Author's interview with Jack Gerber, chief psychologist of the Philadelphia prison system and owner of the Rorschach Discussion List, January 15, 2003.

34   *"although each included some highly valuable components"*: Exner, *The Rorschach: A Comprehensive System*, xi.

34   *"empirically defensible"*: Ibid., 3.

34   *"Until proponents of the Rorschach can produce evidence"*: Jensen, "Rorschach," 238.

35   *"Exner has almost single-handedly rescued the Rorschach"*: American Psychological Foundation, "Award for Distinguished Professional Contributions, John E. Exner Jr., Citation," *American Psychologist*, April 1998.

35   *it is the second most popular personality test available:* Cited in James Wood, Howard N. Garb, and Scott O. Lilienfeld, "The Rorschach Test Is Scientifically Questionable," *Harvard Mental Health Letter*, December 1, 2001.

35   *eight out of ten clinical psychologists said they included it in their test batteries at least "occasionally"*: Cited in ibid.

35   *93 percent of APA-approved graduate programs teach the test:* Cited in Philip Erdberg, "Rorschach Assessment," *Handbook of Psychological Assessment*, 3rd ed., ed. Gerald Goldstein and Michel Hersen (Pergamon, 2000), 447.

35   *90 percent of clinical practitioners in the field believe that psychology students should be skilled in Rorschach assessment:* Cited in Donald J. Viglione and Mark J. Hilsenroth, "The Rorschach: Facts, Fiction, and Future," *Psychological Assessment*, December 2001.

35   *"Basic issues regarding the reliability and validity of the Comprehensive System"*:
      James M. Wood, M. Teresa Nezworski, and William J. Stejskal, "The
      Comprehensive System for the Rorschach: A Critical Examination,"
      Psychological Science, January 1996.

36   *"There is currently no scientific basis for justifying the use of Rorschach scales"*:
      John Hunsley and J. Michael Bailey, "The Clinical Utility of the Rorschach:
      Unfulfilled Promises and an Uncertain Future," *Psychological Assessment*,
      September 1999.

36   *"meager support"*: Ibid.

36   *an immediate moratorium on the administration of the Rorschach:* Howard N.
      Garb, "Call for a Moratorium on the Use of the Rorschach Inkblot Test in
      Clinical and Forensic Settings," *Assessment*, December 1999. (Garb is now
      Chief of the Psychology Research Service at the Wilford Hall Medical
      Center, on Lackland Air Force Base in San Antonio, Texas.)

36   *"phrenology was in vogue"*: William M. Grove, R. Christopher Barden,
      Howard N. Garb, and Scott O. Lilienfeld, "Failure of Rorschach-
      Comprehensive-System-Based Testimony to Be Admissible Under the
      Daubert-Joiner-Kumho Standard," *Psychology, Public Policy, and Law*, June
      2002.

36   *"terrorists" and "assassins"*: Cited in Wood et al., *What's Wrong With the
      Rorschach?*, 264.

36   *"a bunch of hooey"*: Author's interview with Barry Ritzler, February 5, 2003.

36   *"I tell my students who've had half a semester of Rorschach instruction"*: Ibid.

36   *"this so-called controversy"*: Author's interview with Irving Weiner, January
      28, 2003.

36   *"The Rorschach is a wonderful old test"*: Quoted in Peter Hegarty,
      "Homosexual Signs and Heterosexual Silences: Rorschach Research on
      Male Homosexuality From 1921–1969," *Journal of the History of Sexuality*,
      summer 2003.

36   *"If psychologists used tea leaves instead of the Rorschach"*: Quoted in Rosie
      Mestel, "Rorschach Tested: Blot Out the Famous Method? Some Experts
      Say It Has No Place in Psychiatry," *Los Angeles Times*, May 19, 2003.

37   *"I didn't know then that the Rorschach was a hoax"*: Author's interview with
      James Wood, January 6, 2003.

37   *"essentially zero validity"*: Howard N. Garb, James M. Wood, Scott O.
      Lilienfeld, and M. Teresa Nezworski, "Effective Use of Projective
      Techniques in Clinical Practice: Let the Data Help with Selection and
      Interpretation," *Professional Psychology: Research and Practice*, October
      2002.

37   *"a marked tendency to overvalue personal worth"*: John E. Exner Jr., *The
      Rorschach: Basic Foundations and Principles of Interpretation*, 4th ed. (John
      Wiley, 2002), 472.

37   *"can be expected to manifest many more dependency behaviors":* Ibid., 493.

37   *only 20 percent of Comprehensive System scales examined:* Ken R. Vincent and
      Marsha J. Harman, "The Exner Rorschach: An Analysis of Its Clinical
      Validity," *Journal of Clinical Psychology,* July 1991.

37   *"overpathologizes":* Author's interview with Wood.

37   *"If Rorschach scores for a normal adult are interpreted according to Exner's
      norms":* Garb et al., "Effective Use of Projective Techniques in Clinical
      Practice."

38   *Less than a quarter of these works, however, take the form of science's gold
      standard:* Grove et al., "Failure of Rorschach-Comprehensive-System-Based
      Testimony to Be Admissible Under the Daubert-Joiner-Kumho Standard."

38   *more than half are unpublished studies from the Rorschach Workshops:* Ibid.

38   *Since 1968, the Rorschach Workshops have produced more than a thousand
      studies:* John E. Exner Jr., "A Comment on 'The Comprehensive System for
      the Rorschach: A Critical Examination,'" *Psychological Science,* January
      1996.

38   *many of these have never been published—and some have not even been* written:
      Grove, et al., "Failure of Rorschach-Comprehensive-System-Based
      Testimony to Be Admissible Under the Daubert-Joiner-Kumho Standard."

38   *"I make no apology":* Exner, "A Comment on 'The Comprehensive System
      for the Rorschach: A Critical Examination.'"

38   *"really didn't want to take the time":* Author's interview with John E. Exner Jr.,
      February 24, 2004.

38   *When Wood and others asked to see some of this research:* Wood, Nezworski,
      and Stejskal, "The Comprehensive System for the Rorschach: A Critical
      Examination."

38   *On at least one occasion:* Grove at al., "Failure of Rorschach-Comprehensive-
      System-Based Testimony to Be Admissible Under the Daubert-Joiner-
      Kumho Standard."

38   *"It's outrageous":* Author's interview with Scott Lilienfeld, November 20,
      2002.

39   *The screening process for applicants to Roman Catholic seminaries and religious
      orders:* Thomas M. Batsis, "Roman Catholic Vocation Directors' Attitudes
      Regarding Psychological Assessment of Seminary and Religious Order
      Applicants," *Consulting Psychology Journal: Practice and Research,* summer
      1993.

39   *32 percent of psychologists reported using the Rorschach in criminal forensic
      evaluations:* Cited in Chris Piotrowski, "Use of the Rorschach in Forensic
      Practice," *Perceptual & Motor Skills,* February 1996.

39   *the test ranked third among forty instruments employed by forensic psychologists:*
      Cited in ibid.

39   *John Hinckley Jr. (who saw skulls, bones, empty eye sockets, and shrunken*

heads): Laura A. Kiernan, "Psychologist Says Hinckley's Tests Similar to Those of the Severely Ill," *Washington Post*, May 21, 1982.

39   *"were normal to the point of being mundane"*: Jim Stingl, "Parents Blame Each Other, Psychologist Says," *Milwaukee Journal*, February 7, 1992.

39   *a 1999 survey of forensic psychologists found that the test was used in almost a third of emotional-injury assessments*: Marcus T. Boccaccini and Stanley L. Brodsky, "Diagnostic Test Usage by Forensic Psychologists in Emotional Injury Cases," *Professional Psychology: Research and Practice*, June 1999.

39   *psychologists have warned that crucial information about the Rorschach*: Mark A. Ruiz, Evan B. Drake, Aviva Glass, David Marcotte, and Wilfred G. van Gorp, "Trying to Beat the System: Misuse of the Internet to Assist in Avoiding the Detection of Psychological Symptom Dissimulation," *Professional Psychology: Research and Practice*, June 2002.

39   *Estimates of the rate of deliberate deception on tests taken in a legal context*: Author's interview with Paul Lees-Haley, forensic psychologist, October 31, 2002.

39   *"an attorney should provide a client with as much specific information as possible"*: Martha W. Wetter and Susan K. Corrigan, "Providing Information to Clients About Psychological Tests: A Survey of Attorneys' and Law Students' Attitudes," *Professional Psychology: Research and Practice*, October 1995.

39   *A 2001 survey of psychologists who conduct child custody evaluations*: Francella A. Quinnell and James N. Bow, "Psychological Tests Used in Child Custody Evaluations," *Behavioral Sciences and the Law*, September 2001.

40   *the second most frequently used test for this purpose*: Ibid.

40   *"It's not fair to be separated from your family"*: Quoted in Ellen Barry, "Study Finds Web of Deceit on Mental Tests," *Boston Globe*, June 15, 2002.

40   *"If you research the Rorschach"*: Author's interview with Waylon, November 11, 2002.

40   *"clearly fails to meet the standards for admissibility"*: Grove et al., "Failure of Rorschach-Comprehensive-System-Based Testimony to Be Admissible Under the Daubert-Joiner-Kumho Standard."

40   *"In our opinion, the adjudicated rights of citizens should not turn"*: Ibid.

40   *"The use of Rorschach interpretations in establishing an individual's legal status"*: Robyn M. Dawes, *Rational Choice in an Uncertain World* (Harcourt Brace Jovanovich, 1988), 234.

40   *a majority rated the Rorschach "unacceptable" for use*: Stephen J. Lally, "What Tests Are Acceptable for Use in Forensic Examinations? A Survey of Experts," *Professional Psychology: Research and Practice*, October 2003.

41   *"I use the Rorschach a lot less than I used to"*: Author's interview with Thomas Grisso, October 22, 2002.

41   *"under assault"*: Elena J. Eisman, Robert R. Dies, Stephen E. Finn, Lorraine

D. Eyde, Gary G. Kay, Tom W. Kubiszyn, Gregory J. Meyer, and Kevin L. Moreland, "Problems and Limitations in Using Psychological Assessment in the Contemporary Health Care Delivery System," *Professional Psychology: Research and Practice*, April 2000.

41 *"The changing of hearts and minds among Rorschach diehards"*: Author's interview with John Hunsley, January 27, 2003.

41 *"seriously flawed and should not be used"*: Erica Goode, "What's in an Inkblot? Some Say, Not Much," *New York Times*, February 20, 2001.

41 *"I wouldn't have had my picture in* The New York Times*"*: Author's interview with Weiner.

41 *"is not a test"*: Irving B. Weiner, "The Rorschach Inkblot Method (RIM) Is Not a Test: Implications for Theory and Practice," *Journal of Personality Assessment*, June 1994.

42 *the next "guru" of the Rorschach*: Author's interview with Ritzler.

42 *"has to do with different views of human nature"*: Author's interview with Gregory Meyer, January 9, 2003. (Meyer is on leave as associate professor of psychology at the University of Alaska at Anchorage.)

42 *"the Dracula of psychological tests"*: Carol Tavris, "Mind Games: Psychological Warfare Between Therapists and Scientists," *The Chronicle of Higher Education*, February 28, 2003.

43 *"It's an inkblot"* Quoted in Francis X. Clines, "A Sharp Focus on World of Rorschach," *New York Times*, September 3, 1981.

CHAPTER THREE: MINNESOTA NORMALS

45 *"This is the unknown field"*: Starke R. Hathaway, videotaped interview conducted by James N. Butcher, "An Interview With Starke Hathaway," recorded March 1973.

45 *"one first had to get his attention"*: Harrison G. Gough, "Along the Way: Recollections of Some Major Contributors to Personality Assessment," *Journal of Personality Assessment*, spring 1988.

45 *"that man who wrote the book about psychopaths"*: Ibid.

46 *"You had to watch your language around him"*: Author's interview with Leona Dahlstrom, February 18, 2003.

46 *"mind reading"*: James N. Butcher, "Starke Rosecrans Hathaway: Biography of an Empiricist," in *Portraits of Pioneers in Psychology*, vol. 4, ed. Gregory A. Kimble and Michael Wertheimer (American Psychological Association, 2000), 239.

46 *"I took little interest in them"*: Starke R. Hathaway, "Through Psychology My Way," in *The Psychologists: Autobiographies of Distinguished Living Psychologists*, ed. T. S. Krawiec (Clinical Psychology, 1978), 110.

47 *"We had many devices"*: Hathaway, "An Interview With Starke Hathaway."

47 *"from anywhere we wished"*: Ibid.

47   *"If you were in one of our new rooms"*: Ibid.

47   *"As we went on grand rounds"*: Starke R. Hathaway, quoted in Sarnoff A. Mednick, Jerry Higgins, and Jack Kirschenbaum, *Psychology: Explorations in Behavior and Experience* (Wiley, 1975), 350.

47   *"sheer frustration"*: Starke R. Hathaway, "Personality Inventories," in *Handbook of Clinical Psychology*, ed. Benjamin B. Wolman (McGraw-Hill, 1965), 457.

47   *a mortality rate as high as 10 percent*: Max Fink, "What Was Insulin Coma Therapy?" Public Broadcasting System, www.pbs.org/wgbh/amex/nash/filmmore/ps_ict.html.

48   *"lost personality"*: Quoted in Ben Shephard, *A War of Nerves: Soldiers and Psychiatrists in the Twentieth Century* (Harvard University Press, 2001), xviii.

48   *"Does the sight of blood make you sick or dizzy?"*: Quoted in Richard S. Lazarus, *Personality* (Prentice-Hall, 1979), 286.

48   *"Do you nearly always feel that you have strength or energy enough for your work?"*: Quoted in ibid.

48   *"Are you often frightened in the middle of the night?"*: Quoted in Lewis R. Aiken, *Assessment of Adult Personality* (Springer, 1997), 7.

48   *"No existing personality test was worth anything at all"*: Starke R. Hathaway, videotaped interview conducted by W. Grant Dahlstrom, "Measuring the Mind: Psychological Testing: A Conversation With Starke Hathaway," Center for Creative Leadership, 1976.

49   *"Do you usually feel well and strong?"*: Quoted in Aiken, *Assessment of Adult Personality*, 7.

49   *"Are you happy most of the time?"*: Quoted in Lazarus, *Personality*, 286.

49   *"men who were afraid"*: Hathaway, "Personality Inventories," 461.

49   *"Are you critical of others?"*: Quoted in Roger L. Greene, *The MMPI-2: An Interpretive Manual*, 2nd ed. (Allyn and Bacon, 1999), 4.

49   *"Do you daydream frequently?"*: Quoted in ibid.

49   *"Psychology was not a reality with him"*: Hathaway, "A Conversation With Starke Hathaway."

50   *"McKinley was not wholly an advantage to me"*: Ibid.

50   *"We permitted the patients to design their own test"*: Hathaway, "Measuring the Mind."

50   *research was usually conducted with only a handful of subjects*: Kurt Danziger, *Constructing the Subject: Historical Origins of Psychological Research* (Cambridge University Press, 1990), 69.

50   *"since we are all using our minds"*: Quoted in Solomon Diamond, "Francis Galton and American Psychology," in *Psychology: Theoretical-Historical Perspectives*, ed. Robert W. Rieber and Kurt D. Salzinger (American Psychological Association, 1998), 92.

51   *"It is usually no more necessary"*: Quoted in ibid.

51   *"testing visitors and anybody else"*: Hathaway, "A Conversation With Starke
      Hathaway."

51   *Hathaway found 724 presumably sane subjects*: Starke R. Hathaway and J.
      Charnley McKinley, "Construction of the Schedule," in *Basic Readings on the
      MMPI: A New Selection on Personality Measurement*, ed. W. Grant
      Dahlstrom and Leona Dahlstrom (University of Minnesota Press, 1980), 9.

51   *"Minnesota Normals"*: For a description of this group, see Charles S.
      Newmark and David M. McCord, "The Minnesota Multiphasic Personality
      Inventory-2," in *Major Psychological Assessment Instruments*, ed. Charles S.
      Newmark (Allyn and Bacon, 1996), 4.

52   *"Frequently the authors can see no possible rationale"*: J. Charnley McKinley
      and Starke R. Hathaway, "Scales 3 (Hysteria), 9 (Hypomania), and 4
      (Psychopathic Deviate)," in *Basic Readings on the MMPI*, 43.

52   *"who-gives-a-damn-why-it-works attitude"*: George A. Miller and Robert
      Buckhout, *Psychology: The Science of Mental Life* (Harper & Row, 1973), 384.

52   *"galloping empiricism"*: Quoted in Garth J. O. Fletcher, "The Scientific
      Credibility of Commonsense Psychology," in *Fifty Years of Personality
      Psychology*, ed. Kenneth H. Craik, Robert Hogan, and Raymond N. Wolfe
      (Plenum, 1993), 252.

53   *"a Joycean soliloquy in Whitmanic rhythms"*: Peter Carlson, "Ode to the
      Minnesota Multiphasic Personality Inventory," *Washington Post*, September
      14, 1986.

53   *MMPI items*: "List of MMPI Items," Appendix L in W. Grant Dahlstrom,
      George Schlager Welsh, and Leona E. Dahlstrom, *An MMPI Handbook,
      Volume 1: Clinical Interpretation*, revised ed. (University of Minnesota Press,
      1972), 430–437.

54   *"I remember being in McKinley's office"*: Hathaway, "A Conversation With
      Starke Hathaway."

54   *"unduly awkward and impractical"*: Quoted in Hathaway, "Through
      Psychology My Way," 117.

54   *"We were beggars, not choosers"*: Hathaway, "A Conversation With Starke
      Hathaway."

54   *"an easily applicable measuring device"*: Quoted in Arthur L. Benton,
      "Minnesota Multiphasic Personality Inventory, Revised Edition," in *The
      Third Mental Measurements Yearbook*, ed. Oscar Krisen Buros (Buros Institute
      of Mental Measurements, 1949), 105.

55   *"got a little notoriety"*: Hathaway, "A Conversation With Starke Hathaway."

55   *at least 90 percent of the Minnesota Normals*: Cited in Alan F. Friedman,
      James T. Webb, and Richard Lewak, *Psychological Assessment With the MMPI*
      (Lawrence Erlbaum, 1989), 10.

55   *Answering "true" to "Evil spirits possess me at times"*: Cited in ibid.

55   *responding "false" to "I believe in law enforcement"*: Cited in ibid.

55   *"I do not always tell the truth"*: Cited in ibid., 9.

55   *"I gossip a little at times"*: Cited in ibid.

55   *"but for a person to have six or eight of them"*: Paul E. Meehl and Starke R. Hathaway, "The K Factor as a Suppressor Variable in the MMPI," in *Basic Readings on the MMPI*, 96.

56   *high scores on the Lie Scale are not infrequently obtained by members of the clergy*: Cited in Newmark and McCord, "The Minnesota Multiphasic Personality Inventory-2," 13.

56   *the "Minnesota Way"*: Cited in Howard E. A. Tinsley, "The Minnesota Counseling Psychologist as a Broadly Trained Applied Psychologist," in *Assessing Individual Differences in Human Behavior: New Concepts, Methods, and Findings*, ed. David John Lubinski and Rene V. Dawis (Davies-Black, 1995), 341.

56   *"Multers"*: James N. Butcher, foreword in *The MMPI: A Practical Guide*, John Robert Graham (Oxford University Press, 1977), vii.

56   *"By using the inventory, a physician may know"*: "Truth & Consequences," *Time*, May 3, 1943.

56   *"This picture aroused a certain amount of amusement"*: Hathaway, "A Conversation With Starke Hathaway."

56   *"is already the most widely popular test"*: "Truth & Consequences."

56   *"is used routinely by hundreds of private clinics"*: J. Arthur Myers, "John Charnley McKinley, Teacher, Clinician, Contributor of Knowledge, Administrator and Benefactor of Mankind: A Personal Appreciation," *The Journal-Lancet*, November 1946.

56   *"The university printing office was doing nothing but Multiphasics"*: Hathaway, "A Conversation With Starke Hathaway."

57   *"the Corporation was glad to get what they had turned down earlier"*: Ibid.

57   *Within fifteen years, the MMPI would become*: University of Minnesota Press, "Minnesota Multiphasic Personality Inventories: Overview," www.upress.umn.edu/tests/mmpi_overview.html.

57   *McKinley made Hathaway promise to help him kill himself*: Hathaway, "A Conversation With Starke Hathaway."

57   *the odd and awful effect of destroying his ability to express emotion*: Ibid.

57   *"Later that evening I sat in the big medical amphitheater"*: Ibid.

58   *"an automatic, mechanical, clerical kind of task"*: Quoted in Yossef S. Ben-Porath and James N. Butcher, "The Historical Development of Personality Assessment," *Clinical Psychology: Historical and Research Foundations*, ed. C. Eugene Walker (Plenum, 1991), 145.

58   *the MMPI was given at least as often to normal people as to psychiatric patients*: Cited in Anne Anastasi and Susana Urbina, *Psychological Testing*, 7th ed. (Prentice-Hall, 1996), 352.

59   *"I have never seen anything to equal"*: Associated Press, "Ervin Calls Peace

Corps Tests an Invasion of Citizens' Privacy," *New York Times*, September 24, 1966.

59   *"Clearly, the government should not send out an investigator"*: Sam J. Ervin, "Why Senate Hearings on Psychological Tests in Government," *American Psychologist*, November 1965.

59   *"I loved my father and my mother"*: William H. Whyte, *The Organization Man* (Simon and Schuster, 1956), 197.

59   *More explicit critiques*: Martin L. Gross, *The Brain Watchers* (Random House, 1962), and Banesh Hoffmann, *The Tyranny of Testing* (Crowell-Collier Press, 1962).

59   *"The Snoops"*: Cited in Roderick D. Buchanan, "On Not 'Giving Psychology Away': The Minnesota Multiphasic Personality Inventory and Public Controversy Over Testing in the 1960s," *History of Psychology*, August 2002.

59   *"The 'I Love My Mother' Tests"*: Cited in ibid.

59   *reports of public burning of test data*: Cited in ibid.

60   *Ervin had introduced a bill*: Associated Press, "Ervin Calls Peace Corps Tests an Invasion of Citizens' Privacy."

60   *"barrage is the most serious attack that has ever been launched"*: Michael Amrine, "The 1965 Congressional Inquiry into Testing: A Commentary," *American Psychologist*, November 1965.

60   *"I hope you will see"*: Starke R. Hathaway, "MMPI: Professional Use by Professional People," *American Psychologist*, March 1964.

60   *"peeping toms"*: Amrine, "The 1965 Congressional Inquiry Into Testing."

60   *"but there is no corresponding legislative pressure"*: W. Grant Dahlstrom, "Invasion of Privacy: How Legitimate Is the Current Concern Over This Issue?," in *MMPI: Research Developments and Clinical Applications*, ed. James N. Butcher (McGraw-Hill, 1969), 266.

60   *"To change even a comma in an item"*: Hathaway, "MMPI: Professional Use by Professional People."

60   *"if I could"*: Ibid.

60   *"as one cannot make an omelet"*: Raymond B. Cattell, Herbert W. Eber, and Maurice Tatsuoka, *Handbook for the Sixteen Personality Factor Questionnaire* (Institute for Personality and Ability Testing, 1970), xxiii.

60   *it grew out of the accusers' own (presumably warped) personalities*: Paul Meehl, for example, suggested that concern about personality tests was the product of a psychological need for "inviolacy": Paul E. Meehl, "Comments on the Invasion of Privacy Issue," *MMPI: Research Developments and Clinical Applications*, 266.

61   *"Help stop psychological sex tests"*: "Pickets at APA Headquarters Protest Psychological Tests," *American Psychologist*, November 1965.

61   *"the real issue, which is that the test wasn't devised for this purpose"*: Malcolm D. Gynther, "Minnesota Multiphasic Personality Inventory," in *The Seventh*

Mental Measurements Yearbook, ed. Oscar Krisen Buros (University of
Nebraska Press, 1972), 240.

61   *"We thought, 'Uh-oh, this must be that test'"*: Author's interview with Art
     Staples, December 12, 2002.

61   *"There was nothing we could really do"*: Ibid.

61   *"We had been told that if you did not pass the test"*: Author's interview with
     Scott Hadley, December 9, 2002.

61   *"People were looking around at each other"*: Author's interview with Staples.

62   *"These questions had no relation to what we did for a living"*: Author's interview
     with Hadley.

62   *"How was I supposed to answer that?"*: Quoted in Stacy Finz, "Texas
     Company Settles Over Nosy Questions to Employees," *San Francisco
     Chronicle*, July 8, 2000.

62   *"restless and impatient"*: Jeffrey A. Ross, legal brief filed in *Staples* v. *Rent-A-
     Center, Inc.*, May 14, 1999.

62   *"tendency to retreat from reality"*: Ibid.

62   *"independent and hard-headed"*: Ibid.

62   *"resistant to rules and codes"*: Ibid.

62   *"one chapter at a time, with a significant person in his life"*: Ibid.

62   *"He makes assumptions without checking them out"*: Ibid.

62   *"Stupid pop psychology"*: Author's interview with Hadley.

63   *"I thought I was a pretty good person"*: Author's interview with Staples.

63   *employed by 86 percent of clinical psychologists*: Wayne Camara, Julie Nathan,
     and Anthony Puente, "Psychological Test Usage in Professional Psychology:
     Report to the APA Practice and Science Directorates," American
     Psychological Association, May 1998, 19.

63   *administered, by one estimate, to some 15 million Americans each year*: Eugene
     E. Levitt and Edward E. Gotts, *The Clinical Application of MMPI Special
     Scales*, 2nd ed. (Lawrence Erlbaum, 1995), 1.

63   *The MMPI is used by 60 percent of police departments*: David A. Decicco,
     "Police Officer Candidate Assessment and Selection," *FBI Law Enforcement
     Bulletin*, December 2000.

63   *91 percent of psychologists screening applicants to Roman Catholic seminaries and
     religious orders*: Thomas M. Batsis, "Roman Catholic Vocation Directors'
     Attitudes Regarding Psychological Assessment of Seminary and Religious
     Order Applicants," *Consulting Psychology Journal: Practice and Research*,
     summer 1993.

63   *The company agreed to a $2-million settlement*: Cited in Finz, "Texas Company
     Settles Over Nosy Questions to Employees."

63   *"These are questions you wouldn't even answer for your own mother"*: Quoted
     in Constance L. Hays, "Trying to Get a Job? Check Yes or No," *New York
     Times*, November 28, 1997.

63   *"It doesn't take Einstein to figure out"*: Quoted in "Store Settles Suit on Psychological Test," *Chicago Tribune*, July 11, 1993.

64   *"killing a gnat with an atomic bomb"*: Quoted in Joan M. Cheever, "Chain Settles Suit Over Psychological Testing," *National Law Journal*, July 26, 1993.

64   *evidence indicating that the PsychScreen had a 61 percent false-positive rate*: Brad Seligman, legal brief filed in *Soroka v. Dayton Hudson Corporation*, June 1990.

64   *Seligman wrested a $1.3-million settlement from the company*: Cited in *Chicago Tribune*, "Store Settles Suit on Psychological Test."

64   *"I believe everything is turning out just the way the Bible said it would"*: Quoted in Bernadette Tansey, "County Settles Suit Filed by Drug Test Takers," *San Francisco Chronicle*, October 31, 1998.

64   *"Pornography and obscenity have become serious problems"*: Quoted in American Civil Liberties Union, "Northern California County Settles Challenge to Use of Written 'Drug Test,'" press release, October 30, 1998.

64   *"chemically dependent"*: Quoted in Mike McKee, "ACLU Challenges Psychological Tests for GA Recipients," *Recorder*, March 30, 1995.

64   *the test incorrectly classified 44 percent of all applicants as addicts*: Cited in ibid.

64   *the county agreed to pay $1.2 million to the mislabeled test takers*: Cited in Brenda Sandburg, "Drug Test Costs Contra Costa $1.2 Million," *Recorder*, November 2, 1998.

64   *"Workers usually come last as far as most companies are concerned"*: Quoted in Susan Sward, "Security Firm Settles Suit on Applicant Test," *San Francisco Chronicle*, June 5, 1998.

64   *"Most companies make too much profit"*: Quoted in American Civil Liberties Union-North California (ACLU-NC), "Nation's Largest Security Guard Firm to Pay Up to $2.1 Million to Settle Class Action Against Employee 'Litmus Test,' " press release, June 4, 1998.

64   *"The drinking age should be lowered"*: Quoted in Sward, "Security Firm Settles Suit on Applicant Test."

64   *"Marijuana should be legalized"*: Quoted in ACLU-NC, "Nation's Largest Security Guard Firm to Pay Up to $2.1 Million to Settle Class Action Against Employee 'Litmus Test.' "

64   *"a true-or-false pledge of allegiance to corporate America"*: Author's interview with Brad Seligman, February 14, 2003.

64   *"Anyone who believes employers are not perfect"*: Quoted in McKee, "ACLU Challenges Political Questions on Guard Test."

64   *Burns agreed to pay up to $2.1 million*: Cited in Sward, "Security Firm Settles Suit on Applicant Test."

65   *"This country needs higher moral standards"*: From the Job Candidate Profile, quoted in "Sample Questions," Behavioral Science Technology, Inc., www.jobcandidateprofile.com/sample-questions.htm.

65   *"I guess I know some pretty undesirable types"*: From the Substance Abuse
      Subtle Screening Inventory-2, quoted in McKee, "ACLU Challenges
      Psychological Tests for GA Recipients."

65   *"Illegal use of marijuana is worse than drinking liquor"*: From the Substance
      Abuse Subtle Screening Inventory-2, quoted in Ray Delgado, "Firm That
      Probed Job Seekers' Lives Settles Lawsuit," *San Francisco Examiner*, June 5,
      1998.

65   *"I have never wanted to buy things I couldn't afford"*: From the Step One
      Survey, quoted in "Pre-Employment Screening," Texoma Management
      Consultants, www.texomamanagement.com/PreEmploymentScreening.htm.

65   *"Most people would lie to get what they want"*: From the Substance Abuse
      Subtle Screening Inventory-2, quoted in ACLU-NC, "Nation's Largest
      Security Guard Firm to Pay Up to $2.1 Million to Settle Class Action
      Against Employee 'Litmus Test.' "

65   *"desire to follow rules, policies, and procedures"*: PAN-Inc., "Behavior
      Forecaster Accurately Predicts Crucial On-the-Job Behaviors,"
      www.pan-inc.com/forecaster/forecast1.htm.

65   *"customer service attitude"*: James W. Bassett, "Investigate Prospective
      Employees Before Hiring in Order to Avoid Personnel Problems," *Nation's
      Restaurant News*, April 17, 2000.

65   *"computer abuse"*: Hiring Solutions, "Introduction to the Counter-
      Productive Behavior (CPB) Index,"
      www.hiringsolutions.net/files/firstviewtechmanlinks.pdf.

65   *"personal and/or transportation problems"*: Insight Worldwide, "About the
      Test," www.insightww.com/insight.asp?page=home.

66   *"counterproductive behavior"*: Hiring Solutions, "Introduction to the
      Counter-Productive Behavior (CPB) Index."

66   *"alienated attitudes"*: PAN-Inc., "Ready, Aim, HIRE!"
      www.paninc.com/pass3/pass3_1.htm.

66   *"Litigious Profile" or a "Corporate Stalker Profile"*: Cited in Glen Fox, "Hogan
      Development Survey," in *The Fourteenth Mental Measurements Yearbook*, ed.
      James C. Impara and Barbara S. Plake (Buros Institute of Mental
      Measurements, 2001), 547.

66   *"compares the applicant's responses with those of two distinctly different groups"*:
      Smart Moves Consulting, "Step One Survey,"
      www.smartmovesconsulting.com/job_app_screening.php.

66   *"whether job applicants think like trusted employees or convicted felons"*: KLO
      People Dynamics, "An Integrity Test for the 21st Century,"
      www.peopledynamics.net/integrty.htm.

66   *"Which one physically hurt an employee?"*: Insight Worldwide, "About the
      Test."

66   *"invasion of privacy—or rather, what the courts deem to be an invasion of*

privacy": David Arnold, "Psychological Testing in the Wake of 9/11," *Test Publisher*, spring 2002.

66   *testing companies around the country reported increased interest in personality tests following 9/11*: See Torri Minton, "Don't Get Psyched Out: More Companies Considering Pre-Employment Tests," *San Francisco Chronicle*, October 21, 2001; Rebecca Theim, "Psychometric Testing: More Companies Administer Pre-Employment Screening to Assess a Job Candidate's Aptitude, Honesty and Even Personality," *Chicago Tribune*, March 6, 2002.

66   *30 percent of companies now administer personality tests*: Cited in Daniel McGinn, "Testing, Testing," *Newsweek*, June 9, 2003.

67   *"the construct of honesty or integrity remains vague"*: Mark L. Rieke and Stephen J. Guastello, "Unresolved Issues in Honesty and Integrity Testing," *American Psychologist*, June 1995.

67   *are administered by an estimated five thousand to six thousand U.S. organizations and taken by as many as five million Americans each year*: Wayne J. Camara and Dianne L. Schneider, "Integrity Tests: Facts and Unresolved Issues," *American Psychologist*, February 1994.

67   *95.6 percent of people who fail integrity tests are incorrectly classified as dishonest*: U.S. Congress Office of Technological Assessment, "The Use of Integrity Tests for Pre-Employment Screening," OTA-SET-442, U.S. Government Printing Office, 1990.

67   *an error rate far worse than that of the notoriously unreliable polygraph machine*: Benjamin Kleinmuntz, "True Lies: The Dishonesty of Honesty Tests," *The Humanist*, July 1995.

67   *"After all, if a candidate's integrity"*: Maryanne T. Preston, "Evaluating Your Employee Selection and Retention Plan," www.wst.nu/preston/hs-article-eval.htm.

67   *"almost no evidence at all is available"*: American Psychological Task Force on the Prediction of Dishonesty and Theft in Employment Settings, "Questionnaires Used in the Prediction of Trustworthiness in Pre-Employment Selection Decisions: An A.P.A. Task Force Report," American Psychological Association, 1991.

67   *more than half of integrity-test publishers do not require any training or other qualifications*: Camara and Schneider, "Integrity Tests: Facts and Unresolved Issues."

68   *"Maybe the real function of the tests is not to convey information"*: Barbara Ehrenreich, "What Are They Probing For?" *Time*, June 4, 2001.

68   *"I used to like to play drop-the-handkerchief"*: "List of MMPI Items," 430.

68   *"Horses who don't pull should be kicked or beaten"*: Ibid., 435.

68   *endorsed by only 9 percent of the Depression-era farmers in Hathaway's normal sample*: Cited in Anne Brataas, "Tough Break for Minnesota:

Personality Test Has Passed the 'Normals' By," *Chicago Tribune*, October 29, 1989.

68   *as many as eight out of ten test takers answered "true"*: Cited in ibid.

69   *it revealed with unerring accuracy which were black and which were white*: James N. Butcher, "Revising Psychological Tests: Lessons Learned From the Revision of the MMPI," *Psychological Assessment*, September 2000.

69   *"Are they ever going to restandardize that thing?"*: Raymond D. Fowler, foreword in *Essentials of MMPI-2 and MMPI-A Interpretation*, ed. James N. Butcher and Carolyn L. Williams (University of Minnesota Press, 1992), xiii.

69   *the idea had been raised at the 1969 symposium*: James N. Butcher, "Discontinuities, Side Steps, and Finding a Proper Place: An Autobiographical Account," *Journal of Personality Assessment*, June 2003.

69   *"almost a sacred text"*: Quoted in Luse, "Testing Sanity."

69   *articles and books currently numbering around fourteen thousand*: Author's interview with James Butcher, April 10, 2003.

69   *New "Normals" were chosen*: For a description of this process, see Ben-Porath and Butcher, "The Historical Development of Personality Assessment."

69   *"It never really did tell us anything"*: Quoted in Brataas, "Tough Break for Minnesota: Personality Test Has Passed the 'Normals' By."

69   *added new scales*: Ben-Porath and Butcher, "The Historical Development of Personality Assessment."

69   *Eighty-four percent of the items in the MMPI*: Robert P. Archer, "Minnesota Multiphasic Personality Inventory-2," in *The Eleventh Mental Measurements Yearbook*, ed. Jack J. Kramer and Jane Close Conoley (Buros Institute of Mental Measurements, 1992), 558.

69   *"in but slightly altered form"*: Butcher, "Starke Rosecrans Hathaway: Biography of an Empiricist," 244.

70   *"the MMPI-2 will go the way of 'New Coke'"*: Irving Gottesman, quoted in Yossef S. Ben-Porath, "MMPI-2 Items," *MMPI Newsletter*, August 1990.

70   *"withdrawn from service"*: Butcher, "Revising Psychological Tests."

70   *more than 90 percent of psychologists conducting evaluations in child custody and emotional injury cases*: Francella A. Qunnell and James N. Bow, "Psychological Tests Used in Child Custody Evaluations," *Behavioral Sciences and the Law*, September 2001.

70   *more than 90 percent of psychologists conducting evaluations in emotional-injury cases*: Marcus T. Boccaccini and Stanley L. Brodsky, "Diagnostic Test Usage by Forensic Psychologists in Emotional Injury Cases," *Professional Psychology: Research and Practice*, June 1999.

70   *the world's most frequently used clinical personality test*: James N. Butcher, Fanny M. Cheung, and Jeeyoung Lim, "Use of the MMPI-2 With Asian Populations," *Psychological Assessment*, September 2003.

70   *The original was translated into 115 languages:* Jane E. Brody, "Widely Used Mental Test Undergoing Treatment," *New York Times*, August 19, 1986.

70   *the MMPI-2 is fast catching up, with about 50:* Nichol Nelson, "U. Press Extends Scope to Children's, Regional Books," *Minnesota Daily*, October 8, 1998.

70   *"like translating poetry":* Author's interview with Butcher.

70   *"They may hate Americans":* Butcher, personal communication.

70   *"There are some things about humans that are universal":* Quoted in Luse, "Testing Sanity."

70   *"The damn thing works":* Quoted in Brataas, "Tough Break for Minnesota: Personality Test Has Passed the 'Normals' By."

70   *"if you want to know what's wrong with somebody":* Quoted in Luse, "Testing Sanity."

71   *"There are no right or wrong answers":* Hathaway and McKinley, "Construction of the Schedule," 9.

71   *"It's really crazy when you start thinking":* Author's interview with Louise Douce, October 18, 2002.

72   *"was like pulling teeth":* Author's interview with Butcher.

72   *"a personal cult":* Hathaway, "Through Psychology My Way," 111.

72   *"At times I have become impatient":* Ibid., 117.

72   *"people still write and try to telephone Hathaway":* Butcher, "Starke Rosecrans Hathaway: Biography of an Empiricist," 244.

72   *"Stone Age ax":* Hathaway, "Measuring the Mind."

72   *"I fear that the aged MMPI will be tolerated":* Starke R. Hathaway, "Where Have We Gone Wrong? The Mystery of the Missing Progress," in *Objective Personality Assessment: Changing Perspectives,* ed. James N. Butcher (Academic Press, 1972), 23.

72   *"we are stuck":* Ibid., 40.

72   *"the mystery of the missing progress":* Ibid., 22.

72   *"With so many competent efforts":* Ibid., 23.

72   *"those students who think differently":* Ibid., 42.

72   *"I have never had the conviction that I had real insight":* Hathaway, "Through Psychology My Way," 117.

73   *"a true visionary" and "a great pioneer":* Butcher, conclusion in "A Conversation With Starke Hathaway."

73   *"a bug in a cup":* W. Grant Dahlstrom, Paul E. Meehl, and William Schofield, "Obituary: Starke Rosencrans Hathaway," *American Psychologist,* July 1986.

73   *"Everyone knows the word 'ghost'":* Hathaway, "Where Have We Gone Wrong?," 24.

CHAPTER FOUR: DEEP DIVING

75   *"majored in the three R's"*: Quoted in Calvin S. Hall and Gardner Lindzey, *Theories of Personality*, 3rd ed. (Wiley and Sons, 1957), 223.

75   *"spent more time than was considered proper"*: Henry A. Murray, "What Should Psychologists Do About Psychoanalysis?" *Journal of Abnormal and Social Psychology*, April 1940.

76   *"sanguine surplus"*: Henry A. Murray, "The Case of Murr," in *A History of Psychology in Autobiography*, vol. 5, ed. Edwin G. Boring and Gardner Lindzey (Appleton-Century-Crofts, 1967), 285.

76   *"marrow of misery and melancholy"*: Ibid., 300.

76   *"a gratuitous answer to an unspoken prayer"*: Quoted in M. Brewster Smith and James William Anderson, "Henry A. Murray (1893–1988)," *American Psychologist*, August 1989.

76   *"Do you favor Freud or Jung?"*: Quoted in Claire Douglas, *Translate This Darkness: The Life of Christiana Morgan* (Simon & Schuster, 1993), 267.

76   *Christiana suggested that he go to Zurich*: In 1926, Christiana herself became one of Jung's patients; see ibid.

77   *"We talked for hours, sailing down the lake"*: Murray, "The Case of Murr," 153.

77   *"had few intellectual interests, almost nil"*: Quoted in James William Anderson, "The Life of Henry A. Murray: 1893–1988," in *Studying Persons and Lives*, ed. Albert I. Rabin, Robert A. Zucker, Robert A. Emmons, and Susan Frank (Springer, 1990), 318.

77   *"talked alike and thought alike"*: Quoted in ibid.

77   *"deep diving"*: Quoted in Forrest G. Robinson, *Love's Story Told: A Life of Henry A. Murray* (Harvard University Press, 1992), 173.

77   *"dark years"*: Quoted in B. R. Hergenhahn, *An Introduction to the History of Psychology* (Wadsworth, 2001), 488.

77   *"He must have seen that the way to treat me"*: Quoted in Paul Roazen, "Interviews on Freud and Jung With Henry A. Murray in 1965," *Journal of Analytical Psychology*, February 2003.

77   *"I saw things that my philosophy had never dreamt of"*: Murray, "What Should Psychologists Do About Psychoanalysis?"

77   *"I had experienced the unconscious"*: Ibid.

77   *"dirty old man"*: Quoted in Denis Brian, *The Voice of Genius: Conversations With Nobel Scientists and Other Luminaries* (Perseus, 2002), 314.

77   *"bent of empathy"*: Henry A. Murray, "Preparations for the Scaffold of a Comprehensive System," in *Psychology: A Study of a Science*, vol. 3, ed. Sigmund Koch (McGraw-Hill, 1959), 8.

77   *"when it came to chicken embryos"*: Murray, "The Case of Murr," 290.

78   *about the position's paltry $1,800 salary*: Ibid., 287.

78   *"At first I was taken aback"*: Murray, "What Should Psychologists Do About Psychoanalysis?"

78   *"Academic psychology has contributed practically nothing"*: Quoted in James William Anderson, "Henry A. Murray and the Creation of the Thematic Apperception Test," in *Evocative Images: The Thematic Apperception Test and the Art of Projection*, ed. Lon Gieser and Morris I. Stein (American Psychological Association, 1999), 25.

78   *"Nowadays it is the mounting ambition"*: Henry A. Murray, "Historical Trends in Personality Research," in *Perspectives in Personality Research*, ed. Henry P. David and J. C. Brengelmann (Springer, 1960), 6.

79   *the defiant "id" of psychology at Harvard*: Saul Rosenzweig, "E. G. Boring and the Zeitgeist: *Eruditione Gesta Beavit*," *The Journal of Psychology*, May 1970.

79   *"I was a very obnoxious person"*: Quoted in Anderson, "The Life of Henry A. Murray: 1893–1988," 319.

79   *an antagonism that only intensified*: See, e.g., Ross Stagner, "Fifty Years of the Psychology of Personality: Reminiscences," in *Fifty Years of Personality Psychology*, ed. Kenneth H. Craik, Robert Hogan, and Raymond N. Wolfe (Plenum, 1993), 27.

79   *"Things have come in so fast"*: Quoted in Robinson, *Love's Story Told*, 152.

79   *"to understand man and human nature"*: Quoted in ibid., 173.

79   *"wisteria outside, hysteria inside"*: Murray, "The Case of Murr," 305.

79   *"a world of small rooms"*: Leopold Bellak, "Projective Techniques in the Computer Age," *Journal of Personality Assessment*, June 1992.

80   *"redolent with charisma"*: M. Brewster Smith, "Allport and Murray on Allport's Personality: A Confrontation in 1946–1947," in *Fifty Years of Personality Psychology*, 63.

80   *"almost shattering vitality"*: Hiram Haydn, "Henry A. Murray," *The American Scholar*, winter 1969.

80   *psychologists, psychiatrists, psychoanalysts*: David G. Winter, "'Toward a Science of Personality Psycgology': David McClelland's Development of Empirically Derived TAT Measures," *History of Psychology*, May 1998.

80   *"like bold explorers"*: M. Brewster Smith, "Toward Humanizing Social Psychology," *The Psychologists*, vol. 1, ed. T. S. Krawiec (Oxford University Press, 1972), 218.

80   *"infectious zest"*: Dedication in *The Study of Lives: Essays on Personality in Honor of Henry A. Murray*, ed. Robert W. White (Atherton Press, 1963).

80   *"It was a tall order for science"*: Robert W. White, "Exploring Personality the Long Way: The Study of Lives," in *Further Explorations in Personality*, ed. Albert I. Rabin (John Wiley and Sons, 1981), 6.

80   *"I have never called myself a Freudian"*: Henry A. Murray, interviewed by Mary Harrington Hall, "A Conversation With Henry A. Murray," *Psychology Today*, September 1968.

80   *"the greatest depth psychologist"*: Quoted in Robinson, *Love's Story Told*, 112.

81   *"the Baleen"*: Murray, "Preparations for the Scaffold of a Comprehensive System," 52.

81   *"the Skipper"*: White, "Exploring Personality the Long Way," 4.

81   *"a person is different in different contexts"*: Quoted in Anderson, "The Life of Henry A. Murray: 1893–1988," 322.

81   *"Armed with questionnaires"*: Quoted in Anderson, "Henry A. Murray's Early Career," 152.

81   *"which we should be creeping up on"*: Murray, "Preparations for the Scaffold of a Comprehensive System," 8.

81   *"in the human being, imagination is more fundamental"*: Henry A. Murray, "In Nomine Diaboli," *The New England Quarterly*, December 1951.

81   *"No one can have a just idea"*: Quoted in Philip H. DuBois, *A History of Psychological Testing* (Allyn and Bacon, 1970), 100.

81   *writing down seventy-five words on slips of paper*: For a description of Galton's experiment, see Raymond E. Fancher, *Pioneers of Psychology*, 2nd ed. (W. W. Norton, 1990), 235–36.

82   *"lay bare the foundations of a man's thoughts"*: Quoted in Boris Semeonoff, *Projective Techniques* (John Wiley and Sons, 1976), 11.

82   *a list of one hundred words*: Carl G. Jung, "The Association Method," *American Journal of Psychology*, April 1910.

82   *"do not see the spectacles which they wear on their noses"*: Ibid.

82   *"Experiments such as these allow an unexpected amount"*: Quoted in DuBois, *A History of Psychological Testing*, 102.

82   *the "real facts" of human nature*: Murray, "The Case of Murr," 293.

82   *"musical reverie test"*: Henry A. Murray, "Techniques for a Systematic Investigation of Fantasy," *Journal of Psychology*, January 1937.

82   *"literary composition test"*: Ibid.

82   *"odor imagination test"*: Ibid.

83   *"the experimenters came to regard this test"*: Henry A. Murray, *Explorations in Personality: A Clinical and Experimental Study of Fifty Men of College Age* (Oxford University Press, 1938), 535.

83   *"handsome lady who always wore fantastic Indian jewelry"*: Quoted in Douglas, *Translate This Darkness*, 195.

83   *"aflame" with an awareness of their intimacy*: Quoted in ibid., 200.

83   *A red bracelet meant*: Quoted in ibid.

83   *"It was a secret from nobody"*: David C. McClelland, quoted in Robinson, *Love's Story Told*, 443.

83   *"being in love with your work and your lover"*: Quoted in Anderson, "The Life of Henry A. Murray: 1893–1988," 318.

83   *"a developing and enduring love affair"*: Murray, "A Conversation With Henry A. Murray."

83   *"method for investigating fantasies"*: Christiana D. Morgan and Henry A. Murray, "A Method for Investigating Fantasies: The Thematic Apperception Test," *Archives of Neurology and Psychiatry*, vol. 34, 1935.

84   *the team had collected about two thousand photographs and illustrations*: Henry A. Murray, videotaped interview conducted by Richard Evans, "Notable Contributors to the Psychology of Personality," 1964.

84   *"stimulating power"*: Quoted in Wesley G. Morgan, "Origin and History of the Thematic Apperception Test Images," *Journal of Personality Assessment*, October 1995.

84   *Only one of these was sketched from life*: Author's interview with Wesley Morgan, April 15, 2003.

84   *"A woman has her hands squeezed around the throat"*: Quoted in Morgan, "Origin and History of the Thematic Apperception Test Images."

84   *"On the floor against a couch is the huddled form of a boy"*: Quoted in ibid.

84   *"A woman is clutching the shoulders of a man"*: Quoted in ibid.

84   *"I am going to show you some pictures"*: Henry A. Murray and the Staff of the Harvard Psychological Clinic, *Thematic Apperception Test Manual* (Harvard University Press, 1943), 46.

85   *a real-life prodigy, violinist Yehudi Menuhin*: Jorgen Jahnke and Wesley G. Morgan, "A True TAT Story," in *A Pictorial History of Psychology*, ed. Wolfgang G. Bringmann, Helmut E. Lueck, Rudolf Miller, and Charles E. Early (Quintessence, 1997), 376.

85   *"surrounded by a halo of frayed tempers"*: White, "Exploring Personality the Long Way," 11.

85   *"Harry's enthusiastic interpretation of the TAT"*: Robert White, quoted in Lon Gieser and Morris I. Stein, "An Overview of the Thematic Apperception Test," *Evocative Images*, 7.

85   *"knew where to find the skeletons"*: Nevitt Sanford, "What Have We Learned About Personality?" in *A Century of Psychology as Science*, ed. Sigmund Koch and David E. Leary (American Psychological Association, 1992), 494.

85   *"We found out things in two hours"*: Murray, "Notable Contributors to the Psychology of Personality."

85   *"This woman has lost her husband"*: Quoted in Anderson, "Henry A. Murray's Early Career," 145.

86   *"projective methods"*: Lawrence K. Frank, "Projective Methods for the Study of Personality," *Journal of Psychology*, October 1939.

86   *"to obtain from the subject 'what he can or will not say' "*: Ibid., 14.

86   *"You will have to listen carefully"*: Quoted in Woodrow Wilbert Morris, "Other Projective Methods," in *An Introduction to Projective Techniques*, ed. Harold H. Anderson and Gladys L. Anderson (Prentice-Hall, 1951), 534.

86   *"sadistic murderer"* and *"practicing male homosexual"*: Cited in Semeonoff, *Projective Techniques*, 15.

87 *"The flowering of the projective technique of studying personality"*: From the *Test Service Bulletin* of The Psychological Corporation, quoted in Morris, "Other Projective Methods," 513.

87 *"anarchy" in "the realm of projective techniques"*: Quoted in John E. Exner, Jr., "Searching for Projection in the Rorschach," *Journal of Personality Assessment*, fall 1989.

87 *"it can do no harm"*: Quoted in Murray, "What Should Psychologists Do About Psychoanalysis?"

87 *"protest movement"*: Edwin S. Shneidman, "Projective Techniques," in *Handbook of Clinical Psychology*, ed. Benjamin B. Wolman (McGraw-Hill, 1965), 504.

87 *"the 'aha' experience of seeing things hang together"*: Bellak, "Projective Techniques in the Computer Age."

87 *"heady wine"*: Robert I. Watson, "Historical Review of Objective Personality Testing: The Search for Objectivity," in *Objective Approaches to Personality Assessment*, ed. Bernard M. Bass and Irwin A. Berg (D. Van Nostrand, 1959), 13.

87 *"The patterns of the imagination and the patterns of public conduct"*: Henry A. Murray, "Uses of the Thematic Apperception Test," *The American Journal of Psychiatry*, February 1951.

88 *a green Hindu shirt and a black velvet skirt*: Cited in Douglas, *Translate This Darkness*, 261.

88 *"is as distressing as the reopening of an old wound"*: Henry A. Murray and Clyde Kluckhohn, "Outline of a Conception of Personality," in *Personality in Nature, Society, and Culture*, revised edition, ed. Henry A. Murray and Clyde Kluckhohn (Alfred A. Knopf, 1953), 5.

88 *"is like a tiny coral isle growing in a sea of dreams"*: Murray, "What Should Psychologists Do About Psychoanalysis?"

88 *"no less than a magic set of optics"*: Edwin S. Shneidman, "The Thematic Apperception Test: A Paradise of Psychodynamics," in *Evocative Images*, 97.

89 *"exposes so much to a discerning experimenter"*: Murray, *Explorations in Personality*, 728.

89 *"Usually, he comes in, talks about a few pictures, and leaves"*: Murray, "Techniques for a Systematic Investigation of Fantasy," 130.

89 *"The individual rarely has any understanding of himself"*: Frank, "Projective Methods for the Study of Personality."

89 *"should certainly not be enlightened as to the real purpose of the tests"*: Murray, "Techniques for a Systematic Investigation of Fantasy," 122.

89 *"a plausible but fictitious objective"*: Murray, *Explorations in Personality*, 27.

90 *"jungle without boundaries"*: Murray, "A Conversation With Henry A. Murray."

90 *"This man is trying to write a book"*: Quoted in Anderson, "Henry A.

Murray and the Creation of the Thematic Apperception Test," *Evocative Images*, 28.

90   *"There is no end to it"*: Quoted in David Riesman, "Professor Murray Describes Department of Abnormal Psychology," *Harvard Crimson*, January 12, 1929.

90   *"Too soon the season came"*: Murray, "A Conversation With Henry A. Murray."

91   *"paranoid type with delusions of persecution and of grandeur"*: Quoted in Louise E. Hoffman, "American Psychologists and Wartime Research on Germany, 1941–1945," *American Psychologist*, February 1992.

91   *"The organization has been recruiting too many men"*: Quoted in Leonard Handler, "*Assessment of Men*: Personality Assessment Goes to War by the Office of Strategic Services Assessment Staff," *Journal of Personality Assessment*, June 2001.

91   *"covert mental processes"*: Murray, *Explorations in Personality*, 728.

91   *"I must leave—cutting everything off in the middle"*: Quoted in Robinson, *Love's Story Told*, 272.

91   *"Would you like to work with me?"*: Quoted in James Grier Miller, "My Role in the Assessment Program of the Office of Strategic Services," *Behavioral Science*, October 1996.

91   *"would be willing to use sexual means to obtain information"*: Ibid.

91   *"a very strange soldier"*: Ibid.

91   *"He simply disregarded regulations"*: Ibid.

92   *"is the destruction of free inquiry"*: Quoted in Robinson, *Love's Story Told*, 275.

92   *he devised his own procedures*: Inspiration for some of the procedures implemented at Station S came from the activities of Britain's War Office Selection Boards. See Scott Highhouse, "Assessing the Candidate as a Whole: A Historical and Critical Analysis of Individual Psychological Assessment for Personnel Decision Making," *Personnel Psychology*, Summer 2002.

92   *"belongings test"*: The O.S.S. Assessment Staff, *Assessment of Men: Selection of Personnel for the Office of Strategic Services* (Rinehart, 1948), 92.

92   *"interrogation test"*: Ibid., 133.

92   *"an unstable chair which rocked with any nervous movement"*: Miller, "My Role in the Assessment Program of the Office of Strategic Services."

92   *"leaderless group situations"*: Henry A. Murray and Donald W. MacKinnon, "Assessment of OSS Personnel," *Journal of Consulting Psychology*, March–April 1946.

92   *"construction test"*: Ibid.

92   *"Hey there, you, be careful"*: Quoted in Handler, "*Assessment of Men*: Personality Assessment Goes to War by the Office of Strategic Services Assessment Staff."

92   *"No candidate ever completed this task"*: Murray and MacKinnon, "Assessment of OSS Personnel."

93   *a party held on the last night:* The O.S.S. Assessment Staff, *Assessment of Men,* 348.

93   *"for researches into normal personality"*: Quoted in Douglas W. Bray, "Centered on Assessment," *Personnel Psychology,* Summer 1995.

93   *"the final validity is a question mark"*: Quoted in Scott Highhouse, "Assessing the Candidate as a Whole."

93   *"a total flop"*: Martin L. Gross, *The Brain Watchers* (Random House, 1962), 241.

93   *"Obviously the test of cruel war proved more challenging"*: Ibid.

93   *"to any organization employing large numbers of people"*: Leonard W. Doob, *Saturday Review,* May 19, 1948.

94   *"I couldn't wait to try it!"*: Bray, "Centered on Assessment."

94   *"The assessment center technique has shown itself a better indicator"*: William C. Byham, "Assessment Centers for Choosing Managers," *Harvard Business Review,* July-August 1970.

94   *"Suddenly, big companies—Ford, Shell—called"*: Quoted in Adam Hanft, "Smarter Hiring, the DDI Way," *Inc.,* March 1, 2003.

95   *By 1981, 44 percent of state, federal, and local governments:* Phillip E. Lowry, "A Survey of the Assessment Center Process in the Public Sector," *Public Personnel Management,* fall 1996.

95   *"He was completely unaware that his example"*: Bray, "Centered on Assessment."

95   *The average assessment center:* Cited in Frank L. Schmidt and John E. Hunter, "The Validity and Utility of Selection Methods in Personnel Psychology: Practical and Theoretical Implications of 85 Years of Research Findings," *Psychological Bulletin,* September 1998.

95   *DDI has annual revenues of $100 million:* Hanft, "Smarter Hiring, the DDI Way."

95   *more than 15 million people in seventy countries:* Ibid.

95   *62 percent of them used assessment centers:* Lowry, "A Survey of the Assessment Center Process in the Public Sector."

95   *created TAT cards depicting Chinese citizens:* Caroline C. Murray, "Harry's Compass," foreword in Gieser and Stein, *Evocative Images,* x.

95   *he helped develop a set especially for the U.S. Navy:* Dennie L. Briggs, "A Modification of the Thematic Apperception Test for Naval Enlisted Personnel (N-TAT)," *Journal of Psychology,* vol. 37, 1954.

96   *Morgan-Murray Thematic Apperception Test:* Morgan, "Origin and History of the Thematic Apperception Test Images."

96   *"need for achievement"*: This aspect of the work of psychologist David C. McClelland is discussed in David Cohen, *Psychologists on Psychology* (Taplinger, 1977).

97   *"power motive imagery"*: David G. Winter, "Leader Appeal, Leader
        Performance, and the Motive Profiles of Leaders and Followers: A Study of
        American Presidents and Elections," *Journal of Personality and Social
        Psychology*, January 1987.

97   *"a new kind of routine seems to be emerging"*: Quoted in Gardner Lindzey,
        Projective Techniques and Cross-Cultural Research (Appleton-Century-Crofts,
        1961), 4.

97   *"very early became everybody's favorite adopted baby"*: Shneidman, "Projective
        Techniques," 507.

97   *Sixty percent of clinical psychologists use the TAT*: Wayne Camara, Julie
        Nathan, and Anthony Puente, "Psychological Test Usage in Professional
        Psychology: Report to the APA Practice and Science Directorates,"
        American Psychological Association, May 1998.

97.   *more than three-quarters of accredited clinical psychology doctoral programs*:
        Edward D. Rossini and Robert J. Moretti, "Thematic Apperception Test
        (TAT) Interpretation Practice Recommendations From a Survey of Clinical
        Psychology Doctoral Programs Accredited by the American Psychological
        Association," *Professional Psychology: Research and Practice*, August 1997.

97   *it has stayed among the top ten most frequently used psychological tests*: Wayne J.
        Camara, Julie S. Nathan, and Anthony E. Puente, "Psychological Test
        Usage: Implications in Professional Psychology," *Professional Psychology:
        Research and Practice*, April 2000.

97   *"a reigning member of psychology's personality assessment triumvirate"*: Gieser
        and Stein, "An Overview of the Thematic Apperception Test," in Gieser
        and Stein, *Evocative Images*, 6.

97   *A 1993 survey of psychologists*: John E. Pinkerman, Jack P. Haynes, and
        Thomas Keiser, "Characteristics of Psychological Practice in Juvenile Court
        Clinics," *American Journal of Forensic Psychology*, vol. 2, iss. 2, 1993.

97   *"woefully short of professional and scientific test standards"*: John Hunsley,
        Catherine M. Lee, and James M. Wood, "Controversial and Questionable
        Assessment Techniques," in *Science and Pseudoscience in Clinical Psychology*,
        ed. Scott O. Lilienfeld, Steven Jay Lynn, and Jeffrey M. Lohr (Guilford,
        2003), 53.

97   *people who are hungry*: Cited in Scott O. Lilienfeld, "Projective Measures of
        Personality and Psychopathology: How Well Do They Work?," *Skeptical
        Inquirer*, September 1, 1999.

98   *"If I could have one device only"*: Leopold Bellak, "My Perceptions of the
        Thematic Apperception Test in Psychodiagnosis and Psychotherapy," in
        Evocative Images, 133.

98   *"a unique ability to stimulate rich and useful responses"*: Ibid.

98   *"one feels as if one is a discoverer"*: Morris I. Stein, "A Personological
        Approach to the Thematic Apperception Test," in *Evocative Images*, 129.

98 *"What might be happening here?"*: Author's reporting.

99 *"Be smart, get a new start with Ivory soap"*: Cited in Rebecca Piirto, "Measuring Minds in the 1990s," *American Demographics*, December 1990.

99 *"put a tiger in your tank"*: Cited in Lynne Ames, "Tending the Flame of a Motivator," *New York Times*, August 2, 1998.

99 *"a little girl becomes a lovely lady"*: Cited in Robert Krulwich, "The Secret Life of Barbie," ABC News, June 11, 1998.

99 *"Don't ask the murderer if he committed the crime"*: Quoted in Richard Block, "Advertising in Suspense," *Campaign*, March 25, 1994.

99 *"We Bring Good Things to Life"* and Visa's *"Everywhere You Want to Be"*: Cited in Piirto, "Measuring Minds in the 1990s."

100 *"We got a very clear image that a blemish meant social isolation"*: Quoted in ibid.

100 *"The print ad featured a beat-up jalopy"*: Author's interview with Sharon Livingston, November 24, 2002.

100 *The McCann-Erickson advertising agency*: Cited in Rebecca Piirto, "Beyond Mind Games," *American Demographics*, December 1991.

100 *"A lot of their feelings about the roach"*: Quoted in ibid.

101 *"strange life of objects"*: Quoted in Barbara B. Stern, "The Importance of Being Ernest: A Tribute to Dichter," *Journal of Advertising Research*, July 1, 2002.

101 *"is possibly a very direct and new and revolutionary way"*: Quoted in ibid.

101 *"the Aristocrat of Motor Oils"*: Cited in Morgan, "Origin and History of the Thematic Apperception Test Images."

101 *"Americans have fashioned a cosmetic culture"*: Murray, "What Should Psychologists Do About Psychoanalysis?"

101 *"surfaces for depths, gadgets for great ideas"*: Henry A. Murray, introduction in *Pierre; or, The Ambiguities*, Herman Melville (Hendricks House, 1949), xix.

101 *"In this country, we're so interested in gadgetry"*: Murray, "A Conversation With Henry A. Murray."

101 *"better mousetrap"*: Ibid.

101 *"an inert question for me now"*: Ibid.

102 *"Human personality,"* he warned in 1959, has become *"the problem of our time"*: Murray, "Preparations for the Scaffold of a Comprehensive System," 11.

102 *"unfinished and unfinishable"*: Quoted in Anderson, "The Life of Henry A. Murray: 1893–1988," 327.

102 *"one of the Devil's cunningest contrivances"*: Henry A. Murray, "The Personality and Career of Satan," *Journal of Social Issues*, October 1962.

102 *"disquieted by the once-born, unripe confidence"*: Quoted in Ian A. M. Nicholson, *Inventing Personality: Gordon Allport and the Science of Selfhood* (American Psychological Association, 2003), 184.

103 *"I am a species of Pagan"*: Murray, "A Conversation With Henry A. Murray."

103 *"Await the unforeknown. Expect the unforeseeable"*: Quoted in Robinson, *Love's Story Told*, 362.

CHAPTER FIVE: FIRST LOVE

105 *"I went to school very little"*: Center for Applications of Psychological Type, "The Story of Isabel Briggs Myers," www.capt.org/The_MBTI_Instrument/Isabel%20Myers.cfm.

105 *her nickname was "Joy"*: Cited in Frances Wright Saunders, *Katharine and Isabel: Mother's Light, Daughter's Journey* (Consulting Psychologists, 1991), 171.

105 *"A Little Girl's Letter"*: Peter B. Myers, preface in *Gifts Differing: Understanding Personality Type*, Isabel B. Myers with Peter B. Myers (Davies-Black, 1995), 207.

105 *"gifted," "a genius"*: Quoted in Saunders, *Katharine and Isabel*, 9.

105 *"knowing her as I do"*: Quoted in ibid., 27.

105 *"Research was what he cared about most"*: Quoted in Center for Applications of Psychological Type, "The Story of Isabel Briggs Myers."

106 *"Katharine did everything but breathe"*: Quoted in Saunders, *Katharine and Isabel*, 140.

106 *"I wasn't having a very good time"*: Quoted in ibid., 27.

106 *"figuring out Chief"*: Quoted in ibid., 58.

106 *she settled on four categories*: Myers and Myers, *Gifts Differing*, 207.

107 *"a very personal reason"*: Carl G. Jung, *C. G. Jung Speaks: Interviews and Encounters*, ed. William McGuire and R. F. C. Hull (Princeton University Press, 1977), 435.

107 *"In attempting to answer this question"*: Carl G. Jung, editorial note in *Psychological Types* (Princeton University Press, 1971), v.

107 *"to find my own bearings"*: Jung, *C. G. Jung Speaks*, 435.

107 *"It took me quite a long time to discover"*: Ibid., 341.

107 *"This is it!"*: Quoted in Myers and Myers, *Gifts Differing*, 207.

107 *adopted Jung's book as her "Bible"*: Cited in Saunders, *Katharine and Isabel*, 59.

107 *"Isabel seems to stand the test"*: Quoted in ibid., 31.

108 *"Mother Briggs," as Chief now called her*: Cited in ibid., 38.

108 *"slow, plodding logic"*: Isabel B. Myers, *Murder Yet to Come* (Center for Applications of Psychological Type, 1995), 12.

109 *"perfectly impossible"*: Quoted in Saunders, *Katharine and Isabel*, 87.

109 *"whanging them over the back of the neck"*: Quoted in ibid.

109 *"Fitting the Worker to the Job"*: Frank J. Taylor, *Reader's Digest*, January 1942.

109 *"extraordinarily interesting potentialities"*: Quoted in Saunders, *Katharine and Isabel*, 1.

109 *"potential troublemakers"*: Cited in Loren Baritz, *The Servants of Power: A History of the Use of Social Science in American Industry* (Wesleyan University Press, 1960), 159.

109 *"Character analysis"*: For descriptions of this practice, see Baritz, *The Servants of Power*, 69, and Donald S. Napoli, *Architects of Adjustment: The History of the Psychological Profession in the United States* (Kennikat, 1981), 48.

109 *"the laborer's attitude toward industrial relations"*: Eliott Frost, quoted in Baritz, *The Servants of Power*, 70.

110 *"the darkest days of World War II"*: Quoted in Danielle Poirier, "Isabel Briggs Myers, PhD," *MBTI Newsletter*, October 2, 2001.

111 *"Do you prefer to (a) eat to live, or (b) live to eat?"*: Quoted in Saunders, *Katherine and Isabel*, 109.

111 *"straws in the wind"*: Cited in Mary H. McCaulley, "The Myers-Briggs Type Indicator: A Measure for Individuals and Groups," *Measurement and Evaluation in Counseling and Development*, January 1990.

111 *"brought on an observable social change"*: Peter B. Myers interviewed by Thomas G. Carskadon, "Eminent Interview: Peter Briggs Myers," *Journal of Psychological Type*, vol. 61, 2002.

111 *"magnificent idea"*: Myers and Myers, *Gifts Differing*, 24.

111 *"down to everyday life"*: Quoted in Saunders, *Katharine and Isabel*, 110.

112 *"from a critique of my own psychological peculiarity"*: Carl G. Jung, foreword in the first Swiss edition of *Psychological Types*, xi.

112 *"to apply to each type at its best"*: Myers and Myers, *Gifts Differing*, 75.

112 *the descriptions Myers developed for each type*: Descriptions are taken from Isabel Briggs Myers, *Introduction to Type: A Guide to Understanding Your Results on the Myers-Briggs Type Indicator*, 6th ed. (Consulting Psychologists, 1998), 9.

113 *Ernst Kretschmer introduced an influential theory*: For descriptions of Kretschmer's work, see Brian W. P. Wells, *Body and Personality* (Longman Group, 1983), and Brendan A. Maher and Winifred B. Maher, "Personality and Psychopathology: A Historical Perspective," *Journal of Abnormal Psychology*, February 1994.

113 *"to tell them apart, not as Jim and Joe"*: William H. Sheldon with the collaboration of S. S. Stevens, *The Varieties of Temperament: A Psychology of Constitutional Differences* (Harper and Brothers, 1942), 2.

114 *when they resurfaced half a century later*: See Ron Rosenbaum, "The Great Ivy League Nude Posture Photo Scandal," *New York Times Magazine*, January 15, 1995.

114 *"mastiff will change into a spaniel or a collie"*: Ibid., 8.

114 *"the use of mental tests for practical psychological diagnosis"*: Quoted in Napoli, *Architects of Adjustment*, 21.

114 *"a blacklist of charlatans and ignoramuses"*: Quoted in ibid., 49.

115   *"for kindly sending me your interesting questionnaire"*: Quoted in Saunders, *Katharine and Isabel*, 120-21.

115   *"A thousand Thanks!"*: Quoted in ibid., 112.

115   *"someday I am going to have"*: Quoted in ibid., 113.

115   *"to really get interested"*: Quoted in ibid., 158.

115   *"more amusing, more interesting and more of a daily adventure"*: Quoted in Center for Applications of Psychological Type, "Mission & History of CAPT," www.capt.org/About_CAPT/History_and_Mission.cfm.

115   *"It is not too much to hope"*: Myers and Myers, *Gifts Differing*, 201.

116   *"In the early days of colonial America"*: Ibid., 58.

116   Frederick *"Speedy Fred" Taylor*: See John Fabian Witt, "Speedy Fred Taylor and the Ironies of Enterprise Liability," *Columbia Law Review*, January 2003.

116   *"Science Finds, Industry Adopts, Man Conforms"*: Quoted in Thomas Hardy Leahey, *A History of Psychology* (Prentice-Hall, 1992), 371.

117   *"cycloid," "schizoid," "autistic"*: Doncaster G. Humm and Guy W. Wadsworth Jr., "The Humm-Wadsworth Temperament Scale Preliminary Report," *Personnel Journal*, April 1934.

117   *"It will not do to assume"*: David Riesman, *The Lonely Crowd: A Study of the Changing American Character* (Yale University Press, 1950), 29.

117   *"Is the individual's innermost self any business"*: William H. Whyte, *The Organization Man* (Simon & Schuster, 1956), 201.

117   *"with a future and rights of its own"*: Quoted in Saunders, *Katharine and Isabel*, 112.

118   *"is clearly my destiny"*: Quoted in ibid., 125.

119   *"A veil of suspicion hangs about it"*: Quoted in ibid., 134.

119   *"like I sent for the Marines, and they came over the hill shooting at me!"*: Quoted in Mary McCaulley, "MBTI Past and Present: A History," videotaped speech recorded March 1996.

119   *"misinterpretations, distortions, and omissions"*: Quoted in Saunders, *Katharine and Isabel*, 135.

119   *"Larry Stricker, Damn Him"*: Cited in ibid.

119   *"cut off the dog's tail"*: Quoted in ibid., 136.

119   *"the little old lady in tennis shoes," "that horrible woman"*: Cited in ibid., 155.

119   *"Mrs. Myers has dedicated her life"*: Quoted in ibid., 137.

119   *"perfect high-energy diet"*: Cited in ibid., 136.

120   *"a very small fly on the wall"*: Winton Manning, quoted in ibid., 153.

120   *"That's just how I feel"*: Quoted in ibid., 150.

121   that *"it's okay to be my kind of person"*: Quoted in ibid.

121   *"I feel like it X-rayed my soul!"*: Mary McCaulley, "Isabel Briggs Myers As I Knew Her," audiotaped speech recorded July 1999.

121   *"everyone who has fallen in love with the Indicator"*: Quoted in Saunders, *Katharine and Isabel*, 152.

121 *"When I discovered your work"*: Quoted in ibid., page 172.

121 *"You have set a foundation"*: Quoted in ibid., 173.

121 *"No one is going to call my work tacky!"*: Quoted in McCaulley, "MBTI Past and Present: A History."

121 *"a chewing-gum-and-string kind of operation"*: Ibid.

121 *"to promote personal development"*: Center for Applications of Psychological Type, "Mission & History of CAPT."

121 *"Jungian disciples"*: Quoted in Saunders, *Katharine and Isabel*, 169.

121 *sales of the Indicator tripled*: Cited in ibid., 211.

122 *reaching one million by the end of the decade*: "An Appreciation of Isabel Briggs Myers," *The Best of the Bulletin of Psychological Type*, vol. 1, 1998.

122 *"Isabel is the only author we've ever had"*: John D. Black, "On Isabel Briggs Myers' 82nd Birthday," *The Best of the Bulletin of Psychological Type*, vol. 1, 1998.

122 *Myers was toasted as an intellectual "giant"*: Ibid.

122 *a necklace*, INFP *spelled out in gold letters*: Cited in Saunders, *Katharine and Isabel*, 179.

122 *"I really should have burst the bubble"*: Quoted in ibid., 180.

122 *two dozen people have gathered at the 92nd Street Y*: Author's reporting.

123 *"In the middle of a large pile of debris"*: Shoya Zichy, *Women and the Leadership Q: Revealing the Four Paths to Influence and Power* (McGraw-Hill, 2000), xiii.

123 *"I spent fifteen years in an industry"*: Author's interview with Shoya Zichy, November 1, 2002.

123 *"It's all very clear when you look at my type"*: Ibid.

123 *"more and more I gravitated to the work I should have been doing"*: Ibid.

124 *"I'm endlessly interested in what I do"*: Author's reporting.

125 *eighty-nine of the Fortune 100*: "CPP celebrates 60th Anniversary of Myers-Briggs Assessment," PR Newswire, October 28, 2003.

125 *"the world's most popular personality assessment"*: Ibid.

125 *"She seemed to be in her chair working"*: Quoted in Saunders, *Katharine and Isabel*, 171.

125 *"apprentices"*: Katherine Myers interviewed by Walter Joseph Geldar, "Katherine Downing Myers and Whole MBTI Type," February 1998, http://tap3x.net/EMBTI/j4kmyers.html.

125 *"guardians" of what Myers called "my baby"*: Katherine D. Myers interviewed by Thomas G. Carskadon, "Eminent Interview: Katherine Downing Myers," *Journal of Psychological Type*, vol. 61, 2002.

125 *"extending the benefits of psychological type"*: Myers & Briggs Foundation, "The Foundation: Objectives and Mission," www.myersbriggs.org/foundation/objectives_goals.cfm.

125 *"one of the few authentic geniuses"*: Quoted in Deborah G. Thompson, "1997

International APT Conference in Boston," *Georgia Association for Psychological Type Newsletter*, August 1997.

126 *"build understanding and transform lives"*: Consulting Psychologists Press, "Myers-Briggs Type Indicator," www.cpp.com/products/mbti/index.asp.

126 *the Management By Strengths system*: MBS Inc., "Management By Strengths . . . A Team Building Program," www.strengths.com.

126 *"It's shorter" than the original, she says, "but just as accurate"*: Author's reporting.

126 *"I use the Myers-Briggs as a foundation for my counseling"*: Author's interview with Norma Zuber, October 21, 2002.

126 *many major corporations*: Cited in John B. Murray, "Review of Research on the Myers-Briggs Type Indicator," *Perceptual and Motor Skills*, June 1990.

126 *"Cloning humans isn't an option"*: Quoted in Associated Press, "AP Top Technology Headlines," July 13, 2000.

127 *six months to "become ENFJs"*: Cited in Rowan Bayne, *The Myers Briggs Type Indicator: A Critical Review and Practical Guide* (Chapman & Hall, 1995), 95.

127 *"People tend to react to each other based on race and gender"*: Nancy Hutchens quoted in Lena Williams, "Companies Capitalizing on Worker Diversity," *New York Times*, December 15, 1992.

127 *Texaco settled a race discrimination suit*: Cited in Helen Lippman, "Harnessing the Power of Diversity," *Business & Health*, June 1999.

127 *"type-preference conflict"*: Richard Silveira, "Know Your People Better—Use Myers-Briggs Type Indicator Testing," *Proceedings of the United States Naval Institute*, November 2003.

128 *"not only helps students with their reasoning"*: "Myers-Briggs Personality Test Now Part of UA Law School's Academic Support Efforts," University of Alabama press release, September 18, 1997.

128 *"People of different types take on different kinds of volunteer opportunities"*: Author's interview with Lynne Baab, April 16, 2003.

129 *"That an employee's personality needs to 'fit' the duties of the job"*: Omnia Group, "The Beauty of Benchmarking," www.omniagroup.com/news/template.asp?article=beauty.

129 *"Administrator" personality, "Counselor-Advisor" personality*: Omnia Group, "Not Ideal But Workable," www.omniagroup.com/news/template.asp?article=not.

129 *employees are given a framed copy of their personality profile*: Cited in Kris Maher, "Web-Based Tools Help Find the Right Person for the Job," *Wall Street Journal*, November 26, 2002.

130 *"called it the 'aha' reaction"*: Peter B. Myers, preface in *Gifts Differing*, xiii.

130 *"one of her greatest pleasures in giving feedback"*: Ibid.

130 *"The type community is like Machu Picchu"*: Author's interview with Shoya Zichy, December 3, 2002.

131 *"ENTJs are Life's Natural Leaders," "INTPs Incubate Ideas"*: Otto Kroeger Associates, "Typewatching Tee-Shirts," www.typetalk.com/store/store_products_tshirt.htm.

131 *"we must continue trying out type descriptors and questions"*: Kathy Myers, "Katherine Downing Myers and Whole MBTI Type."

131 *"finding best-fit type"*: See, e.g., Myers & Briggs Foundation, "About the MBTI Instrument," www.myersbriggs.org/about_mbti/bestfit.cfm.

131 *"a deficit of type development"*: Myers and Myers, *Gifts Differing*, 177.

131 *"falsification of type"*: Ibid.

131 *"real selves"*: Ibid.

131 *"own ideal path of type development"*: McCaulley, "The Myers-Briggs Type Indicator: A Measure for Individuals and Groups."

132 *"It lets people know that they're not alone"*: Author's interview with Zuber.

132 *"Is there anything that you haven't accomplished"*: Author's reporting.

132 *"An act of irresponsible armchair philosophy"*: John E. Barbuto, "A Critique of the Myers-Briggs Type Indicator and Its Operationalization of Carl Jung's Psychological Types," *Psychological Reports*, April 1997.

132 *"Too slick and simple"*: Robert J. Gregory, *Psychological Testing: History, Principles, and Applications* (Allyn & Bacon, 1996), 536.

132 *"A party game"*: Robert Hogan, quoted in "Personality Test Winning Over All Types," *Baltimore Sun*, July 14, 1990.

133 *"a Jungian horoscope"*: Thomas G. Carskadon, "MBTI Characterizations: A Jungian Horoscope?," unpublished paper.

133 *the more than 7,800 studies that they say have been conducted*: Center for Applications of Psychological Type, "Research," www.capt.org/Research/Home.cfm.

133 *"was a good intuitive thinker in the afternoon"*: Alida S. Westman and Francis M. Canter, "Diurnal Changes on the Myers-Briggs Type Indicator: A Pilot Study," *Psychological Reports*, April 1984.

133 *One of the most thorough appraisals*: In the Mind's Eye: Enhancing Human Performance, ed. Daniel Druckman and Robert A. Bjork (National Academy Press, 1991), 95–101.

134 *"Barnum effect"*: The phenomenon was named by Paul E. Meehl in "Wanted—a Good Cookbook," *American Psychologist*, June 1956.

134 *a circus should have "a little something for everybody"*: Quoted in James M. Wood, M. Teresa Nezworski, Scott O. Lilienfeld, and Howard N. Garb, "The Rorschach Inkblot Test, Fortune Tellers, and Cold Reading," *Skeptical Inquirer*, July-August 2003.

134 *lifted from an astrology book*: Bertram R. Forer, "The Fallacy of Personal Validation: A Classroom Demonstration of Gullibility," *Journal of Abnormal and Social Psychology*, vol. 44, 1949.

135 *"Pollyanna principle"*: For more about this phenomenon, see Adrian

Furnham and Sandra Schofield, "Accepting Personality Test Feedback: A
Review of the Barnum Effect," *Current Psychological Research and Reviews*,
summer 1987.

135   *descriptions drawn from the Myers-Briggs literature*: Myers, *Introduction to Type*,
       13.

135   *"There's a sucker born every minute"*: Quoted in Wood et al., "The Rorschach
       Inkblot Test, Fortune Tellers, and Cold Reading."

136   *"World of Type"*: Association for Psychological Type, "APT XV 2004
       International Conference,"
       www.aptinternational.org/conference/index.cfm?pg=confinfo.htm.

136   *"type is nothing static"*: Jung, C. G. *Jung Speaks*, 435.

136   *"it is often very difficult to find out"*: Jung, *Psychological Types*, 3.

137   *"a few basic, observable differences"*: Myers and Myers, *Gifts Differing*, 1.

137   *"the fisherman calmly fishing for minnows"*: Angelo Spoto, *Jung's Typology in
       Perspective* (Sigo, 1989), 134.

137   *"Every individual is an exception to the rule"*: Quoted in Robert I. Watson, *The
       Great Psychologists: From Aristotle to Freud* (J. B. Lippincott, 1963), 496.

137   *fitting such individuals into a rigid system is "futile"* Jung, *Psychological Types*,
       xiv.

137   *"stick labels on people at first sight"*: Ibid.

137   *"Everyone," he sighed, "is in love with his own ideas"*: Ibid., 541.

CHAPTER SIX: CHILD'S PLAY

139   *Exchange between T. Justin Moore and Kenneth B. Clark*: Witness testimony
       filed in *Dorothy E. Davis, et al., v. County School Board of Prince Edward
       County, Virginia*, Civil Action Number 1333, February 1952.

139   *"I have come to the conclusion that prejudice"*: Ibid.

140   *"Some human beings may react by withdrawing"*: Ibid.

140   *"chicken shacks"*: Cited in Donald P. Baker, "Closed: Fifty Years Ago in
       Virginia, Integration Came Down to This," *Washington Post*, March 4, 2001.

140   *"the delicate, complex areas"*: Witness testimony, *Davis v. County School Board*.

141   *"Dr. Clark, are there any methods which are scientifically accurate"*: Ibid.

141   *"the most promising methods"*: Ibid.

141   *"Then we ask them questions"*: Ibid.

141   *"Can't you abbreviate, Dr. Clark?"*: Ibid.

142   *"stir up and foment critical situations"*: Ibid.

142   *"the Chinaman and the Indian have, in their own way, pride of race?"*: Ibid.

142   *"the Negro," "a suntanned white man"*: Ibid.

142   *"just as good as any high school in Virginia"*: Ibid.

142   *"every one of them" have twenty years' experience and a PhD in education*: Ibid.

142   *"have brand-new buses to ride to school every day in"*: Ibid.

142   *"I insist that, Mr. Moore"*: Ibid.

142   *"No amount of that kind of material attempt at equality"*: Ibid.

143   *calling it "dirty" and "bad"*: Ibid.

143   *"A great many of the children react as if I were the devil in hell"*: Ibid.

143   *"the flagrant damage to the self-esteem"*: Ibid.

143   *"Jesus Christ, those damned dolls!"*: Quoted in Richard Kluger, *Simple Justice: The History of Brown v. Board of Education and Black America's Struggle for Equality* (Vintage Books, 1977), 321.

144   *"If a Negro child goes to a school"*: Witness testimony, *Davis v. County School Board*.

144   *the "idealistic person"*: Ibid.

144   *"none too bright," "He was about a C student"*: Quoted in Kluger, *Simple Justice*, 502.

144   *provided a revealing "self-portrait"*: Quoted in Woodrow Wilbert Morris, "Other Projective Methods," in *An Introduction to Projective Techniques*, ed. Harold H. Anderson and Gladys L. Anderson (Prentice-Hall, 1951), 523.

144   *"any substantial validity"*: Quoted in Kluger, *Simple Justice*, 501.

144   *"In summary," he proclaimed, "the testimony of all our experts"*: Summation filed in *Dorothy E. Davis, et al. v. County School Board of Prince Edward County, Virginia*, Civil Action Number 1333, February 1952.

144   *"We do know that a perfectly terrible situation would be created"*: Ibid.

144   *"It indisputably appears from the evidence"*: Original opinion filed in *Dorothy E. Davis, et al. versus County School Board of Prince Edward County, Virginia*, Civil Action Number 1333, March 1952.

145   *"In this milieu we cannot say"*: Ibid.

145   *"these oxlike men"*: Quoted in Franz Samelson, "From 'Race Psychology' to 'Studies in Prejudice': Some Observations on the Thematic Reversal in Social Psychology," in *A History of Psychology: Original Sources and Contemporary Research*, 2nd ed., ed. Ludy T. Benjamin Jr. (McGraw-Hill, 1997), 634.

145   *leading some social scientists to urge restrictions on immigration*: See ibid.

145   *its first appearance in the* Psychological Index: Cited in ibid., 633.

145   *"lacking in filial affection"*: Quoted in Ludy T. Benjamin Jr., "American Psychology's Social Agenda: The Issue of Race," in *A History of Psychology*, 611.

146   *American Indians were "decidedly inferior" to whites*: Quoted in Thomas Russell Garth, *Race Psychology: A Study of Racial Mental Differences* (Whittlesey House, 1931), 162.

146   *"have no basis in biological heredity"*: Gunnar Myrdal, *An American Dilemma: The Negro Problem and Modern Democracy*, vol. 2 (Harper and Brothers, 1944), 956.

146   *"more indolent, less punctual, less careful"*: Ibid., 959.

146   *"They know that all the striving they may do"*: Ibid.

146   *"underlying antidemocratic trends in the personality"*: Theodor W. Adorno, Else
       Frenkel-Brunswik, Daniel J. Levinson, and Sanford R. Nevitt, *The
       Authoritarian Personality* (Harper and Row, 1950), 223.

146   *"America is getting so far"*: Ibid., 226.

147   *"Too many people today"*: Ibid.

147   *"The sexual orgies of the old Greeks"*: Ibid.

147   *the item that yielded some of the most useful information*: Ibid., 246.

147   *"Obedience and respect for authority"*: Ibid., 226.

147   *"The majority of mankind quite readily take any shape"*: Ruth F. Benedict,
       Patterns of Culture (Houghton Mifflin, 1934), 196.

147   *"Human nature is almost unbelievably malleable"*: Margaret Mead, *Sex and
       Temperament in Three Primitive Societies* (Morrow, 1935), 280.

148   *"He is the little creature of his culture"*: Benedict, *Patterns of Culture*, 2.

148   *"At Howard University was the first time"*: Witness testimony, *Davis v. County
       School Board*.

148   *"an education in race relations"*: Ibid.

148   *"in order to see if we could not get them to treat us"*: Ibid.

148   *"a quite different person"*: Ibid.

148   *"a very intense feeling of race"*: Ibid.

148   *"To hell with medical school"*: Quoted in John P. Jackson Jr., *Social Scientists for
       Social Justice: Making the Case Against Segregation* (New York University
       Press, 2001), 31.

148   *"systematic understanding of the complexities of human behavior"*: Quoted in
       Nat Hentoff, "The Integrationist," *The New Yorker*, August 23, 1982.

149   *"there is no adequate proof of fundamental race differences"*: Quoted in
       Benjamin, "American Psychology's Social Agenda," 612.

149   *a case study of an eighteen-year-old race riot participant*: Kenneth B. Clark and
       James Barker, "The Zoot Effect in Personality: A Race Riot Participant,"
       Journal of Abnormal and Social Psychology, April 1945.

150   *"To separate [black schoolchildren] from others of similar age"*: Opinion of U.S.
       Supreme Court, *Brown v. Board of Education of Topeka*, May 17, 1954.

150   *"tremendous exhilaration"*: Quoted in Ludy T. Benjamin and Ellen M. Crouse,
       "The American Psychological Association's Response to *Brown v. Board of
       Education*: The Case of Kenneth B. Clark," *American Psychologist*, January
       2002.

150   *"we were in the clouds"*: Quoted in ibid.

150   *"the greatest compliment ever paid to psychology"*: Quoted in ibid.

150   *"the doll man"*: Quoted in Kluger, *Simple Justice*, 315.

151   *"psychologist for society"*: Quoted in Keppel, *The Work of Democracy: Ralph
       Bunche, Kenneth B. Clark, Lorraine Hansberry, and the Cultural Politics of
       Race* (Harvard University Press), 1995, 131.

151   *"public therapy"*: Kenneth B. Clark, "Social Conflict and Problems of Mental Health," *Journal of Religion and Health*, vol. 8, iss. 3, 1969.

151   *"American children can be saved"*: Kenneth B. Clark, *Prejudice and Your Child* (Wesleyan University Press, 1988; originally published 1955 by Beacon Press), 130.

151   *"The fascinating thing, the thing which we did not expect"*: Witness testimony, *Davis v. County School Board.*

151   *"this was the first time we had evidence"*: Ibid.

152   *"activity play therapy"*: "Dr. David M. Levy, 84, A Psychiatrist, Dies," *New York Times*, March 4, 1977.

152   *"get under the desk and play with the child"*: Mrs. Max Ascoli, quoted in ibid.

152   *"children's emergent awareness of themselves"*: Ruth E. Horowitz, "Racial Aspects of Self-Identification in Nursery School Children," *The Journal of Psychology*, January 1939.

152   *"Give me the doll that you like best"*: Kenneth B. Clark and Mamie P. Clark, "Racial Identification and Preference in Negro Children," in Theodore M. Newcomb and Eugene L. Hartley, *Readings in Social Psychology* (Henry Holt, 1947), 619.

153   *two-thirds of the black children tested*: Ibid., 624.

153   *"It seems justifiable to assume from these results"*: Ibid., 625.

153   *"conform with the accepted racial values"*: Ibid., 626.

153   *"It is clear that the Negro child"*: Kenneth. B. Clark and Mamie P. Clark, "Emotional Factors in Racial Identification and Preference in Negro Children," *Journal of Negro Education*, vol. 19, 1950.

153   *"The earliest drawing test"*: This technique, now known as the Goodenough-Harris Drawing Test, is still in use as a measure of intelligence.

154   *recalls his mother as "a witch"*: Author's interview with Robert Machover, October 2, 2002.

154   *"My mother had X-ray vision about drawings"*: Ibid.

154   *"an intimate tie-up"*: Karen Machover, *Personality Projection in the Drawing of the Human Figure: A Method of Personality Investigation* (Charles C. Thomas, 1949), 4.

154   *"intellectual or perhaps moral vanity"*: Karen Machover, "Drawing of the Human Figure: A Method of Personality Investigation," in *An Introduction to Projective Techniques*, 354.

154   *"restraining yet socially decorative devices"*: Ibid., 357.

155   *"you could not turn your head to see who was after you"*: Quoted in Machover, *Personality Projection in the Drawing of the Human Figure*, 57.

155   *"was admittedly associated with sadistic fantasies"*: Ibid., 49.

155   *"homosexual panic"*: Ibid., 15.

155   *"masculine protest"*: Ibid., 71.

155 *a practice she described as "reparations"*: Thomas Fagan, "Karen Machover (1902–1996)," *American Psychologist*, July 1997.

155 *"boxing people into categories"*: Author's interview with Robert Machover.

155 *"to persuade a nine-year-old girl to answer questions"*: John N. Buck, "Chronological Milestones in the Development of the H-T-P," in *Advances in the House-Tree-Person Technique: Variations and Applications*, ed. John N. Buck and Emanuel F. Hammer (Western Psychological Services, 1969), ix.

159 *"I noticed that the most successful athletes"*: Author's interview with Don Lowry, December 6, 2002.

159 *"All of a sudden I had an awareness"*: Ibid.

159 *"The reaction was phenomenal"*: Ibid.

159 *"Where's the action?," "Do you need a hug?"*: Author's reporting.

161 *"from Harvard to the ghettos"*: True Colors Communications Group, "The True Colors Story," www.truecolors.org/About/AboutTCStory.htm.

161 *"a pretty far-out guy"*: Author's interview with Lowry.

161 *"Type affects everything"*: Author's interview with Paul Tieger, April 9, 2003.

161 *"It's helpful to start getting an awareness of type"*: Ibid.

161 *"what their strengths are"*: Author's interview with Thomas Oakland, November 21, 2002.

161 *"Wouldn't it have been great to have had that"*: Ibid.

162 *"left-brain dominant" or "right-brain dominant"*: Kenneth A. Kiewra and Damien McShane, "Style of Learning and Thinking," in *The Eleventh Mental Measurements Yearbook*, ed. Jack J. Kramer and Jane Close Conoley (Buros Institute of Mental Measurements, 1992), 888.

162 *"is not aware of any instrument"*: Robert D. Brown, "Learning Styles Inventory," in *The Fourteenth Mental Measurements Yearbook*, ed. James C. Impara and Barbara S. Plake (Buros Institute of Mental Measurements, 2001), 679.

162 *"Being attentive to and responding to"*: Ibid.

162 *"propose many possible uses"*: Robert J. Drummond, "Murphy-Meisgeier Type Indicator for Children," in *Test Critiques*, vol. 7, ed. Daniel J. Keyser and Richard C. Sweetland (Test Corporation of America, 1991), 519.

162 *"may be a futile and unwarranted exercise"*: Jeffrey Jenkins, "Learning Preference Inventory," in *The Eleventh Mental Measurements Yearbook*, 457.

162 *"great caution in making educational prescriptions"*: Brown, "Learning Styles Inventory," 679.

162 *"cannot be recommended for use"*: Michael W. Pratt, "Learning Style Identification Scale," in *The Ninth Mental Measurements Yearbook*, ed. James V. Mitchell (Buros Institute of Mental Measurements, 1985), 839.

162 *"a psychometric disaster"*: Thomas R. Knapp, "Learning Style Inventory," in *The Thirteenth Mental Measurements Yearbook*, ed. James C. Impara and Barbara S. Plake (Buros Institute of Mental Measurements, 1998), 608.

162   *"no redeeming values"*: Jan N. Hughes, "Learning Style Inventory," in *The Eleventh Mental Measurements Yearbook*, 461.

162   *"too simplistic" and "not well supported"*: Kiewra and McShane, "Style of Learning and Thinking," 889.

162   *"Nope. These are biologically-based qualities"*: Author's interview with Oakland.

163   *"Children typically say, 'My gosh' "*: Ibid.

163   *"Just as each snowflake, tree, and star"*: The Psychological Corporation, "Student Styles Questionnaire," promotional brochure.

163   *gifted students are 29 percent more likely*: Kristen Harmel, "Gifted Students Are More Imaginative and Emotional, UF Study Shows," University of Florida press release, July 17, 2000.

163   *"blacks and Hispanics generally prefer a practical approach"*: Cathy Keen, "Temperament May Make Learning Easy as A, B, C, Says UF Researcher," University of Florida press release, October 22, 1996.

163   *"are more likely than whites to base their decisions"*: Ibid.

163   In order *"to be more effective in life"*: Author's interview with Oakland.

163   *"It doesn't pigeonhole or get offensive"*: Quoted in Ann Dickerson, "Defining Students' Styles of Learning," *Atlanta Journal and Constitution*, May 13, 1999.

164   *more than two-thirds of child protection workers*: Cited in Gerald P. Koocher, Gail S. Goodman, Sue C. White, William N. Friedrich, Abigail B. Sivan, and Cecil R. Reynolds, "Psychological Science and the Use of Anatomically Detailed Dolls in Child Sexual-Abuse Assessments," *Psychological Bulletin*, September 1995.

164   *about a third of law enforcement officers and mental health professionals*: Cited in ibid.

164   *consistently ranked among the instruments psychologists use most often*: Wayne J. Camara, Julie S. Nathan, and Anthony E. Puente, "Psychological Test Usage: Implications in Professional Psychology," *Professional Psychology: Research and Practice*, April 2000.

164   *projective drawing tests are being used* more *often than before*: Francella A. Quinnell and James N. Bow, "Psychological Tests Used in Child Custody Evaluations," *Behavioral Sciences and the Law*, September 2001.

164   *85 percent of graduate programs in clinical psychology*: Chris Piotrowski and Christine Zalewski, "Training in Psychodiagnostic Testing in APA-Approved PsyD and PhD Clinical Psychology Programs," *Journal of Personality Assessment*, October 1993.

164   *"Children who have not been abused"*: While researchers cannot be absolutely sure that all children in a "normal" sample have not been abused, many attempt to ensure that this is the case by questioning parents or by asking parents to sign a statement declaring that they have no knowledge of any

such abuse. Alternatively, researchers may refer to abused and apparently
non-abused children as "referred" and "non-referred" samples, or as
"clinical" and "community" samples.

164 *touching, rubbing, poking, and pinching body parts:* Cited in John Hunsley,
Catherine M. Lee, and James M. Wood, "Controversial and Questionable
Assessment Techniques," in *Science and Pseudoscience in Clinical Psychology,*
ed. Scott O. Lilienfeld, Steven Jay Lynn, and Jeffrey M. Lohr (Guilford,
2003), 57.

164 *placing the dolls "in a position suggestive of sexual intercourse":* Cited in ibid, 58.

164 *75 percent spontaneously undressed the dolls:* Cited in Koocher et al.,
"Psychological Science and the Use of Anatomically Detailed Dolls."

164 *71 percent touched the male doll's penis:* Cited in ibid.

164 *used by almost a quarter of clinicians:* Wayne Camara, Julie Nathan, and
Anthony Puente, "Psychological Test Usage in Professional Psychology:
Report to the APA Practice and Science Directorates," American
Psychological Association, May 1998.

164 *"no objective evidence to suggest":* Robert C. Reinehr, "Children's
Apperception Test," in *The Thirteenth Mental Measurements Yearbook,* 234.

165 *"The use of the technique as a method":* Ibid.

165 *"an historical anachronism":* Howard M. Knoff, "Children's Apperception
Test," in *The Thirteenth Mental Measurements Yearbook,* 233.

165 *"despite its following, the CAT should not be available":* Ibid.

165 *"embarrassing," "phrenology for the twentieth century":* Robert J. Gregory,
Psychological Testing: History, Principles, and Applications, 3rd ed. (Allyn and
Bacon, 1999), 468.

165 *"more properly belongs in a museum":* F. M. Gresham, " 'What's Wrong With
This Picture?' Response to Motta et al.'s Review of Human Figure
Drawings," *School Psychology Quarterly,* fall 1993.

165 *the "sign" approach has no solid evidence behind it:* See Sophia Kahill,
"Human Figure Drawing in Adults: An Update of the Empirical Evidence,
1967–1982," *Canadian Psychology,* October 1984; Walter G. Klopfer and
Earl S. Taulbee, "Projective Tests," *Annual Review of Psychology,* 1976;
Howard B. Roback, "Human Figure Drawings: Their Utility in the
Clinical Psychologist's Armamentarium for Personality Assessment,"
Psychological Bulletin, July 1968; and Clifford H. Swensen, "Empirical
Evaluations of Human Figure Drawings: 1957–1966," *Psychological
Bulletin,* July 1968.

165 *global assessments of the sketches are likely to pass judgment on artistic ability and
general intelligence:* Dale B. Harris, "The Draw-A-Person," in *The Seventh
Mental Measurements Yearbook,* vol. 1, ed. Oscar Krisen Buros (Gryphon,
1972), 403.

165 *"one of the worst horrors ever perpetrated":* Albert Ellis, "The House-Tree-

Person Technique," in *The Fourth Mental Measurements Yearbook*, ed. Oscar Krisen Buros (Gryphon, 1953), 178.

165 *"incredible naïveté, fanaticism, and arrant disregard"*: Ibid., 179.

165 *More recent efforts:* See Howard N. Garb, James M. Wood, Scott O. Lilienfeld, M. Teresa Nezworski, "Effective Use of Projective Techniques in Clinical Practice: Let the Data Help With Selection and Interpretation," *Professional Psychology: Research and Practice*, October 2002; Merith Cosden, "Draw A Person Screening Procedure for Emotional Disturbance," in *The Twelfth Mental Measurements Yearbook*, ed. Jane Close Conoley and James C. Impara (Buros Institute of Mental Measurements, 1995), 321-322.

165 *27 percent of clinicians use the Draw-a-Person Test:* Camara, Nathan, and Puente, "Psychological Test Usage in Professional Psychology."

165 *34 percent use the House-Tree-Person Test:* Ibid.

165 *"illusory correlation":* Loren J. Chapman and Jean P. Chapman, "Genesis of Popular But Erroneous Psychodiagnostic Observations," *Journal of Abnormal Psychology*, June 1967.

165 *around nine out of ten psychologists:* David Smith and Frank Dumont, "A Cautionary Study: Unwarranted Interpretations of the Draw-A-Person Test," *Professional Psychology: Research and Practice*, June 1995.

166 *a classic 1967 experiment:* Chapman and Chapman, "Genesis of Popular But Erroneous Psychodiagnostic Observations."

166 *"Again and again, the DAP signs have failed to hold up":* Loren J. Chapman and Jean P. Chapman, "Test Results Are What You Think They Are," *Psychology Today*, November 1971.

166 *"I know that paranoids don't seem to draw big eyes":* Quoted in ibid.

166 *"by seeking to prove that they are not as inferior":* Witness testimony, *Davis* v. *County School Board.*

166 *came to be called the "lost generation":* See, e.g., Susan Bagby, "The Robert R. Moton Museum: A Center for the Study of Civil Rights in Education," *Organization of American Historians Newsletter*, May 2000.

167 *"within ten years or so":* Quoted in Studs Terkel, *Race: How Blacks and Whites Think and Feel About the American Obsession* (The New Press, 1992), 334.

167 *"too small to test the reaction to a new soap":* Ernest van den Haag in association with Ralph Ross, *Passion and Social Constraint* (Stein and Day, 1963), 283.

167 *"the best conclusion that can be drawn":* Ernest van den Haag, "Social Science Testimony in the Desegregation Cases—A Reply to Professor Kenneth Clark," *Villanova Law Review*, fall 1960.

167 *"I would not have the constitutional rights of Negroes":* Edmond Cahn, "Jurisprudence," *N.Y.U. Law Review*, January 1955.

167 *"either laughed or tried to appear casual":* Quoted in Jackson, *Social Scientists for Social Justice*, 154.

167   *"Man's relations with his fellow man"*: Kenneth B. Clark, "The Desegregation Cases: Criticism of the Social Scientists' Role," *Villanova Law Review*, winter 1959–1960.

167   *"I believe that to be taken seriously"*: Kenneth B. Clark, *Dark Ghetto: Dilemmas of Social Power* (Harper and Row, 1965), xxi.

168   *"Should social scientists play a role"*: Clark, "The Desegregation Cases."

168   *"fundamental changes in the power alignments"*: Ibid.

168   *"To be quite candid about the success of my attempts"*: Quoted in Keppel, *The Work of Democracy*, 131.

168   *"moral schizophrenia"*: Quoted in Terkel, *Race*, 334.

168   *"I fear the disease has metastasized"*: Quoted in Jackson, *Social Scientists for Social Justice*, 212.

168   *"Thirty years after Brown, I must accept the fact"*: Quoted in Benjamin and Crouse, "The American Psychological Association's Response to *Brown* v. *Board of Education*."

169   *"With your cynicism, your pessimism, as intense as it is"*: Quoted in Terkel, *Race*, 337.

169   *"It's always been about the children"*: Quoted in Ken Woodley, "The Rainbow . . . Before Me," *The Farmville Herald*, April 25, 2001.

169   *"Look not at the face nor the color"*: Quoted in ibid.

CHAPTER SEVEN: THE STRANGER

171   *"intellectually indigestible"*: Raymond B. Cattell, "Raymond B. Cattell," in *A History of Psychology in Autobiography*, vol. 6, ed. Gardner Lindzey (Prentice-Hall, 1974), 88.

171   *"by processes with which no self-respecting scientist"*: Raymond B. Cattell, *A New Morality from Science: Beyondism* (Pergamon, 1972), 28.

171   *"since better truth-finding processes now exist"*: Ibid., 28–29.

171   *"of the same metal as science itself"*: Raymond B. Cattell, "Ethics and the Social Sciences—The 'Beyondist' Solution," *The Mankind Quarterly Monograph*, July 1981.

171   *"elegant equations"*: Cattell, *A New Morality from Science*, xv.

171   *he admired the rigor of men like Dmitri Mendeleev*: Dennis Child, "Raymond Bernard Cattell (1905–1998)," *British Journal of Mathematical and Statistical Psychology*, November 1998.

172   *more than fifty books and five hundred scholarly articles and chapters*: Ibid.

172   *he was ranked near the top of a list of the most eminent psychologists*: Steven J. Haggbloom, Renee Warnick, Jason E. Warnick, Vinessa K. Jones, Gary L. Yarbrough, Tenea M. Russell, Chris M. Borecky, Reagan McGahhey, John L. Powell III, Jamie Beavers, and Emmanuelle Monte, "The 100 Most Eminent Psychologists of the 20th Century," *Review of General Psychology*, June 2002.

172   *"is on the job night and day"*: Cattell, "Raymond B. Cattell," 74.

172   *so lost in thought that he could find his car*: Ibid., 75.

172   *"utilizing the quiet of the night"*: Raymond B. Cattell, "Travels in Psychological Hyperspace," in *The Psychologists*, vol. 2, ed. T. S. Krawiec (Oxford University Press, 1974), 108.

172   *she often didn't have time to finish one cassette*: Child, "Raymond Bernard Cattell (1905–1998)."

172   *"Dr. Cattell writes faster than I can read"*: Quoted in Richard Goresuch, "Eulogies [for] Raymond Bernard Cattell," www.cattell.net/devon/rbceul.htm.

172   *"Dr. Cattell has already written a paper on it"*: Quoted in ibid.

172   *"on Christmas day and other unlikely times"*: Cattell, "Raymond B. Cattell," 71.

172   *"the best recreation is a change of work"*: Cattell, "Travels in Psychological Hyperspace," 115.

172   *spent a single day painting one landscape*: Ivan Scheier, "Remembering Raymond Bernard Cattell," www.cattell.net/devon/rbcpers.htm.

172   *he shot only nine holes, running from one to the next*: Ibid.

172   *Cattell would walk briskly around a local park*: Child, "Raymond Bernard Cattell (1905–1998)."

172   *he would swim the sidestroke while facing one of his graduate students*: Ibid.

172   *"Busy as I was, she had to put up with neglect"*: Cattell, "Raymond B. Cattell," 68.

172   *"From overwork, snatched meals, and a cold attic"*: Cattell, "Travels in Psychological Hyperspace," 89.

172   *"It bred asceticism and impatience with irrelevance"*: Ibid., 90.

172   *even his friends called him "aristocratic"*: Desmond Cartwright, "A Ray of Light: Raymond Bernard Cattell," www.StThomasU.ca/~jgillis/trides.htm.

173   *He adored bawdy limericks, London music hall ditties, and English folk songs*: Ralph Mason Dreger and Irwin A. Berg, "Raymond Bernard Cattell (1905–1998)," www.StThomasU.ca/~jgillis/tridre.htm; Devon Cattell, "Remembering Raymond Bernard Cattell," www.cattell.net/devon/rbcpers.htm.

173   *a swimming pool that was a one-inch-to-the-mile copy*: Irwin A. Berg, "Raymond B. Cattell: The Man, His Explorations and His Impact on Psychology," in *Multivariate Personality Research: Contributions to the Understanding of Personality in Honor of Raymond B. Cattell*, ed. Ralph Mason Dreger (Claitor's, 1972), xxxix; Janus Wehmer, "Remembering Raymond Bernard Cattell," www.cattell.net/devon/rbcpers.htm.

173   *"The researcher's life is a long wrestling with difficulties alone"*: Cattell, "Raymond B. Cattell," 91.

173   *he once devised a test of one's sense of humor*: Raymond B. Cattell, "Principles of Design in 'Projective' or Misperceptive Tests of Personality," in *An*

Introduction to Projective Techniques, ed. Harold H. Anderson and Gladys L. Anderson (Prentice-Hall, 1951), 77–78.

173   *the mating erg, the pugnacity erg, the food-seeking erg:* See Raymond B. Cattell, *Personality: A Systematic, Theoretical, and Factual Study* (McGraw-Hill, 1950), 199.

173   *"psychological hyperspace":* Cattell, "Travels in Psychological Hyperspace," 85.

174   *"lexical hypothesis":* See, e.g., Lewis R. Goldberg, "The Structure of Phenotypic Personality Traits," *American Psychologist*, January 1993.

174   *Francis Galton was probably the first to speculate on it:* See, e.g., D. B. Bromley, *Personality Description in Ordinary Language* (John Wiley and Sons, 1977), 64.

174   *"distinguish the behavior of one human being from that of another":* Gordon W. Allport and Henry S. Odbert, *Trait-Names: A Psycho-Lexical Study* (*Psychological Review Company*, 1936), 24.

174   *Charles Spearman devised the method:* For a review, see Robert I. Watson, "Historical Review of Objective Personality Testing: The Search for Objectivity," in *Objective Approaches to Personality Assessment*, ed. Bernard M. Bass and Irwin A. Berg (D. Van Nostrand, 1959), 6–7.

175   *"The headmaster divided his time":* Cattell, "Raymond B. Cattell," 63.

175   *"ferment of social and political ideas":* Raymond B. Cattell, "The Voyage of a Laboratory, 1928–1984," *Multivariate Behavioral Research*, April–July 1984.

175   *"a certain shock at the poverty and poor morale":* Cattell, "Travels in Psychological Hyperspace," 88.

175   *"soon my laboratory bench began to seem small":* Cattell, "Raymond B. Cattell," 64.

175   *"Like the timely flash of a bell buoy":* Ibid.

175   *"As I packed up my flasks and condensers":* Ibid.

175   *"it was said with some truth":* Cattell, "Travels in Psychological Hyperspace," 87.

175   *"My choice seemed to me justified":* Cattell, "Raymond B. Cattell," 64.

175   *"do-gooders," "social workers":* Raymond B. Cattell, "Interview With Raymond B. Cattell," *Eugenics Bulletin*, spring-summer 1984.

175   *"to make up by the warmth of their hearts":* Quoted in Berg, "Raymond B. Cattell: The Man, His Explorations and His Impact on Psychology," xxxix.

175   *"soft-nosed":* Ibid., xv.

176   *"Through all the experiences of the merely 'fringe' jobs in psychology":* Cattell, "Travels in Psychological Hyperspace," 90.

176   *"unraveling the structures of temperament and motivation":* Cattell, "The Voyage of a Laboratory, 1928–1984."

176 *"the riddle of the universe"*: Robert J. Throckmorton, "Remembering Raymond Bernard Cattell," www.cattell.net/devon/rbcpers.htm.

176 *"there being then six men in Britain"*: Cattell, *A New Morality From Science*, xi.

176 *"The broken marriage and the bleak future"*: Cattell, "Raymond B. Cattell," 69.

176 *"the wrench of a tooth extraction"*: Cattell, "Travels in Psychological Hyperspace," 90.

176 *"a beauty of a more abstract and placeless kind"*: Ibid., 91.

176 *"close to that which great religions have called being 'reborn' "*: Ibid.

177 *"the literally long-suffering subject"*: Ibid., 106.

177 *"Every day for nine weeks"*: Ibid.

177 *"there is a kind of absentmindedness about the scientist"*: "Editorial," in *Human Affairs*, ed. R. B. Cattell, J. Cohen, and R. M. W. Travers (Macmillan, 1937), 8.

177 *"There is no place like home"*: Cattell, "Travels in Psychological Hyperspace," 129.

177 *"the small community of three or four research associates at a time"*: Ibid.

177 *"all aspects of human personality which are or have been of importance"*: Raymond B. Cattell, "The Description of Personality: Basic Traits Resolved Into Clusters," *Journal of Abnormal and Social Psychology*, October 1943.

177 *"the chaotic jungle of human behavior"*: Raymond B. Cattell, *The Scientific Analysis of Personality* (Pelican, 1965), 56.

177 *"whether the dark blobs which he sees"*: Ibid.

178 *"Sacred Illiac"*: Cattell, "Raymond B. Cattell," 74.

178 *"natural elements"*: Cattell, *The Scientific Analysis of Personality*, 325.

178 *"logically equivalent to an element in the physical world"*: Ibid.

178 *"New concepts need new terms"*: Quoted in Berg, "Raymond B. Cattell: The Man, His Explorations and His Impact on Psychology," xxix.

178 *"precisely referred to only by abandoning the battered, changing coinage of popular language"*: Cattell, "Raymond B. Cattell," 90.

178 *"Autia," "Harria," "Parmia," "Zeppia"*: See Raymond B. Cattell and Paul Kline, *The Scientific Analysis of Personality and Motivation* (Academic, 1977), 342–44.

178 *"to leave out no aspect of the total personality"*: Quoted in Starke R. Hathaway, "Personality Inventories," in *Handbook of Clinical Psychology*, ed. Benjamin B. Wolman (McGraw-Hill, 1965), 467.

178 *"Do you tend to get angry"*: Cited in Charles M. Harsh, "The Sixteen Personality Factor Questionnaire," in *The Fourth Mental Measurements Yearbook*, ed. Oscar Krisen Buros (Gryphon Press, 1953), 147.

178 *from "worrying suspiciousness" to "calm trustfulness"*: Cited in ibid.

179   *coining the term* eugenics *in 1883 from the Greek word for "good in birth"*:
        Cited in Richard A. Soloway, *Demography and Degeneration: Eugenics and the
        Declining Birthrate in Twentieth-Century Britain* (University of North
        Carolina Press, 1990), xvi.

179   *"to increase the contribution of the more valuable classes"*: Quoted in William
        H. Tucker, *The Science and Politics of Racial Research* (University of Illinois
        Press, 1994), 45.

179   *"the galaxy of genius" that might be created*: Quoted in ibid., 46–47.

179   *a government-sponsored eugenic competition*: See, e.g., Raymond E. Fancher,
        Pioneers of Psychology, 2nd ed. (W. W. Norton, 1990), 229.

179   *"an accurate measurement of every one's intelligence"*: Quoted in Tucker, *The
        Science and Politics of Racial Research*, 73.

179   *"Perfect justice," Spearman predicted, "is about to combine with maximum
        efficiency"*: Quoted in ibid.

180   *"English Children Getting More and More Stupid!," "Ban Balmy Babies!"*:
        Quoted in Soloway, *Demography and Degeneration*, 215.

180   *"start a chain reaction leading to a formal government investigation"*: Cattell,
        "Raymond B. Cattell," 67.

180   *"One may ask why so much trouble has been taken"*: Raymond B. Cattell,
        Beyondism: Religion From Science (Praeger, 1987), 213.

180   *"I was astonished when I came to America"*: Cattell, "Interview with Raymond
        B. Cattell."

180   *"the tang of inhumanity"*: Cattell, *Beyondism*, 199.

180   *"actually, in the history of human movements"*: Ibid.

180   *"I never dreamed that it would take so long"*: Cattell, "Travels in Psychological
        Hyperspace," 88.

180   *Cattell encouraged his graduate students to have more children*: See John R.
        Nesselroade, "Open Letter to Prof. Cattell from Prof. John R. Nesselroade,
        www.StThomasU.ca/~jgillis/awalifnes.htm.

181   *"would surely eliminate very rapidly"*: Cattell, "Travels in Psychological
        Hyperspace," 88.

181   *"Beyondism is based on the principle that evolution is good"*: Raymond B.
        Cattell, "Open Letter to the APA," December 13, 1997, posted at
        www.stanford.edu/~cattell/openletter.htm.

181   *Galton had also mused on the possibility of basing a religion on evolutionary
        principles*: See, e.g., Soloway, *Demography and Degeneration*, 80–81.

181   *"the Evolutionary Purpose"*: Cattell, *Beyondism*, 258.

181   *a "grand experiment"*: Cattell, *A New Morality From Science*, 106.

181   *"the variation and natural selection which now take place"*: Ibid., 92.

181   *"cooperating with Nature"*: Quoted in Tucker, *The Science and Politics of Racial
        Research*, 242.

181   *"genetic and cultural patterns"*: Cattell, A *New Morality From Science*, 216.

181   *"qualified elites"*: Cattell, *Beyondism*, 260.

181   *"are apparently the exact opposite"*: Quoted in Tucker, *The Science and Politics of Racial Research*, 242.

182   *"outright transfer of gains from one group to another"*: Cattell, A *New Morality From Science*, 216.

182   *"The wider intergroup morality requires"*: Ibid., 196.

182   *"genthanasia"*: Ibid., 219.

182   *"a moribund culture is ended"*: Ibid.

182   *"triumphs and the tragedies"*: Cattell, *Beyondism*, 95.

182   *"Here is the need for all the compassion we can summon"*: Ibid.

182   *he built a house shaped like a sailboat*: John Horn, "Raymond Bernard Cattell (1905–1998)," *American Psychologist*, January 2001.

182   *reminded him of his native Devonshire*: See ibid.

182   *science seemed to be moving in his direction*: Cattell, *Beyondism*, 221.

183   *"With good fortune we shall before long see"*: Ibid., 256.

183   *"By far the most systematic and rigorous attack"*: Hathaway, "Personality Inventories," 466.

183   *"neologic gobbledegook"*: Lewis R. Goldberg, Warren T. Norman, and Edward Schwartz, "The Comparative Validity of Questionnaire Data (16PF Scales) and Objective Test Data (O-A Battery), in Predicting Five Peer-Rating Criteria," *Applied Psychological Measurement*, spring 1980.

183   *"so abstruse," remarked one observer, as to be "little understood"*: Robert B. Ewen, *An Introduction to Theories of Personality*, 4th ed. (Lawrence Erlbaum, 1993), 318.

183   *"If the worthiness of a theory is to be assessed"*: Ibid., 337.

183   *has been translated into or adapted for use in more than fifty languages*: Brent Edward Wholeben, "Sixteen Personality Factor Questionnaire," in *Test Critiques*, vol. 5, ed. Daniel J. Keyser and Richard C. Sweetland (Test Corporation of America, 1985), 597.

183   *frequently administered, especially for career counseling and employee selection*: See, e.g., James N. Butcher, G. Cynthia Fekken, and Joshua Taylor, "Objective Personality Assessment with Adults," in *Comprehensive Clinical Psychology*, vol. 4, ed. Cecil R. Reynolds (Elsevier, 1998), 423.

183   *second in use only to the MMPI*: Robert J. Gregory, *Psychological Testing: History, Principles, and Applications*, 3rd ed. (Allyn and Bacon, 1999), 483.

183   *acclaimed as the father of the biggest development in personality testing*: Goldberg, "The Structure of Phenotypic Personality Traits."

184   *Fiske applied factor analysis to a pool of personality descriptors*: Donald W. Fiske, "Consistency of the Factorial Structures of Personality Ratings from

Different Sources," *Journal of Abnormal and Social Psychology*, vol. 44, 1949.

184   *Tupes and Christal . . . located five factors:* Ernest C. Tupes and Raymond E. Christal, "Stability of Personality Trait Rating Factors Obtained Under Diverse Conditions," United States Air Force Wright Air Development Center Technical Note, Number 58–61, 1958.

184   *Norman reported he'd found five factors:* Warren T. Norman, "Toward an Adequate Taxonomy of Personality Attributes: Replicated Factor Structure in Peer Nomination Personality Ratings," *Journal of Abnormal and Social Psychology*, June 1963.

184   *In 1981, John Digman:* John M. Digman and Naomi K. Takemoto-Chock, "Factors in the Natural Language of Personality: Re-Analysis, Comparison, and Interpretation of Six Major Studies," *Multivariate Behavioral Research*, April 1981.

184   *Goldberg named the factors "the Big Five":* Lewis R. Goldberg, "Language and Individual Differences: The Search for Universals in Personality Lexicons," in *Review of Personality and Social Psychology*, vol. 2, ed. Ladd Wheeler (Sage, 1981), 141–165.

184   *the correlation, or statistical relationship, between personality tests and people's actual behavior:* Walter Mischel, *Personality and Assessment* (Lawrence Erlbaum, 1968), 38.

184   *"Most traditional clinical assessments":* Ibid., 279.

185   *"It is as if we live in two independent worlds":* Ibid., 1.

185   *"acknowledged in the abstract":* Ibid., 10.

185   *"Unlike rats and other lower organisms":* Ibid.

185   *"to a grossly oversimplified view":* Ibid., 301.

185   *universally described as "dark":* See, e.g., Jerry S. Wiggins, epilogue in *Personality Assessment Via Questionnaires*, ed. Alois Angleitner and Jerry S. Wiggins (Springer-Verlag, 1986), 225.

185   *"experiencing a major crisis":* Dan P. McAdams, "Conceptual History," in *Handbook of Personality Psychology*, ed. Robert Hogan, John Johnson, and Stephen Briggs (Academic Press, 1997), 19.

185   *"paralyzed in agonizing reflection":* Lewis R. Goldberg and Gerard Saucier, "So What Do You Propose We Use Instead? A Reply to Block," *Psychological Bulletin*, March 1995.

185   *"mired in Mischellian mud":* Dan P. McAdams, "A Psychology of the Stranger," *Psychological Inquiry*, vol. 5, iss. 2, 1994.

185   *"mini-theories," "theories of the middle range":* See, e.g., Robert Hogan, "Reinventing Personality," *Journal of Social and Clinical Psychology*, spring 1998.

186   *"Machiavellianism":* Richard Christie and Florence L. Geis, *Studies in Machiavellianism* (Academic, 1970).

186   *"Nowadays almost everyone is an interactionist"*: Albert Bandura, "The
      Changing Icons in Personality Psychology," in *Psychology at Iowa: Centennial
      Essays*, ed. Joan H. Cantor (Lawrence Erlbaum, 1991), 121.
186   *"big and bluff, like a bear"*: Author's interview with Lewis Goldberg, June 9,
      2003.
186   *"Jeff," as he's known, "is sweet and quiet"*: Ibid.
186   *"an astonishingly fruitful research collaboration"*: Jack Block, "A Contrarian
      View of the Five-Factor Approach to Personality Description," *Psychological
      Bulletin*, March 1995.
187   *"I believe that the 'new morality' of permissiveness is no morality at all"*: Quoted
      in Samuel Juni, "Revised NEO Personality Inventory," in *The Twelfth Mental
      Measurements Yearbook*, ed. Jane Close Conoley and James C. Impara (Buros
      Institute of Mental Measurements, 1995), 866.
187   *"I would rather be known as 'merciful' than as 'just'"*: Quoted in ibid., 867.
187   *"I'm not crafty or sly"*: Quoted in ibid., 866.
187   *"I have never literally jumped for joy"*: Quoted in ibid., 867.
187   *"Some people think of me as cold and calculating"*: Quoted in ibid., 866.
187   *"I have fewer fears than most people"*: Quoted in ibid., 867.
187   *"I am dominant, forceful, and assertive"*: Quoted in ibid.
187   *"I often feel helpless and want someone else to solve my problems"*: Quoted in ibid.
187   *"After decades of debate"*: Quoted in Yossef S. Ben-Porath and James N.
      Butcher, "The Historical Development of Personality Assessment," in
      Clinical Psychology: Historical and Research Foundations, ed. C. Eugene
      Walker (Plenum, 1991), 144.
187   *"both necessary and reasonably sufficient"*: Robert R. McCrae and Paul T.
      Costa Jr., "Clinical Assessment Can Benefit From Recent Advances in
      Personality Psychology," *American Psychologist*, September 1986.
188   *"just right"*: Robert R. McCrae and Oliver P. John, "An Introduction to
      the Five-Factor Model and Its Applications," *Journal of Personality*, June
      1992.
188   *"is an empirical fact"*: Ibid.
188   *"Those who use the Myers-Briggs Type Indicator"*: Paul T. Costa Jr. and Robert
      R. McCrae, "Solid Ground in the Wetlands of Personality: A Reply to
      Block," *Psychological Bulletin*, March 1995.
188   *"The research leading to the Big Five structure"*: Gerard Saucier and Lewis R.
      Goldberg, "The Language of Personality: Lexical Perspectives on the Five-
      Factor Model," in *The Five-Factor Model of Personality: Theoretical
      Perspectives*, ed. Jerry S. Wiggins (Guilford, 1996), 59.
188   *"an explosion of interest"*: Oliver P. John and Richard W. Robins, "Gordon
      Allport: Father and Critic of the Five-Factor Model," in *Fifty Years of
      Personality Psychology*, ed. Kenneth H. Craik, Robert Hogan, and Raymond
      N. Wolfe (Plenum, 1993), 233.

188   *"nonhuman species"*: Samuel D. Gosling and Oliver P. John, "Personality Dimensions in Nonhuman Animals: A Cross-Species Review," *Current Directions in Psychological Science*, June 1999.

188   *"It is unclear why there were only three canine factors"*: Thomas W. Draper, "Canine Analogs of Human Personality Factors," *The Journal of General Psychology*, July 1995.

189   *five personality factors found among brands*: Jennifer L. Aaker, "Dimensions of Brand Personality," *Journal of Marketing Research*, July 1997.

189   *"you can account for 99 percent of the differences in human behavior"*: Pierce Howard, quoted in Steve Bates, "Personality Counter: Measuring Personality," *HR Magazine*, February 2002.

189   *Costa and McCrae have identified six "personality styles"*: See Carlen Henington, "NEO-4," in *The Fourteenth Mental Measurements Yearbook* (Buros Institute of Mental Measurements, 2001), 830.

189   *"the magic five"*: Fritz Ostendorf and Alois Angleiter, "Enthusiasts Contra Pessimists," *Psychological Inquiry*, vol. 5, iss. 2, 1994.

189   *"poised on the brink of a solution"*: Goldberg, "The Structure of Phenotypic Personality Traits."

190   *"Human beings are fundamentally rational"*: Robert R. McCrae, "Trait Psychology and the Revival of Personality and Culture Studies," *The American Behavioral Scientist*, September 2000.

190   *"people generally understand themselves"*: Robert R. McCrae and Paul T. Costa Jr., "Toward a New Generation of Personality Theories: Theoretical Contexts for the Five-Factor Model," in *The Five-Factor Model of Personality*.

190   *"candor and cooperation"*: Quoted in Block, "A Contrarian View of the Five-Factor Approach to Personality Description."

190   *"It is probably not meaningful or profitable to ask why"*: McCrae and John, "An Introduction to the Five-Factor Model and Its Applications."

190   *"Genetic factors are expected to play a major role"*: National Institutes of Aging, "Laboratory of Personality and Cognition," www.grc.nia.nih.gov/branches/lpc/lpcfb2000.pdf.

190   *"Barring such events as dementia and major depressive episodes"*: Quoted in Rowan Bayne, *The Myers-Briggs Type Indicator: A Critical Review and Practical Guide* (Chapman & Hill, 1995), 88.

190   *personality is fixed once our twenties are past*: See McCrae, "Trait Psychology and the Revival of Personality and Culture Studies."

190   *"In most of us, by the age of thirty"*: Quoted in Paul T. Costa Jr. and Robert R. McCrae, "Set Like Plaster: Evidence for the Stability of Adult Personality," in *Can Personality Change?*, ed. Todd F. Heatherton and Joel Lee Weinberger (American Psychological Association, 1994), 21.

190   *"it keeps different social strata from mixing"*: Quoted in Ross Stagner, "Fifty

Years of the Psychology of Personality: Reminiscences," in Craik, Hogan, and Wolfe, *Fifty Years of Personality Psychology*, 24.

191   *"They thought they had changed, but they hadn't"*: Quoted in Marina Pisano, "The Changing Face of Personality," *San Antonio Express-News*, July 6, 2003.

191   *"individuals are knowledgeable and intelligent observers"*: McCrae and Paul T. Costa Jr., "Toward a New Generation of Personality Theories."

191   *"The Five-Factor Model may be a human universal"*: National Institutes of Aging, "Laboratory of Personality and Cognition."

191   *"very similar five-factor solutions"*: McCrae, "Trait Psychology and the Revival of Personality and Culture Studies."

191   *"The fact that the five factors are found in many different cultures"*: Paul T. Costa Jr. and Robert R. McCrae, "Four Ways Five Factors Are Basic," *Personality and Individual Differences*, June 1992.

191   *the five qualities most important to human survival*: See, e.g., David M. Buss, "Social Adaptation and Five Major Factors of Personality," in Wiggins, *The Five-Factor Model of Personality*.

191   *our brains are wired to ask five key questions* See Goldberg, "Language and Individual Differences," 161.

191   *"while the contents of the wagon are examined"*: Block, "A Contrarian View of the Five-Factor Approach to Personality Description."

192   *"imperialistic"*: Dan P. McAdams, "A Psychology of the Stranger."

192   *"the trait kingdom to come"*: Dan P. McAdams, "Alternative Futures for the Study of Human Individuality," *Journal of Research in Personality*, September 1996.

192   *"We must all be a little more humble"*: Lawrence A. Pervin, "Further Reflections on Current Trait Theory," *Psychological Inquiry*, vol. 5, iss. 2, 1994.

192   *"They have a commercial, proprietary inventory"*: Author's interview with Jack Block, April 11, 2003.

192   *"There are lots of fads in psychology"*: Ibid.

192   *"is a social phenomenon"*: Juni, "Revised NEO Personality Inventory," 864.

192   *subjects instructed to "fake good"*: Michael R. Bagby and Margarita B. Marshall, "Positive Impression Management and Its Influence on the Revised NEO Personality Inventory: A Comparison of Analog and Differential Prevalence Group Designs," *Psychological Assessment*, September 2003.

192   *as many as 88 percent of job applicants*: Joseph G. Rosse, Mary D. Stetcher, Janice L. Miller, and Robert A. Levin, "The Impact of Response Distortion on Preemployment Personality Testing and Hiring Decisions," *Journal of Applied Psychology*, August 1998.

192   *the ease with which the NEO PI-R can be manipulated*: See, e.g., Butcher, Fekken, and Taylor, "Objective Personality Assessment with Adults," 420.

192   *"getting carried away"*: Juni, "Revised NEO Personality Inventory," 866.

193   *"the rigid logic of the method"*: Block, "A Contrarian View of the Five-Factor Approach to Personality Description."

193   *"no statistical procedure should be treated as a mechanical truth generator"*: Quoted in ibid.

193   *"It is my belief"*: Ibid.

193   *"the Big Five is a model"*: Author's interview with Goldberg.

193   *"is reproduced better in some languages"*: Gerard Saucier and Lewis R. Goldberg, "Lexical Studies of Indigenous Personality Factors: Premises, Products, and Prospects," *Journal of Personality*, December 2001.

193   *appears better able to predict behavior*: See Harry C. Triandis and Eunkook M. Suh, "Cultural Influences on Personality," *Annual Review of Psychology*, 2002.

194   *"the most impressive achievement"*: Costa and McCrae, "Solid Ground in the Wetlands of Personality: A Reply to Block."

194   *"is indeed crucial information"*: McAdams, "A Psychology of the Stranger."

194   *"a psychology of the stranger"*: Dan P. McAdams, "The Five-Factor Model in Personality: A Critical Appraisal," *Journal of Personality*, June 1992.

194   *One of these is* contingent *information*: See McAdams, "A Psychology of the Stranger."

195   *"In a remarkable seventy-year career"*: "Gold Medal Award for Life Achievement in Psychological Science, Raymond B. Cattell, Citation," *American Psychologist*, August 1997.

195   *"before it knew of the information"*: Quoted in Philip J. Hilts, "Racism Accusations and Award Is Delayed," *New York Times*, August 15, 1997.

195   *"monitors campus racism and serves as a resource center"*: "Short Resume of Barry Mehler," www.ferris.edu/htmls/academics/syllabi/mehlerbarry/drm/res.htm.

195   *"the potential awardee has a lifetime commitment"*: Quoted in Hilts, "Racism Accusations and Award Is Delayed."

196   *"seal of approval to a man"*: Quoted in ibid.

196   *"blue-ribbon panel"*: Quoted in ibid.

196   *"As a result of an award I never requested"*: Cattell, "Open Letter to the APA."

196   *"I am not and have never been a racist"*: Quoted in Sue Ellen Christian, "Psychologists Navigate Mine Field," *Chicago Tribune*, August 17, 1997.

196   *"my views of eugenics have evolved"*: Quoted in Hilts, "Racism Accusations and Award Is Delayed."

196   *"important policy decisions should be based on scientific information"*: Quoted in Christian, "Psychologists Navigate Mine Field."

197   *"The Big Five makes me think"*: Author's interview with Scott Meier,

associate professor at the State University of New York at Buffalo and
author of *The Chronic Crisis in Psychological Measurement and Assessment: A
Historical Survey* (Academic Press, 1994), May 2, 2003.

CHAPTER EIGHT: UNCHARTED WATERS

199   *the neuroscientist clicks open a richly detailed image:* Author's reporting.

199   *performed this particular experiment in 1999:* Turhan Canli, Zuo Zhao, John E.
Desmond, Eunjoo Kang, James Gross, and John D. E. Gabrieli, "An fMRI
Study of Personality Influences on Brain Reactivity to Emotional Stimuli,"
Behavioral Neuroscience, February 2001.

200   *"neural signature":* Ibid.

200   *"I'm cautious about the overinterpretation of this data":* Author's interview with
Turhan Canli, August 25, 2003.

200   *"If a life-or-death decision was based":* Ibid.

200   *"Personality research in general":* Quoted in Graham Lawton, "Let's Get
Personal," *New Scientist*, September 13, 2003.

201   *MRI scans of children might identify those at risk:* See Carl E. Schwartz,
Christopher I. Wright, Lisa M. Shin, Jerome Kagan, and Scott Rauch,
"Inhibited and Uninhibited Infants Grown Up: Adult Amygdalar Response
to Novelty," *Science*, June 20, 2003, and Bill Hendrick, "The Shyness Trap,"
Atlanta Journal and Constitution, July 22, 2003.

201   *will one day be diagnosed by their brain scans:* Joseph D. Matarazzo,
"Psychological Testing and Assessment in the 21st Century," *American
Psychologist*, August 1992.

201   *the nervous systems of introverts are more sensitive:* See, e.g., Lewis R. Aiken,
Human Differences (Lawrence Erlbaum, 1999), 179.

201   *depressed people have a relatively slower heartbeat:* Ibid., 178.

201   *anxious and neurotic individuals settle down less quickly:* Ibid.

201   *eye movements can provide clues:* Ibid., 179.

201   *neurotics produce fewer antibodies:* Anna L. Marsland, Sheldon Cohen, Bruce
S. Rabin, and Stephen B. Manuck, "Associations Between Stress, Trait
Negative Affect, Acute Immune Reactivity, and Antibody Response to
Hepatitis B Injection in Healthy Young Adults," *Health Psychology*, January
2001.

201   *High levels of the hormone testosterone:* Marvin Zuckerman, "Good and Bad
Humors: Biochemical Bases of Personality and Its Disorders," *Psychological
Science*, November 1995.

201   *members of college fraternities with elevated average testosterone:* James M.
Dabbs, Marian F. Hargrove, and Colleen Heusel, "Testosterone Differences
Among College Fraternities: Well-Behaved Versus Rambunctious,"
Personality and Individual Differences, February 1996.

201   *"appreciative of fantasy, aesthetics, ideas, and values"*: James M. Dabbs and
      Charles H. Hopper, "Cortisol, Arousal, and Personality in Two Groups of
      Normal Men," *Personality and Individual Differences*, vol. 2, iss. 9, 1990.

202   *criminality, drug use, sexual promiscuity, and other "norm-breaking behavior"*:
      See Zuckerman, "Good and Bad Humors," and Britt af Klinteberg, "Biology,
      Norms and Personality: A Developmental Perspective," *Neuropsychobiology*,
      vol. 34, iss. 3, 1996.

202   *about 50 percent of individual differences in personality*: Author's interview
      with Dean H. Hamer, Chief of the Section on Gene Structure and
      Regulation in the Laboratory of Biochemistry of the National Cancer
      Institute, April 16, 2003.

202   *Individuals who inherit one form of the gene*: See Aiken, *Human Differences*,
      179, and Beth Azar, "Searching for Genes that Explain Our Personalities,"
      APA Monitor, September 2002.

202   *people with a particular version of this gene*: Dean H. Hamer, Benjamin D.
      Greenberg, Sue Z. Sabol, and Dennis L. Murphy, "Role of the Serotonin
      Transporter Gene in Temperament and Character," *Journal of Personality
      Disorders*, winter 1999.

202   *"look at all the genes in an organism and predict its behavior"*: Quoted in Robert
      S. Boyd, "People May Be Judged by Their Genes, Scientists Fear," *Times-
      Picayune*, April 19, 1998.

203   *measure, to a fraction of a second, how quickly we punch in (A) or (B)*: See,
      e.g., Frederick M. Siem, "The Use of Response Latencies to Enhance Self-
      Report Personality Measures," *Military Psychology*, vol. 8, iss. 1, 1996.

203   *gauge the degree of pressure applied*: Cited in Yossef S. Ben-Porath and James
      N. Butcher, "The Historical Development of Personality Assessment," in
      Clinical Psychology: Historical and Research Foundations, ed. C. Eugene
      Walker (Plenum, 1991), 146.

203   *even allow the test to modify itself as a person takes it*: See, e.g., Steven P. Reise
      and James M. Henson, "Computerization and Adaptive Administration of
      the NEO PI-R," *Assessment*, December 2000.

203   *"countdown method"*: See, e.g., Richard W. Handel, Yossef S. Ben-Porath,
      and Mimi Watt, "Computerized Adaptive Assessment with the MMPI-2 in
      a Clinical Setting," *Psychological Assessment*, September 1999.

203   *to use computers to test "automatic" or unconscious reactions*: See, e.g., Annie
      Murphy Paul, "Where Bias Begins: The Truth About Stereotypes,"
      Psychology Today, May-June 1998.

203   *known as the Implicit Association Test (IAT)*: Anthony G. Greenwald, Debbie
      E. McGhee, and Jordan L. K. Schwartz, "Measuring Individual Differences
      in Implicit Cognition: The Implicit Association Test," *Journal of Personality
      and Social Psychology*, June 1998.

203   *enter "good" in response to a black face*: See, e.g., Nilanjana Dasgupta, Debbie

E. McGhee, Anthony G. Greenwald, and Mahzarin R. Banaji, "Automatic Preference for White Americans: Eliminating the Familiarity Explanation," *Journal of Experimental Social Psychology*, May 2000.

203   *The test picks up tendencies toward shyness:* Jens B. Asendorpf, Rainer Banse, and Daniel Muecke, "Double Dissociation Between Implicit and Explicit Personality Self-Concept: The Case of Shy Behavior," *Journal of Personality and Social Psychology*, August 2002.

204   *developed a program that calculates the frequency with which individuals use certain types of words:* See, e.g., James W. Pennebaker and Laura A. King, "Linguistic Styles: Language Use as an Individual Difference," *Journal of Personality and Social Psychology*, December 1999.

204   *"People who talk in the present tense":* Author's interview with James Pennebaker, April 11, 2003.

204   *"shamelessly crude":* James W. Pennebaker and Anna Graybeal, "Patterns of Natural Language Use: Disclosure, Personality and Social Integration," *Current Directions in Psychological Science*, June 2001.

205   *"The most replicated associations":* Jonathan Benjamin, Richard P. Ebstein, and R. H. Belmaker, "Personality Genetics, 2002," *Israel Journal of Psychiatry and Related Sciences*, vol. 39, iss. 4, 2002.

205   *"People see pictures of the brain":* Author's interview with Turhan Canli, April 11, 2003.

205   *"new phrenology":* Quoted in Laura Spinney, "The Mind Readers," *New Scientist*, September 21, 2002.

205   *MRI technology is less reliable:* Nikos K. Logothetis, "The Neural Basis of the Blood-Oxygen-Level-Dependent Functional Magnetic Resonance Imaging Signal," *Philosophical Transactions of the Royal Society of London*, Series B, *Biological Sciences*, August 2002.

205   *"I can imagine a day when people will be selling that":* Author's interview with Dean Hamer.

206   *"We never seem to solve our problems":* Gordon W. Allport, "The Open System in Personality Theory," in *Varieties of Personality Theory*, ed. Hendrik M. Ruitenbeek (E. P. Dutton, 1964), 149.

206   *ever-changing "fashions":* Quoted in Richard I. Evans, *Gordon Allport: The Man and His Ideas* (E. P. Dutton, 1970), 83.

206   *"mental thermometers":* Rolf O. Kroger and Linda A. Wood, "Reification, 'Faking,' and the Big Five," *American Psychologist*, December 1993.

207   *"He is such an optimist":* Quoted in E. M. Swift, "Feat of Global Dimensions," *Sports Illustrated*, April 21, 1986.

208   *"From an early age, I was surrounded by boats":* Quoted in William Nasby and Nancy W. Read, "The Voyager and the Voyage," *Journal of Personality*, December 1997.

208   *"Russ really filled the role of my father":* Quoted in ibid.

208   *"I have a natural tendency to put the blinders on"*: Quoted in ibid.

209   *"When he finally told me he wanted to sail around the world"*: Quoted in Swift, "Feat of Global Dimensions."

209   *"You're out of your goddamn mind"*: Quoted in ibid.

209   *"My place in the customary order of things"*: Quoted in Nasby and Read, "The Voyager and the Voyage."

209   *"Sailing a boat alone"*: Quoted in Barbara Lloyd, "American to Sail in Solo Trip," *New York Times*, October 6, 1985.

209   *"I want to come back knowing myself in a deeper way"*: Quoted in *Around Alone*, film directed by Christopher G. Knight, distributed by the New Film Company, 1990.

210   *"Morgan is understood to be a man"*: William Nasby and Nancy W. Read, "The Life Voyage of a Solo Circumnavigator: Integrating Theoretical and Methodological Perspectives," *Journal of Personality*, December 1997.

211   *"I don't think I want to spend much time"*: Dodge Morgan, *The Voyage of American Promise* (Houghton Mifflin, 1989), 135.

211   *"painful postpartum of leaving"*: Quoted in Knight, *Around Alone*.

211   *"The cold reality of six months alone"*: Morgan, *The Voyage of American Promise*, 64.

211   *"It seems I cope better with the loneliness"*: Quoted in Nasby and Read, "The Voyager and the Voyage."

211   *"They like it when I make a fool of myself"*: Quoted in Knight, *Around Alone*.

212   *"A storm, frightening as it often is"*: Quoted in Nasby and Read, "The Voyager and the Voyage."

212   *"I need a sense of progress"*: Quoted in ibid.

212   *"2030: Eat dinner straight from cooking pot"*: Morgan, *The Voyage of American Promise*, 71.

212   *"They are so irrelevant to my world now"*: Ibid., 133.

212   *"surely the psychological pros will be able to learn something useful"*: Ibid.

212   *"I never fitted the general boy assembly"*: Gordon W. Allport, "Gordon W. Allport," in *A History of Psychology in Autobiography*, vol. 5, ed. Edwin G. Boring and Gardner Lindzey (Appleton-Century-Crofts, 1967), 4.

213   *"Floyd's astoundingly neat system"*: Quoted in Ian A. M. Nicholson, *Inventing Personality: Gordon Allport and the Science of Selfhood* (American Psychological Association, 2003), 127.

213   *what he candidly conceded was an "attack"*: Quoted in ibid.

213   *"You seem to be developing a type of Psychology"*: Quoted in ibid.

213   *"He writes to me as he would to an unknown prof"*: Quoted in ibid., 128.

213   *on a career he would proudly describe as "maverick"*: Quoted in ibid., 164.

214   *"I wanted an 'image of man'"*: Allport, "Gordon W. Allport," 15.

214   *"but if it makes one think"*: Quoted in Evans, *Gordon Allport: The Man and His Ideas*, 82.

214   *"Following the lead of the older sciences"*: Gordon W. Allport, "Personality: A Problem for Science or a Problem for Art?" in *The Nature of Personality: Selected Papers* (Greenwood, 1975), 206.

214   *"Personality is never general"*: Ibid.

214   *"the long way around"*: Gordon W. Allport, "The Trend in Motivational Theory," *American Journal of Orthopsychiatry*, January 1953.

214   *"There is something in it to irritate almost everyone"*: Quoted in Thomas F. Pettigrew, "Gordon Willard Allport: A Tribute," *Journal of Social Issues*, fall 1999.

214   *"The letters deal with a mother-son tangle"*: Allport, "Gordon W. Allport," 21.

215   *"wishing that I could take refuge in vague generalizations"*: Quoted in David G. Winter, "Gordon Allport and 'Letters From Jenny,'" in *Fifty Years of Personality Psychology*, ed. Kenneth H. Craik, Robert Hogan, and Raymond N. Wolfe (Plenum, 1993), 153.

215   *"the imprimatur of his own personal experience"*: Ibid., 150.

215   *"the gray-green water rolls by the pilothouse windows"*: Morgan, *The Voyage of American Promise*, 100.

215   *"Breaking waves are washing over the deck"*: Ibid., 98.

215   *"The day wears on painfully"*: Ibid., 100.

216   *"I do not have any Christmas spirit"*: Ibid., 97.

216   *"Happy New Year"*: Quoted in Knight, *Around Alone*.

216   *"Let's see what they have for us"*: Quoted in ibid.

217   *"My world is naturally obvious and simple and direct"*: Morgan, *The Voyage of American Promise*, 110.

217   *"I'm like water drops skittering"*: Quoted in Knight, *Around Alone*.

217   *using cards from the Thematic Apperception Test to study subjects' "intimacy motivations"*: Author's interview with Dan McAdams, May 6, 2003.

218   *a structured protocol for documenting life stories:* The life story interview protocol is available online at www.sesp.northwestern.edu/foley/instruments.htm.

218   *"Although these stories are grounded in reality"*: Author's interview with McAdams.

218   *"I was born prematurely"*: Dan P. McAdams, "Personality, Modernity, and the Storied Self: A Contemporary Framework for Studying Persons," *Psychological Inquiry*, vol. 7, iss. 4, 1996.

218   *a positive relationship between the coherence of individuals' stories and their psychological well-being:* Dana Royce Baerger and Dan P. McAdams, "Life Story Coherence and Its Relation to Psychological Well-Being," *Narrative Inquiry*, vol. 9, iss. 1, 1999.

218   *Sigmund Freud and other pioneers of talk therapy:* Ibid.

218   *"redemption" stories and "contamination" stories:* See, e.g., Foley Center for the Study of Lives, "Overview of Research Programs," www.sesp.northwestern.edu/foley/research.htm.

219   *people who tell redemptive stories tend to be happier and more "generative":* Dan P. McAdams, Jeffrey Reynolds, Martha Lewis, Allison H. Patten, and Phillip J. Bowman, "When Bad Things Turn Good and Good Things Turn Bad: Sequences of Redemption and Contamination in Life Narrative and Their Relation to Psychosocial Adaptation in Midlife Adults and in Students," *Personality and Social Psychology Bulletin,* April 2001.

219   *"coauthors" of their life story:* Dan P. McAdams, "The Psychology of Life Stories," *Review of General Psychology,* June 2001.

219   *"There is no simple, single key":* McAdams, "Personality, Modernity, and the Storied Self."

219   *"Life narratives are about knowledge for knowledge's sake":* Author's interview with McAdams.

219   *"I do not yet know quite what to make of them":* Robert R. McCrae, "Integrating the Levels of Personality," *Psychological Inquiry,* vol. 7, no. 4, 1996.

220   *"tentative, eclectic, and humble":* Allport, "Gordon W. Allport," 7.

220   *"Our knowledge is a drop":* Ibid., 23.

220   *"American Promise, American Promise":* Quoted in Swift, "Feat of Global Dimensions."

220   *"Well, at least I haven't become invisible":* Quoted in ibid.

220   *"I have made up my mind":* Quoted in Christopher L. Tyner, "Dodge Morgan's Solo Sail Gives U.S. a New Seafaring Hero," *Christian Science Monitor,* April 14, 1986.

220   *"You're the first human beings I've seen in a hundred and fifty days!":* Quoted in Tony Chamberlain, "Morgan's Feat Alive in Print," *Boston Globe,* June 28, 1989.

EPILOGUE

223   *among the field's most frequently used instruments:* Wayne J. Camara, Julie S. Nathan, and Anthony E. Puente, "Psychological Test Usage: Implications in Professional Psychology," *Professional Psychology: Research and Practice,* April 2000.

223   *the latest report of the APA Ethics Committee:* "Report of the Ethics Committee, 2002," *American Psychologist,* August 2003.

225   *a development already underway:* See, e.g., Elena J. Eisman, Robert R. Dies, Stephen E. Finn, Lorraine D. Eyde, Gary G. Kay, Tom W. Kubiszyn, Gregory J. Meyer, and Kevin L. Moreland, "Problems and Limitations in Using Psychological Assessment in the Contemporary Health Care

Delivery System," *Professional Psychology: Research and Practice*, April 2000, which acknowledges that "past episodes of indiscriminate use of costly psychological evaluations" contributed to managed care organizations' current reluctance to reimburse psychologists for assessment services.

225   *"If a professional psychologist is 'evaluating' you"*: Robyn M. Dawes, *House of Cards: Psychology and Psychotherapy Built on Myth* (Free Press, 1994), 152–153.

226   *the X-ray is more like a mirror:* Quoted in Richard H. Dana, "Rorschach," in *The Sixth Mental Measurements Yearbook*, ed. Oscar Krisen Buros (Gryphon, 1965), 495.

Index

About the Author

ANNIE MURPHY PAUL is a former senior editor at *Psychology Today*. She writes the monthy *Mind/Body* column for *Shape*, and her articles have appeared in *Salon, Discover, USA Weekend, Self, Fitness,* and *Ladies' Home Journal*, among other publications. A 1999–2000 Rosalyn Carter Mental Health Journalism Fellow, she graduated from Yale University and is currently enrolled in the Mid-Career Master's Program at the Columbia University Graduate School of Journalism. She lives in New York City. Readers can email her at *personalitybook@aol.com*.

DATE			